LIFE ON THE FRINGES

A Feminist Journey Toward
Traditional Rabbinic Ordination

LIFE ON THE FRINGES

A Feminist Journey Toward Traditional Rabbinic Ordination

By

HAVIVA NER-DAVID

Dear Jayne,
I hope you enjoy this book and
find it meaningful. Let me know what
you think. See you at Eish Kodesh!

בהכרה
הביבה

Foreword by Blu Greenberg

JFL BOOKS
A DIVISION OF JEWISH FAMILY & LIFE!

Library of Congress Cataloging-in-Publication Data Available
ISBN 0-9664306-7-0

Jacket design by Jesse M. Kahn of jesse kahn creative
Frontispiece photograph by Debbi Cooper
Interior book design by Sylvia Frezzolini Severance

10 9 8 7 6 5 4 3 2 1

First Edition

Manufactured in the United States of America
Published by JFL Books
A division of Jewish Family & Life!
56 Kearney Road, Suite B
Needham, MA 02494
Tel (781) 449-9894
Fax (781) 449-9825
www.JFLBooks.com

To Jacob,

who has supported the writer, the book,

the life, and the struggle

CONTENTS

◆

Foreword ix

Preface and Acknowledgments xiii

On Language xvi

Introduction 1

ONE   Community: Beginnings 11

TWO   *Brit*: Covenant 20

THREE   *Mitzvot*: Commandments 28

FOUR   God: Believing 66

FIVE   *Halakhah:* Law 81

SIX   *Chuppah*: Marriage 131

SEVEN   *Taharah* and *Tumah*: Purity and Impurity 150

EIGHT   *Mikveh:* The Ritual Bath 177

NINE   *Torah:* Learning 189

TEN   Israel: Building 226

Epilogue 241

Notes 244

FOREWORD

◆

THE ENCOUNTER BETWEEN FEMINISM and Orthodoxy is nothing less than a clash between two worldviews: a contemporary ideology of equality of the sexes and the values of an eternal religion based on a high degree of gender differentiation (which tilts toward hierarchy more often than not). Already, feminism has cut a deep and wide swath into the lives of Orthodox Jewish women. It intersects our theologies, our communal and interpersonal relationships, our very senses of self.

In negotiating this encounter, a thousand tasks present themselves: assessing every act, every statement, every ritual and tradition through a new lens; sifting through sources—and sorting through feelings—for answers; reckoning which battles to engage in and which to let go by with relative serenity; questioning the revealed word and obeying the Commanding Voice; nuancing for the sake of children, parents, or community sensibilities; allowing intellect and personal integrity to speak forcefully to our tradition; discerning when to come closer to God through that tradition and when to distance from inherited assumptions—and assessing the costs of all these choices. Often, these are wrenching steps. Undertaking these tasks together or even separately can exhilarate or sap strength, embolden us or make us feel vulnerable.

In this insightful work, Haviva Ner-David engages deeply with all of these issues. We are grateful to her for this, because as a community we are poised at the beginning of the encounter between feminism and traditional Judaism. I always figured that it would take at least a generation or two to sort it all out. By sharing her intimate journey, she will surely shorten the process for all of us.

There are two primary ways of exploring the many issues before us. One is through the life of the mind, the intellectual argument, discussions of ideology and sources, the drawing of logical conclusions. The other is through the experiential, taking on new forms of ritual and religious behavior. Though these modes are not mutually exclusive, human nature is such that individuals tend to emphasize one over the other. I tend to prefer the first, cautiously waiting to do what is innovative. I prefer to do battle in the realm of ideas, arguing with myself and with others until I find a comfortable place in my mind and soul to support new actions before I jump in.

Ner-David juggles both modes in equal and ample measure, intensely and with passion. She deals with every issue this way, whether it is women's rabbinic ordination, wearing a tallit, observing *niddah*, birth ceremonies for girls, marriage rites, homosexuality, choosing where to daven, raising feminist daughters. She thinks, studies, makes a commitment, acts with forethought, studies the sources again, reflects midway through her journey, agonizes, takes a different step, revisits a conclusion, asks more questions, examines her ambivalences, allows herself to be influenced by the principled behavior of others. All the while she explicates the sources in the way of a master teacher. In her life's actions, she weaves together tradition, knowledge, emotions, and a sense of ethics and justice—not only for herself, but also for all of us.

Throughout this book, there is the ring of truth—no false modesty here, and no airs. Ner-David hides nothing, spares no one, especially herself, in her search for truth. She speaks openly of uncertainty and hesitation. She recognizes always the mix of things—separating from parents interrelated with forging one's own spiritual identity, protective mothering with brave choices, individual need with communal priorities, love with compromise, spirituality with sexuality, a loving desire to come close to God with political anger. After a lofty discourse on faith, she acknowledges all the human power issues; we are left not with a cloying taste in the mouth but with an understanding of a fully human woman shuttling between heaven and earth—as all genuinely religious mortals must do. Maturely, she recognizes that we can all live with multiple truths and be a part of multiple communities, yet still find our own anchor and inner compass as we make our way.

The reader will encounter other heroes in the pages ahead. Ner-David's husband Jacob is one. Strong and egalitarian, he demonstrates that you can be tender and "all man," incredibly supportive and still have a mind of your own. Jacob's model informs those men who currently stand on the sidelines.

Ner-David's parents are also heroes: first, for the struggle to raise open-minded and observant teenage children, and then for allowing their daughter to write so openly about them. One must give them much credit, for there are surely plenty of ways they could have said no. (One more prayer to add to the liturgical lexicon of parents—that our children don't grow up to be writers.) Most important, they are heroes for their part in producing such a sensitive, intelligent, spiritually vital human being.

Leaving no thought unexamined, no Jewish life experience unquestioned, Ner-David takes steps that sometimes make us feel like applauding—and sometimes make us uncomfortable almost to the point of covering our eyes and reading through the slits between our fingers. Wrestling with issues from which we might wish to hide, she pulls us in right behind her, resistant yet sensing our own anticipation, feeling something akin to what we might while watching a precious stone being cut and polished before our very eyes.

Nowhere is the phrase "the personal is political" more apparent than in the unfolding of Ner-David's life. Her journey from smart Jewish child born into a modern Orthodox family to rebellious teenager to ardent feminist-wife-mother-community member will serve as a trail guide for others beginning or midway along parallel journeys. Each woman and man must surely sort out all these issues in a very personal way, but Ner-David's actions and reflections enable others to build upon her inner struggle, bringing all of us to a new place sooner than we thought.

You are about to be taken along on an incredible journey inside the mind and heart of a trailblazer. Good passage.

Blu Greenberg

PREFACE AND ACKNOWLEDGMENTS

THE EVENTS IN THIS BOOK are true. The way that I remember them will surely differ at times from others' own memories. The names and identifying characteristics of some people have been changed to protect their privacy.

I would like to acknowledge Yosef Abramowitz, the publisher of JFL Books, and his wife, Rabbi Susan Silverman, the epitome of true friends. Their belief in this book and in me has made this dream come true. I would also like to acknowledge Rabbi Sue Fendrick, my editor, who through her comments and hard work helped me to turn a manuscript into the book you have before you.

Many thanks to Rabbi Aryeh Strikovsky for his teaching, piety, wisdom, and courage; Dr. Noam Zohar for his teaching, advising, support, moral and religious fortitude, and halakhic proofreading; Richie Lewis and Judith Antonelli for their editorial work and bolstering comments; Debbi Cooper for the natural-yet-professional-looking results of our surprisingly enjoyable photo shoots; and my study partners, Devorah Schoenfeld and Mia Diamond Padwa, for their emotional support, editorial comments, and *hevruta* time.

Acharon acharon haviv ("the last is most beloved"), I would like to thank my family—those related to me through both blood and law—for enriching my life, encouraging my pursuits, and for being there for me as I lived the story you are about to read.

I would like to especially thank my parents, who may disagree with some of my choices but have nevertheless supported my endeavors, no matter how unusual—including the writing of this book, despite its intensely personal nature. I know that it wasn't always easy for them, and that they understand that my intention in replaying the past is not to hurt but to heal and to use my writing as a vehicle for effecting change.

Much of this book was written during the first year that I lived in Israel. It is now finally "coming out into the light" (the very appropriate Hebrew phrase for being published). Much has happened since I completed the original manuscript, most of which I did not even attempt to explore in detail. However, one thing I must especially emphasize is the birth of our second daughter, Meira Shoshana, who, appropriate to her first name, which means "she shines," has already brought much light into our lives.

I am blessed with God's greatest gift: my children, who, within the course of a day, deplete my mental and physical resources only to restore them once again with a smile, a hug, or their mere presence in my life; and with siblings who have had the courage to choose different lifestyles, each following his or her own path, but who nevertheless are supportive of one another's individuality and are there for one another when it truly matters. I am also very fortunate to have found my soulmate, Jacob, who has pushed me to follow my dreams, and who, in true marital partnership, gives of himself to me in so many ways so that I can work towards actualizing those dreams.

Do you remember that day at the beach? It was pouring, and I was holed up inside sitting with my Gemara. Adin was asleep, Michal was out with her grandparents, and you came in from outside, dripping wet, to lure me into the rain.

"Let's go in the ocean!" you said.

"You're crazy," I said, dismissing you and poking my head back into the oversize maroon volume.

"Come on," you urged. "It'll be fun!"

Well, I did think you were crazy, but I agreed anyway. I knew you had a crazy side when I married you, as did you about me.

I'll never forget that day in the ocean. When we started into the stormy waves, crashing powerfully against the shore, I felt released. I felt free for the first time in quite a while—since the kids had been born. Leaving you, the weaker swimmer, behind, I ran out into the waves, going out farther and farther, hearing you calling me, telling me to be careful, to mind the undertow.

When I finally made it out beyond the place where the waves were breaking, I was lifted up onto the ocean's surface, floating, and I let the waves lift me and drop me, lift me and drop me, as I rode them.

Perhaps it was risky, irresponsible, to go out so far in that storm—especially with two small children waiting for me at home—but I made it out and back and now have the memory and the feeling of accomplishment.

Thank you, Jacob, for pushing me into the storm to ride the waves. Even if sometimes I'm out there alone, I know you're at the shore watching and smiling.

ON S'MICHA

As of the date of this book's publication, Rabbi Strikovsky is not certain what title he will give his female students of Jewish law when they finish their courses of study with him (identical to those that his male *s'micha* students pursue, certifying their knowledge in particular areas of law). He is considering using other titles, such as "*Haveira*" (the female equivalent of a talmudic title for a learned teacher). His ambivalence, he says, is due not to halakhic questions about whether a woman of learning may or should be granted s'micha, but to concerns about whether the time is right for women to use the title "*Rav*" or Rabbi.

I hope that, God willing, when I complete a particular area or a more comprehensive course of study, I will be able to use the title "Rabbi". With or without this label, when a woman is formally and publicly recognized for such learning by an Orthodox rabbi, a significant barrier—which stands in the way of honor and authority being given to persons of learning, regardless of gender—will be forever broken. It will be an essential step toward the ultimate goal of complete recognition and acceptance of women as rabbis, leaders, teachers of Torah, and authorities in Jewish law.

ON LANGUAGE

◆

"THE RABBIS" AND "THE SAGES" in this book refer to the revered teachers and students of what is known as "the rabbinic period," which produced the Mishnah, Talmud, and much of midrashic literature, approximately 100–600 C.E.

Unless otherwise specified, references to pages in the Talmud can be assumed to refer to the Babylonian Talmud ("the Bavli"), considered more authoritative for halakhic purposes than the Jerusalem or Palestinian Talmud ("the Yerushalmi"). "The Mishnah" and "the Gemara" refer to the works which together make up the Talmud (often referred to colloquially as "Gemara"). The lowercase "mishnah" refers to a unit within the Mishnah.

Transliteration of Hebrew, Aramaic, and Yiddish words reflects a balance between consistency and familiar usage. With some exceptions, "ch" is used for the letter *chet*, "kh" for an unpointed, guttural *kaf*, and "h" for the letter *heh*.

INTRODUCTION

❖

IT'S A GLORIOUS SUMMER morning in Jerusalem, and I am standing at the window looking out at a cloudless, sapphire blue sky. There is still a chill in the air this early in the day, and the tiles beneath my bare feet feel refreshingly cool. I think of how hot I will soon be as the sun rises higher in the sky and I walk my two children—my three-year-old daughter, Michal, and my one-year-old son, Adin—to *gan* (preschool) on my way to the *yeshiva* where I am studying Talmud this year, our first year living in Israel. By the afternoon, when I pick them up, I will feel the heat from the sidewalk through the soles of my sandals.

This is a city of extremes: mountains and valleys, hot days and cool nights, the *haredim* (ultra-Orthodox) and the *hilonim* (secular Jews). It is an intense city, where emotions fly and everyone believes that he or she has the truth and is willing to fight to defend it; yet there is something about Jerusalem that embraces all of this and everyone. It is a real place, where everything comes to a head. It is a place that both beckons to me and pushes me away, embraces me and seems about to spit me out. It is here that I choose to make my home.

I drape my tallit, my prayer shawl, over my head, and suddenly it is dark. I block out all distractions—the blue sky, the bright sun glaring off the white Jerusalem stone—for a completely private moment with God. I inhale a deep breath of clean morning air, thinking about my life and the kindness that God has bestowed on me. Under my tallit, I recite softly in Hebrew:

How precious is Your lovingkindness, O God! The children of humanity take refuge in the shadow of Your wings. May they be sated from the abundance of Your house; and may You give them to drink from the stream of Your delights. For with You is the source of all life— by Your light we shall see light. Extend Your kindness to those who know You, and Your charity to the upright of heart.[1]

With my white and gray tallit now draped over my shoulders, I take my leather tefillin out of their worn velvet bag; its purple material is so frayed that there are spots which are almost translucent. Along with my first pair of tefillin, this bag once belonged to my husband's great uncle—who, it is fair to say, would not be thrilled to know that I, a woman, am the inheritor of these ritual objects. Although it is not prohibited for women to wear tefillin, traditionally only men have worn them, except for a few exceptions recorded throughout Jewish history. The Talmud tells us that Michal, the daughter of the biblical King Saul and the first wife of King David, "wore tefillin and the Sages did not protest her action."[2] There is also a tradition that the three daughters of Rashi—the eleventh-century French scholar who wrote the most commonly studied commentaries on the Bible and Talmud—wore tefillin, as did Chana Rochel Werbermacher, known as the Maiden of Ludomir. She was a Hasidic woman and mystic with a large following in the Ukraine in the nineteenth century, who after a serious illness took on the mitzvot that are traditionally obligations only for men, and who eventually emigrated to Israel.

Although I know that there have been other women throughout the ages who have chosen to wear tefillin, they have been anomalies and probably could all fit into one room. In the past two decades, especially since women have been given the opportunity to become rabbis in the Conservative movement and must, as a requirement for ordination, assume the obligation to don tefillin every morning when they pray, more women have taken on this practice. However, I cannot think of more than twenty women I know of any denomination who are not Conservative rabbis or rabbinical students and who regularly wear tefillin.

As I wrap the leather straps around my left arm seven times—seven is the number of the lower *sefirot,* or divine emanations, in Kabbalah, Jewish mysticism—I think about the first time that I wore tefillin five years ago. The moment felt so right, integrating my feminist and Jewish selves, which until that point had been like two magnets repelling one another. Yet I also felt as if I were breaking an ancient taboo. Growing up, I had seen only men wearing tefillin; it just wasn't an option for girls, anymore than it was an option for a boy to wear a dress. I played in Little League, wore blue jeans and T-shirts, and even studied Bible and Talmud with the boys, but this symmetry of experience did not extend to the realm of Jewish ritual. In the synagogue, I had to sit behind a *mechitzah*, the partition separating men and women, once I became a bat mitzvah (at age 12, an adult woman in Jewish law). While my brothers could read publicly from the Torah scroll, lead and participate actively in services, count in a minyan (a quorum of ten required for public prayer), and serve as witnesses under Jewish law, I could not. When they reached the age of bar mitzvah, they received their own pairs of tefillin. I got my ears pierced.

It was not until ten years after my bat mitzvah that I obtained tefillin. My husband, Jacob, gave me his spare set. He showed me how to put them on, and I trembled with both excitement and fear as I followed his directions. How could something that made me feel so whole also make me feel like hiding?

The source cited for the origin of the practice of laying tefillin is the ancient biblical text: "And you shall tie them as a sign on your arm, and they shall be an emblem between your eyes."[3] I had grown to feel, after twenty-two years of reciting that verse every day in the Shema, that those words were speaking to me. Despite what I had learned in school and at home, I had come to believe that God did indeed expect me to perform this mitzvah. Reading the verse, I felt myself included in this commandment; it felt like a holy act.

However, I was well aware that the Rabbis had exempted women from wearing tefillin and that mainstream *poskim*, Jewish legal scholars, discouraged women from wearing them. When commenting on the story of Michal, the daughter of King Saul, in the Babylonian Talmud, the *Tosafot* (a school of medieval commentators on the Talmud) bring a counterversion of this midrash (found in *Pesikta Rabbati*, chapter 22, and quoted in the Jerusalem Talmud), which states that the Rabbis *did* protest Michal's actions. In explaining the Jerusalem Talmud's version, the Tosafot suggest that "tefillin require a *guf naki* [clean body], and women are not meticulous enough to be careful [in this regard]."[4] The Rema, Rabbi Moshe Isserles, the Eastern European legal codifier from the sixteenth century whose gloss to the medieval Jewish law code, the *Shulchan Arukh*, is arguably the most influential Ashkenazi compilation of halakhah (Jewish law), writes that we should protest the performing of this mitzvah by women.[5] The *Mishnah B'rurah*, written by Israel Meir ha-Kohen (better known as the Hafetz Hayyim) in nineteenth-century Lithuania, alludes to the statement in the Tosafot about tefillin requiring a clean body as the reason to discourage women from performing this mitzvah.[6]

In accordance with the notion that a woman's body is not clean enough for her to wear tefillin, it has historically been virtually taboo for a woman to do so, despite the fact that the Tosafot suggest this only as an explanation for the counter midrash not quoted in the Babylonian Talmud, not as a binding legal principle. The Rabbis never actually say that it is forbidden for a woman to don tefillin, because it clearly is not, which is illustrated by the version of the Michal story brought by the Babylonian Talmud (a more halakhically authoritative source than the Jerusalem Talmud) in which the Rabbis do not protest her wearing tefillin.

When I read the biblical verse commanding us to wear the signs of God's words on our hands and head, I feel those words speaking to me. Although I may have a traditional exemption from performing this mitzvah because I am a woman, I could not feel religiously authentic if I took advantage of that exemption. Since assuming this obligation, I have found it to be neither a burden nor an action that clashes in any way with my womanhood. On the contrary, I have found that performing this mitzvah enhances my prayer experience immeasurably.

When I put on my tefillin, I feel that my prayer is elevated; I am willing to give up my exemption in order to strive toward higher spiritual levels. If that means that I must be extra careful about my hygiene, I am willing to take upon myself this responsibility, just as a man must. Socially and practically, this may not be the easiest or most simple choice, but spiritually, it is the only choice that makes sense for me.

Having put on both my arm and head tefillin, I recite the following verse, meditating on my personal connection to our *brit*, our covenant with God: "I will betroth you to Me forever; I will betroth you to Me with righteousness, justice, kindness, and mercy. I will betroth you to Me with fidelity, and you will know God."[7]

I wonder: How will I strive to fulfill my part of the brit today? The tefillin remind me that my obligation to help bring God's divine plan into the human world is through the actions of my hands and the thoughts in my head. If my thinking remains holy, I hope, my deeds will be holy.

With small children, I know that it is not easy to always keep my thoughts or my actions so lofty. My life has never seemed so infused with purpose as it has since I first held Michal to my breast, but it is easy to lose sight of this and difficult to keep my mind on a spiritual plane while changing an endless stream of diapers or trying not to lose patience when one child cries in his stroller and the other refuses to walk another inch. This time of reflection, before I am bombarded with everyone else's needs, is especially important to me now that these moments of calm are rare. They help me in the challenge to bring my relationship with God into the nitty-gritty acts of living.

It is most commonly understood that the Rabbis exempted women from performing certain time-bound mitzvot, such as putting on tefillin, because women's time belongs to others—their children and their husbands. They should not feel pressured to take time away from nurturing others in order to fulfill God's will. God will understand. However, I need this time set aside for God. I need to reconnect with my spiritual center before facing the day, and I need to make time for this apart from my other responsibilities, especially those related to caring for my children. If I lose myself in all of this caring, what good am I to others? What good am I to myself? What good am I to God? The words of Hillel the Sage echo in my ears: "If I am not for myself, who will be for me? When I am only for myself, what am I? And if not now, when?"[8]

As I am saying the Shema, Michal joins me, rubbing the sleep from her eyes. Her hair is a mass of chestnut brown waves flying in different directions, and she is wearing one of my T-shirts, which she has adopted as pajamas. The neck of the shirt hangs loosely, revealing one of her shoulders in a way that reminds me of the fact that she is female and that some day she may actually look sensual in such a pose. At the age of three, there is nothing about Michal to indicate that she is a girl except for the fact that she sometimes wears dresses or skirts. Even her long hair does not identify her gender in the *dati* (religious) community, since it is customary not to cut a boy's hair until he is three. Michal has been mistaken for a boy numerous times because she wears a *tallit katan* (the four-cornered garment with tzitzit, ritual fringes, traditionally worn under the clothes of Jewish boys and men).

It is fascinating to me that even when Michal is wearing a ribbon in her hair or a feminine outfit with flowers, people assume that she is a boy because she is wearing tzitzit. Once a woman even made this mistake when Michal was wearing a dress. She looked confused when she noticed the tzitzit poking out from under Michal's dress, but she quickly decided that someone like me, whose head covering identifies me as an observant Jew, would sooner put a dress on my son than tzitzit on my daughter.

I am ambivalent about my decision to give Michal tzitzit. Although I have adopted for myself practices that cross gender lines in the traditional Jewish community in which I live, I am not always sure it is fair for me to put Michal in that position before she is old enough to understand the implications. For this same reason, I have not pushed her to wear a *kippah* (a traditionally male headcovering) all of the time, although she does own one and wears it often when she prays. However, I don't want her to feel that these practices are off-limits to her because she is a girl. I take seriously my responsibility as a Jewish mother to introduce my children to Torah and mitzvot with love, enthusiasm, and careful thought, but with a daughter this job becomes more complicated. How can I best prepare Michal to make decisions about her role and practices as a Jewish woman? Traditional norms give her a bias in one direction. Is it wrong for me to balance the scales, to show her that there is an alternative?

I do not want her to grow up feeling, as a Jewish female, resentful of her religion, or marginalized and irrelevant, both of which I often felt as a child and a young woman. Even if she will be different, and perhaps even feel alienated from those around her or embarrassed at times, I hope that the benefit of growing up experiencing the entirety of her tradition—all of the mitzvot—as her own will outweigh the difficulties she will encounter.

I don't force Michal to wear tzitzit. Each morning, the decision is hers. She sees me wearing them; she sees her father, Jacob, wearing them; and we strongly encourage her to follow in our path. She usually seems happy to say the *brachah* (blessing) and put them on; the joy and pride in her eyes when she kisses the fringes is enough to reinforce my decision. Nevertheless, there are some days when she tells me that she doesn't want to wear her tzitzit, and on those days I let her get dressed without them.

I wonder if her seemingly whimsical decision making is related to her gender. Perhaps she is becoming sensitive to the comments she hears: "Why is she wearing tzitzit? Girls don't wear tzitzit!" Yet she never tells me on those mornings that the reason she does not want to wear tzitzit is that she is a girl; within a few days she always wants to wear them again.

I do not want to make religious issues a point of argument between us. I want Michal to have positive experiences and associations with her Jewish practices, not negative ones. I intend to be as flexible with Adin when he turns three—the age at which a son is traditionally given his first set of tzitzit and his religious education begins—even with mitzvot like tzitzit, which for a man are obligatory. I do not plan to force him to wear tzitzit or a kippah, although I will certainly encourage him to do so. I imagine that it will be easier to convince him, since he sees boys and men around him wearing them. Will I indeed keep to this egalitarian ideal, or will I slip into more conventional gender expectations? Will I be more forceful with Adin when it comes to kippah and tzitzit?

I reach the point in the Shema where I read the verse from Numbers 15:37 in which God commands us, the Jewish people, to wear tzitzit to remind us of the mitzvot (although here too the Rabbis have interpreted this to refer to men only). Suddenly, Michal snaps fully awake. "*Ima*," she orders, "I want to kiss my tzitzit! Wait!"

When Michal returns with her tzitzit, I continue reciting the Shema, and when I say the word "tzitzit," we both kiss our fringes. I wonder if my face is glowing with the pride I feel. As I pray, I insert a thought, an unarticulated request to God, that Michal's enthusiasm for prayer and mitzvot will continue. She sits beside me until I have finished reciting the Shema, and then, as I recite the *Amidah*, during which I must stand, she hides beneath my tallit, as I remember having done with my father.

I am uncomfortable with the fact that my most vivid, intense memories of committed prayer are from watching only my father, not my mother, putting on tefillin and tallit each morning. Although women are, according to most rabbinic opinions, obligated to pray at least twice a day, most of the women in the community in which I grew up did not pray regularly. Sometimes they made it to shul (synagogue) before the communal prayers were over on Shabbat, but they did not feel obligated to do so. They did feel that it was their duty, however, to have a proper Sabbath meal waiting for everyone when they arrived home from shul.

I am convinced that part of what makes men like my father so committed to praying each morning during the workweek is the obligation to put on their tefillin. Somehow, that very physical action gives focus and discipline to the rather intangible act of prayer. I am reassured of my decision to take upon myself these obligations from which I am exempt according to Jewish law, because I too am reaching for that increased intensity and focus in my prayer experience. Michal will have memories of both me and her father praying each morning, swaying back and forth wrapped in our *tallitot* and tefillin.

As I remove my tefillin and rewrap them in the way that Jacob showed me five years ago, Michal exclaims: "*Ima*, I want my own tefillin, too!"

"You'll get your own tefillin when you become a bat mitzvah, when you're twelve years old, if you still want them then. Do you think you will?" I ask. I know that I am being overbearing. I want to make the most of Michal's burst of enthusiasm for prayer and its rituals, since I know that tomorrow could bring exactly the opposite reaction, but I also don't want to overdo it. I don't want her to feel that I'm pressuring her. I want her to take on practices because *she* wants to, but I want to make the choices possible and palatable.

Michal nods her head. "And I want my own tallit, too," she says. I can hear the beginnings of an Israeli accent, after only two months of living in this country, creeping into her Hebrew. "When I get to be an even bigger girl, like you," she adds. I take her into my arms. Maybe what I am trying to impart to my children is actually making an impression. "Of course you can, Michal," I say as I cuddle her. "Of course you can."

And then Michal has had enough. She squirms out of my embrace and becomes instantly occupied, building with some blocks that she finds on the floor from the day before.

How different her childhood will be from mine, I think. She will grow up seeing me and other women wearing tallitot, tefillin, and reading from the Torah. And she lives in a Jewish country: Hebrew will soon be the language of the street for her, not just words in the Bible. Shabbat will be a day of tangible, visible rest and quiet, with the stores closed and noticeably fewer cars on the road. Judaism—with the intensity and heightened meaning it brings to life, its ancient traditions and slow-paced progress—will surround her. Only time will tell what the effects will be of the choices I make as I raise my children.

CHAPTER ONE

◆

Community: Beginnings

It is not good that a person should be alone.
— Genesis 2:18

I LIVE IN JERUSALEM. It is a city of great intensity, where people come in search of spirituality and meaning, and religious groups battle over the definition of truth. I was not born in this boiling pot; I was born in the melting pot of Manhattan, on the very Jewish Upper West Side. When I was two years old, my family, which then included my parents and my four-and-a-half-year-old brother, Jonathan, moved out to suburban Westchester.

In many ways, life in the New York suburbs was placid and idyllic for a child whose grandparents had come from Eastern Europe, avoiding murder at the hands of the Nazis a generation later. We lived a protected and blessed existence, with few worries or tensions that would be apparent to an outsider. Our house had a mezuzah on the front doorpost; our neighborhood had two shuls—one Orthodox and one Conservative; my siblings and I were bused to the closest yeshiva day school, where we learned Jewish subjects half of the day and secular subjects the other half; we lived comfortably as Jews in America.

My family was part of Modern Orthodoxy, a Jewish religious movement[1] which took on this identity and label in New York in the 1920s, though it had roots in nineteenth-century German Judaism and in the beginnings of religious Zionism. Its founders and adherents sought to hold on to Jewish tradition and law while fully integrating modernity into their lives—which meant not only cars and washing machines, but also, more important, an openness to secular knowledge and culture beyond what was absolutely necessary for their day-to-day survival. A Jew could be part of and contribute to the "outside world" while remaining a committed and practicing religious Jew. The two were not mutually exclusive. The Modern Orthodox ideal was a worldly Jew, working as a professional in the secular sphere, enjoying and contributing to secular culture, while also adhering to a traditional Jewish lifestyle—which meant keeping Shabbat, eating only kosher foods, and studying traditional Jewish texts regularly, among other things.

Being open to secular knowledge also meant letting modern ideas seep into and affect Jewish thought and practice. For instance, until the last twenty years or so (when Modern Orthodox institutions in general began to shift more to the right religiously) men and women (and not necessarily only husbands and wives) did ballroom dancing at Modern Orthodox synagogue fundraising dinners. Modernity was not something to fend off, but to embrace with moderation. As Rabbi Emanuel Rackman, one of the first rabbis to call himself Modern Orthodox, has written:

> The Torah does not have to be afraid of modernity. It can cope with modernity. There is no challenge the Torah cannot cope with. We may be able to solve some problems which please moderns. Sometimes when we cannot solve a problem and please moderns, we have to help moderns acquire a new perspective. But [Modern Orthodoxy] as a whole does not fear to cope with any challenge, and will not isolate itself because of challenges.[2]

One of the modern values the movement embraced was a greater degree of personal autonomy. There was no single rabbinical figure to which Modern Orthodox Jews turned to answer all of their Jewish legal questions (as is the case in more right-wing communities, especially among Hasidic Jews), and practices varied within the larger Modern Orthodox "community." My parents and their peers often made decisions on their own as to how to balance modernity with tradition in their own lives. Although this was not an explicit principle within Modern Orthodoxy, it was a de facto reality.

For instance, like many in their Modern Orthodox community, my parents kept a strictly kosher home but ate foods like kosher fish and pasta in nonkosher restaurants, setting aside the area of Jewish law that forbids eating food cooked in the same pot that nonkosher foods are. Although my mother wore a hat in shul, she did not wear one at other times, despite what some consider a halakhic requirement (and others a weighty custom) that a married woman wear a head covering. Although my father wore his kippah while he was at home, at the homes of religious friends, and at shul and religious functions, he did not wear one at work, despite a strong and long-standing tradition of religious Jewish men covering their heads with either a hat, a kippah, or both. While it was out of the question in my parents' community for a woman to sing a solo aloud in the shul sanctuary, it was accepted practice for a man to go to the opera or a Broadway show and hear women singing there (even though rabbinical opinions in the more right-wing Orthodox world forbid a man to hear a woman's singing voice).

It was not clear to me then and is still not clear to me now exactly what the standard for change was. No one, as far as I know, has written a definitive "statement of purpose" for the Modern Orthodox movement. What I do know is that what was considered a core Jewish value or practice was treated as immutable, and what was considered variable and dependent upon social and cultural norms was open for change. The definition of what was a core value and what was not was subjective. There was no formula for making this decision.

As in all legal systems, there are many gray areas. Psychological, sociological, theological, legal, and practical factors all had to be considered. Decisions were made based on conflicting Jewish values as well. For instance, as a child, I attended a number of lifecycle events of relatives and friends in non-Orthodox shuls. It seems to me that in that case the value of k'vod habriyot, respect for human beings, was deemed more important than Orthodox rabbinic sanctions against entering a non-Orthodox synagogue or praying without a mechitzah.

The claim—one I believe to be valid—of the founders of Modern Orthodoxy was that they were not creating a revolution in Judaism. Change has always been a reality of Jewish practice over the centuries. Otherwise, our religion would not have survived. The Modern Orthodox community made changes in tradition to accommodate

modernity, but there was only so far that they would go with this revolution. Any more was considered crossing a line into forbidden terri-
tory, stretching law and tradition so far that it became meaningless; any
less was considered dangerously rigid and backward. In my parents'
eyes, those religiously to the right were narrow-minded, and those to
the left of them were, as my father liked to put it, "so open-minded
their brains will fall out." Judaism, in my parents' minds, would surely
be lost to the grandchildren of their Reform and Conservative peers if
they didn't slow down their pace and style of change.

The community in which I grew up had a foot in each of two
worlds. We adhered to the traditions of generations past, but we were
also looking ahead, moving forward in a changing, progressing world.
As an American Jewish girl growing up as both "modern" and
"Orthodox," I often felt acutely the tensions between these two worlds:
the world of the synagogue, the Rabbis, and mitzvot; and the world of
Disneyland, the Beatles, and equal opportunity. I could wear Levi's
jeans, watch *The Brady Bunch*, and read *The Catcher in the Rye*, as
long as I wore a dress or a skirt for religious occasions, did not watch
any television on Shabbat, and studied Jewish texts (the Bible, Talmud,
and Jewish philosophy) on a regular basis. I looked like my nonreligious Jewish and even my non-Jewish peers, watched the same television programs, read the same books; yet, I knew I was different.

In many ways, the religious path I have chosen for myself is not so
different from the one upon which my parents embarked. I, too, am
striving to build a religious Jewish community based on the ideal of an
ever developing halakhah, incorporating positive contributions from
the modern world. As a woman who grew up in an Orthodox Jewish
community soon after the emergence of the twentieth-century women's
liberation movement, it is not surprising that feminism is the perspective through which I focus my efforts to actualize this ideal.

My parents unwittingly planted the seeds. They put me in the same
classroom with my male peers with an open book of the Talmud before
me. This was a revolutionary step in the Orthodox world at that time,
when most girls did not study Talmud—especially not alongside boys—
but it was as far as they thought they could go. It is my turn to move
the struggle forward.

I push the limits of halakhic innovation far beyond those of my childhood, yet I am also more traditional than my family of origin in other areas. I do not eat cooked food that is "kosher by ingredients" in nonkosher restaurants, and I wear a head covering all the time outside my house. I do without the best restaurants, and I am proud to look like a religiously observant Jew. I am not so eager to fit in with the culture around me, whether in America or in secular Israeli society.

The pressures to look and act like those in the secular and non-Jewish world were much stronger twenty years ago than they are now. Multiculturalism did not exist then, and differences were frowned upon, even discriminated against. The general societal trend is to celebrate cultural and religious difference, at least to some extent, and I am thankful to be developing my own mode of religious expression at a time when I am not made to feel ashamed for being a religious person, rooted in the traditions of my people. Of course, there is still much negative feeling toward religion and religious people, especially here in Israel, where many secular Jews resent the religious establishment (which restricts their lives in certain ways) and then project these negative feelings upon all religious people. However, even here in Israel, I feel this gradually changing. Although there is still much tension between the religious and the secular, there has been movement here toward promoting tolerance and unity. Coupled with a new openness to religion and spirituality among many "secular" Israelis, this has resulted in a shift, even if a subtle one, toward a somewhat more relaxed, even curious, atmosphere surrounding religion.

Along with multiculturalism has come pluralism. Looking and acting like a Jew is no longer the source of shame that it used to be, and we have many more ways of being Jewish. One need not fit into a mold imposed from without or within. Many Jews are returning to tradition, connecting to our past in numerous and varied ways. Although I might have been considered a freak in my parents' generation for wearing a tallit and tefillin, now I am merely an eccentric or an oddity—which *is* progress.

So what am I? Am I an Orthodox Jew? Conservative? Reform? Reconstructionist? Havurah? Many people are uncomfortable with those of us who defy categorization and refuse to be labeled. I find that people I meet are constantly trying to fit me into a familiar category. "So you are Conservative," they say. Or, "You sound like a Reform

Jew, really." Or, "You are Orthodox, but you put on tefillin?!" they ask, mystified. "Well, you can't be Orthodox," they insist, "if you want to be a rabbi." What I tell them is that I identify with and learn from each of these communities in many ways, but I also differ from each of them in significant ways.

The Orthodox community today is often too narrow in its vision, too afraid to take the necessary steps to continue the cautious journey upon which rabbinic Judaism embarked 2,000 years ago. Halakhah is a journey. The word "halakhah" is from the same root as the word "to walk" or "to go" in Hebrew. It defines how we as a community will live a Torah-based life in a world that is changing (both in positive and negative ways). Halakhah must be conservative, as must all legal systems, but it also must progress. Change must happen slowly and in stages in order for a community to feel bound to new practices and to allow time to judge if change will be beneficial or detrimental. But organic change within the halakhic system must happen; it is integral to the system itself. Halakhah should not be used as a means to guard against change, but rather as a means to implement change in a thoughtful manner so that timeless traditional values are not sacrificed in the process. Halakhah is our tool to implement *tikkun* (repair) within our own community as well as in the world as a whole. It is our legal system, but it can also be a powerful tool for shaping individual, communal, and national character.

I do not see these ideals being implemented often enough in the Orthodox world, but the other movements are often too quick to make changes, not cautious enough. I fear that they risk losing continuity with the past and an understanding of the importance of the mitzvot as obligatory. In the Conservative movement, at least its leadership and some core synagogue members in each community are committed to this ideal, but it seems to have failed in the task of transmitting its ideology to its masses. The vast majority of Conservative laypeople are not aspiring to observe halakhah and mitzvot, to at least engage in a serious dialogue with tradition. That is a sign that something is being lost in the transmission.

I am a Jew who takes seriously Torah, halakhah, mitzvot, and a constant spiritual striving to make my life holy. I am a Jew who is in constant pursuit of Torah. As a woman living at the cusp of the twentieth and twenty-first centuries, I struggle with tradition, but I am invested in this way of life. I am committed to bringing Torah into the twenty-first century without sacrificing the beauty and the power of both the everyday details of Jewish practice and the larger moral framework of communal values.

I also want to connect with the greatest number of people in the most effective way—perhaps quixotically—without being hampered by the preconceptions and restrictions that go along with labels. Labels are dangerous, because they make it easier for us to discount those who do not wear the same label that we do, and to demonize the other. I want to embrace the "other"—to take from all Jews and all movements what they have to offer, and to offer to all Jews and all movements what I have to give. I often say that I am postdenominational, since I truly feel that I am one of *c'lal Yisrael*, the entire Jewish people. I will pray in any synagogue, from the strictest *haredi* to the most liberal Reform, and respect the decisions each community has made for itself. A mechitzah that completely cuts women off visually from the service may offend my feminist sensibilities, just as a microphone may not fit into my standards of what is appropriate for Shabbat, but I won't let these differences cut me off from other Jews.

I am a pluralist, but that does not mean that I have no religious identity. I am a halakhic Jew striving to make my life reflect God's will. I am invested in halakhah and the halakhic process, yet I do not always feel that existing Jewish law expresses what God wants from us. We should resist too easily making changes in traditional practice, but progress is an essential, even traditional, part of Judaism.

My relationship with Judaism sometimes feels much like my relationship with those I love most. Commitment is a given; the ties are too strong to sever. There are tensions and struggles, pressure on both sides to change, as well as a realization that some things will not—and should not—change. It is hard work, but preserving the relationship is important.

Judaism cannot be lived only on a personal level. Ideally, a Jew needs community. There are mitzvot that can only be performed in the context of a community—such as public prayer and Torah readings, and, of course, visiting and helping the sick, welcoming guests, and other such interpersonal mitzvot. Community helps to bolster us in our observance. Being the sole Shabbat-observant Jew in a town is not an easy lifestyle. In addition, if one does not live among other observant Jews, certain religious institutions—such as a *mikveh* (ritual bath) or a religious school—will not be built.

In contrast to Groucho Marx's famous line, "I wouldn't want to belong to a club that would have me as a member," most of us want to fit in, to be comfortable and surrounded by others who look and act at least somewhat like we do. It is validating to know that the choices you have made have also been made by others, and it is especially validating to be surrounded by them. Even those of us who prefer living in a heterogeneous atmosphere do like to have a community to identify with, within the larger mix. Most of us, even those who love to travel to many places and meet different kinds of people, do want a place to come home to.

I don't yet completely have this luxury. I find community in many different frameworks, including the Internet. For example, I participate in an e-mail group through which Jewish religious feminists offer one another support, advice, information, and interesting discussions. I belong to four different congregations in my neighborhood: one liberal Orthodox (where women have a separate Torah service and participate in the mixed service within the confines of traditional halakhah); one nondenominational (there is a mechitzah, but women are called up to the Torah and read from the Torah, although they cannot lead the parts of the service that require a minyan, a quorum of, traditionally, ten men); one Reform; and one a women's *tefillah* (prayer) group in which women gather to pray every six weeks on Shabbat, although we do not consider ourselves a minyan. I teach in a yeshiva affiliated with the Conservative movement, and I am studying with an Orthodox rabbi. My oldest daughter is in a nondenominational mixed religious-secular school, my son is in a *gan* run by the Reform movement, and my youngest daughter is cared for in the home of a Sephardi Orthodox woman. In addition, my Rosh Hodesh group, about fifteen women of different Jewish religious identifications, meets once a month on the first day of each Jewish month to celebrate this traditional women's holiday together.

I have also built a community for myself out of my activism. I am heavily involved in Women of the Wall, a group of women from all

Jewish religious denominations that meets to pray as a women's *tefillah* group at the Kotel, the Western Wall, as well as Mevo Satum, an organization dedicated to helping women whose husbands will not give them a Jewish divorce. The amazingly committed, energetic, and spiritual women I have met through these organizations are my community as well; they inspire me in my own personal strivings and bolster my soul when it is weary from struggle. There are friends, colleagues, and acquaintances all around the world with whom I share similar ideas and convictions. Although I may not live in a homogeneous community of religious Jewish feminists who observe halakhah and participate in Jewish life exactly as I do, my religious and feminist needs are met in many different ways. More and more I find that I am not so alone.

CHAPTER TWO

◆

Brit: Covenant

This is My covenant, which you shall keep, between Me
and you and your seed after you. Every male among
you shall be circumcised.
— Genesis 17:10

I WAS BORN IN 1969: the year the first man walked on the moon, the Mets won the World Series, and Golda Meir became the first female prime minister of the State of Israel. I was the second of four children. My older brother, Jonathan, who was born two and a half years before me, had been received with a festive, thoughtful, and highly symbolic celebration. He was welcomed into the brit, the covenant that God made with Abraham that continues through the generations between God and the Jewish people, with much fanfare and ritual. Dressed in a crisp, pure white layette gown with intricate lace and a hand-knit tiny baby blue sweater, he was placed on a satin pillow, like a king on a throne. After the *mohel*, the professional circumciser, cut off my brother's minuscule foreskin—as the Bible reports that God told Abraham to do to himself and the male members of his household, and ordained for all future Jewish males—my father blessed his *bechor*, his firstborn son, in Hebrew: "Just as he has entered into the covenant, so may he enter into the Torah, the marriage canopy, and good deeds."

Like my brothers, I was born a Jew. Unlike my brothers, my sister and I were never formally accepted into the Jewish community. My parents, unlike my grandparents or great-grandparents, did have a party to celebrate the arrivals of their daughters, but there was no religious character to that gathering. There was no ritual to mark my entrance into the Jewish people.

What does it mean to be a Jew and at the same time wonder if I am a full member of the covenant that is at the core of our religion?

In the first book of the Torah, God speaks to Abraham: "And you shall be circumcised in the flesh of your foreskin, and it shall be a sign of the covenant between me and you."[1] Of Sarah, God says, "I will bless her, and I will give you a son from her. I will bless her, and she will be a mother to nations; royal peoples will come from her."[2]

Is Sarah a member of the covenant, or merely a breeder of members of the covenant? She will provide a son for Abraham and be a mother of the Jewish nation, but is she herself a member of the nation? She is a vessel; without her there would be no Jewish people. She is essential to building the nation but peripheral to the religious covenant between that nation and God. As a Jewish woman, descended from Sarah, the archetypal Jewish woman, so am I.

When God instructs Moses to tell the Israelite nation to prepare for the giving of the Torah, Moses says to them, "Be ready for three days; do not go near a woman."[3] Moses defines "the nation" as only the men, but whom did God have in mind? Who makes up the nation that received the Torah? Were my foremothers included? Were they present at Sinai?

When the midrashic commentators describe true revelation at Sinai, women are present. Yet it is still painful to hear that verse read aloud every year in shul. At this pivotal moment in Jewish history—the receiving of the Torah, which is at the core of our mature covenant with God—women's place seems to be in question.

When I ask male rabbis today: "Are women equal members of the brit?", the answer I receive is always affirmative.

"So what do you do with the Torah text itself?" I ask. "It seems clear from Genesis, chapter 17, that the brit is with Abraham and his male descendants. There is no mention of brit in connection with Sarah, nor any ritual to mark her relationship with God—except perhaps becoming pregnant at ninety, but that isn't mentioned in relation to Sarah's personal covenant, nor is it something that women in later generations go through to enter into the covenant. We are told that Sarah will bear a son, Isaac, with whom God will establish a brit, but we never hear of a brit with Sarah herself. She receives a blessing, and becomes a 'mother of nations,' but the covenant itself seems to be reserved for men. If women are indeed members of the brit," I add, "why is there no ritual to mark our entrance into it?"

"Well," these rabbis answer, "women are automatically members of the brit when they are born. They do not need to be circumcised, because they are born whole."

"That's all very nice," I say, "and it pacifies me—for about a minute! If Sarah was born so whole, while Abraham needed completion, why didn't God speak to *her* instead of Abraham? Why didn't God choose *her* instead of Abraham, or at least as an equal partner with Abraham in the covenant? Why didn't God tell her, '*Lechi Lach*,' go forth?!"

Too often the answers sound like apologetics. I don't think that most male rabbis actually believe that women are born more whole than men, and if they do, I don't think that putting us on a pedestal solves many problems. It's no help being told you are superior if your experience is that of a second-class citizen. Actions *do* speak louder than words. But straight answers wouldn't hurt.

Each and every morning, observant Jewish males wake up and say their morning prayers, including the blessing "Blessed are You, Lord, our God, Ruler of the universe, for not having made me a woman."

Each and every morning, observant Jewish females wake up and say their morning prayers, including the following blessing: "Blessed are You, Lord, our God, Ruler of the universe, for having made me according to Divine will."

Each and every morning in school, when we said our morning prayers, the boys would stand up and thank God that they were not girls. Then they would sit down, and we, the girls, would stand up and say our *brachah*—saying, essentially, that we were satisfied with our inferior lot because it was God's will.

Throughout my childhood, on a daily basis, the religious ritual of my community reminded me of my lesser status. Throughout my childhood, on a daily basis, I was reminded of female subjugation, sanctioned in God's name.

Not one of us girls, whose parents raised us to believe that in the secular sphere we could grow up to be doctors and lawyers and judges, protested or even questioned the content of our morning blessing. It was not until later, when I reached adolescence—and saw my male peers at the age of bar mitzvah taking on more mitzvot, while I at the age of bat mitzvah was pushed further to the periphery of religious ritual—that I began to notice this contradiction. I had accepted my inferior religious status while knowing that I would never let my gender inhibit my aspirations in the secular sphere. These two worlds, religious and secular, which my parents had hoped could peacefully coexist, would remain at odds in my consciousness, because my status in each was so different. In the "outside world," as we called it, I perceived myself to be an equal, full participant with unlimited aspirations (although today I realize that even that is not true), while in our own religious community, I felt like a second-class citizen.

Today, when I pray each morning, I thank God for making me a woman. As a woman, I can bear, give birth to, and nourish (from my own body) my children. What incredible experiences and powers for God to have bestowed upon human beings! As a woman, I am also sensitive to injustice in the world. Because I experience that injustice in such a personal and essential way, my drive to help rectify it is especially great.

Thank God for having made me a woman.

One of the biggest differences between the Modern Orthodox community and the ultra-Orthodox community is that in Modern Orthodoxy there is much interaction between girls and boys, whereas ultra-Orthodox communities keep boys and girls separate until the time for *shiduchim*, matchmaking for the purpose of marriage. The arranging of these matches is highly controlled, as is all interaction between the sexes (which is limited in the ultra-Orthodox community). In contrast, in the Jewish day school I attended, boys and girls studied all subjects in coed classes. More important, perhaps, the fact that we learned everything together with the boys meant that we learned everything they did, even Talmud, which until twentieth-century America was rarely taught to girls in an institutional framework. In many Orthodox communities today, even some that are not ultra-Orthodox, women still do not study Talmud in a serious way.

When we were in fifth grade, girls and boys were separated for the first time: the girls were sent to home economics, and the boys to cantillation class. We learned how to cook and sew; the boys learned how to read from the sacred Torah scroll.

The school administration had taken the bold step of allowing us, the girls, to learn Talmud with the boys. They had opened up for us the world of Jewish learning, but they were not ready to allow us access to the Torah scroll itself; they were not willing to give us full entrée into the world of the sacred.

My bat mitzvah celebration was on a Shabbat morning at the shul—like most boys' bar mitzvah celebrations are. My friends and family met at the shul for services, and when the praying and reading from the Torah were over, we went into the social hall for *kiddush*, the blessing over the wine that is said at Shabbat and holiday meals, and *ha-motzi*, the blessing over the bread and the meal, and a catered lunch. After the meal was over, I delivered my *d'var torah*, my interpretive talk.

The particular logistics of this event were extremely important, because it was the first time in the history of our synagogue that a girl was having her bat mitzvah celebration in the shul itself and on Shabbat as an adjunct to the services. The idea of a bat mitzvah celebration in some way parallel to a bar mitzvah celebration is usually traced to the 1920s, when Rabbi Mordechai Kaplan, an Orthodox-ordained rabbi who would become the founder of Reconstructionist Judaism, had his daughter read from the *chumash*, a bound copy of the Torah text, before his congregation. There are in various Jewish communities some earlier examples of the marking of a girl's arriving at the age of mitzvot. Yet in my parents' generation, only boys celebrated their religious coming of age. If a girl did have a bat mitzvah celebration, it did not take place in shul on Shabbat morning, and usually there was no ritual or even learning involved. It consisted of a party, and that was all.

I don't remember if our "radical" approach was at my parents' initiative or my own. My parents saw no reason why they shouldn't celebrate their daughter's bat mitzvah in the shul they had been active in establishing and maintaining. It seemed a natural place to hold the event, for both logistical and emotional reasons. I was willing to be the first one to take this step.

It was crucial that my bat mitzvah not be considered an integral part of the service. That was the condition for being allowed to have it there at all. Our rabbi made clear that my speech would be delivered not in the sanctuary itself but in the social hall, and well after the end of the ritual activities.

I do not want to minimize the importance of the decision to allow me to have my celebration in the shul building. The fact that I was able to deliver a *d'var torah* was a step forward in our community and a product of how far Modern Orthodoxy had already moved. It was only because my parents decided to educate me as seriously in religious subjects as they did my brothers that I was able to write and deliver such a speech. My mother and the other women in her family never had this kind of Jewish education, and I am grateful to have been given the tools to understand and analyze the texts of my tradition. But I soon wanted more. By the age of thirteen, I would yearn to participate in all aspects of Jewish religious life.

The rabbi made his announcement: "The service is now officially over; please join Haviva's family in the social hall for a separate bat mitzvah celebration." This message of exclusion from ritual life became an indelible part of the way I saw my status as a Jew, even within the most liberal of Orthodox communities. *We will go only so far to include you*, I heard between his words. *We will give you what we can to appease you, but there are some boundaries that you can never cross. Unlike your brothers, you will never be a true insider.*

As I struggled in my teenage years with my place as a woman in Judaism, it was this same rabbi who gave me books to read and citations of texts to study. It was this rabbi who conducted my marriage ceremony, who sat with me and my husband-to-be to discuss what it means to build a Jewish home, and who recited blessings under our wedding canopy. It was also this rabbi who only a few years later spoke derisively of me from the pulpit after I had started wearing tefillin and tallit and publicly declared my desire to study to be an Orthodox rabbi.

The Shabbat after my bat mitzvah, I found my soon-to-be permanent seat next to my mother, behind the mechitzah. Once I had turned twelve, I had become a woman. Overnight, apparently, I had become a sexual distraction for the men. Before that time, I was not allowed to participate in the services because I, like the boys my age, was a minor; once I turned twelve, I was not allowed to participate because I was a woman. I was made to sit in the back, separated behind a barrier, on the sidelines of my own religion.

When our first daughter, Michal, was born, Jacob and I wanted her to start her life as a Jew who felt like an equal member of the Jewish people. Although the text of the Torah, the Sages in the Talmud, and the rabbis after them provide no ritual for marking a baby girl's entry into the brit, our tradition still teaches that God's intention is for the covenant to be with all Jews, men and women alike, and we wanted to perform a ritual that would symbolize her participation in this brit with God. We wanted it to be something physical, something she would experience through her body, something akin to *brit milah*, but nothing that would leave a mark on her perfect miniature body or make her experience pain.

On the seventh day after her birth we held a carefully crafted ceremony welcoming Michal into the brit, complete with songs, blessings, and rituals garnered from traditional sources, a variety of birth ceremonies others had done for their newborn daughters, and some of our own innovation and heartfelt creative outpouring at this emotional time. Most of the ceremonies we drew from were from families who are not Orthodox, although we did base a part of our ceremony on the *Zeved HaBat*, a traditional Sephardi ceremony for welcoming a baby girl. When I was born, parties were common, but ceremonies were unheard of. Today, it is becoming more and more acceptable even for Orthodox Jews to have some kind of formal ceremony for newborn girls. For Michal's *brit ha-bat* (covenant of the daughter), as we called it, Jacob and I chose the seventh day rather than the eighth, which is when boys have their *brit milah*, to follow the example of bat mitzvah, which occurs one year earlier for a girl than does bar mitzvah for a boy.

For our third child and second daughter, Meira, we would hold the ceremony on the fifteenth day, having heard of this idea from friends who had their daughter's ceremony on that day. This is based on the biblical notion that a woman is ritually impure for one week after the birth of a boy and for two weeks after the birth of a girl. The biblical text also explains that on the eighth day, the day the mother is once again sexually permitted to her husband after the birth of a boy, the circumcision is performed. There is no parallel ritual mentioned for a girl to be welcomed into the brit, but it would seem to us that if there were to be one, the fifteenth day, the day the mother is once again sexually permitted to her husband after the birth of a girl, would be the appropriate time to have it.

One of the rituals we performed at both of our daughters' ceremonies was dipping their hands into mikveh water. This was meant to evoke the commentary of the Meiri, Rabbi Menachem ben Solomon, who lived in Provence in the late thirteenth and early fourteenth centuries. He suggests that our foremother Sarah immersed herself in a mikveh as a sign of her brit with God at the same time that Abraham and the male members of his household were circumcised.[4]

Two months later, after Michal's umbilical cord had fallen off and the doctor said she could be bathed, and my bleeding had stopped and I had ritually immersed, Jacob and I brought Michal to the mikveh. We undressed her, carefully and lovingly, and dipped her feet in the warm water. "Do you think she'll be okay?" I asked. "Yes," Jacob reassured me. "The doctor said it was fine."

I stood naked, holding her, my tiny bundle, in my arms and walked down the seven steps into the clear blue water of the mikveh. All the feelings of intense emotion, power, responsibility, and love that I experienced the first time I saw my daughter resurfaced as I carried her, step by step, back into God's womb. I thought: *There can be no more appropriate ritual to bring our daughter, the product of our love and partnership with God, into the Jewish people. There can be no more appropriate means than mikveh, the ritual bath in which women throughout Jewish history have been immersing themselves after the cessation of their menstrual flow, for me to initiate my daughter into Jewish womanhood, with all its joys and conflicts, trials and responsibilities.*

As I stood in the mikveh with Michal, I blew into her face so that she would instinctively hold her breath, and then I dunked her. As I let go of her for a split second so that the water would touch every spot on her skin, I put what is most precious to me into the hands of God.

CHAPTER THREE

◆

Mitzvot: Commandments

And it shall constitute for you tzitzit, that you may see it and remember all of the commandments of God and perform them; and not explore after your heart and after your eyes after which you stray. So that you may remember and perform all of my commandments and be holy to your God.
— Numbers 15: 38–39

EVERY MORNING OF MY CHILDHOOD, I saw my father come down the stairs, walk into the library, and take his blue velvet bag from the wooden cabinet. He would take out his woolen blue and white tallit and drape it over his head like a shawl, its tassels dangling from the corners, and mumble some words in Hebrew that I now know were the blessing for wrapping oneself in a tallit followed by a selection from Psalms. Then he would take from this bag a smaller blue velvet bag, which contained his tefillin, two leather boxes with leather straps wound around them. These he would unwind, then wrap one around his arm, place the other on his head, and complete the task by winding the ends of the arm straps around his fingers. As he did these elaborate wrappings and windings, he would recite additional blessings and Hebrew verses. Then he would take out his pocket-size leatherbound *siddur*, a prayer book he kept in his velvet bag and used each morning, and begin his morning *tefillah*.

My father liked to sing his *tefillot* out loud as he paced around the house, or greet people as they came downstairs, and he had the odd habit of looking through his mail and other papers as he paced. He is a fidgety man who needs to putter—even when talking to God.

I loved to watch my father perform this morning ritual. I loved to watch the leather straps being wrapped tightly around his arm—which to me then seemed as muscular as Popeye's—leaving indentations in his skin that would last for at least an hour after he removed the tefillin. Although his singing voice was the butt of many of our childhood jokes, I also loved to listen to his chanting as he paced. There was something calming, almost hypnotic, about the way he wandered and sang. This was something I could count on every morning, no matter what the special circumstances. Even if we were catching an early morning flight for a family trip, there he would be, pacing and chanting, as my mother ran about making sure that we were all packed, and the rest of us rolled out of bed and into the taxi cab like zombies, half asleep.

This was something I knew my father had been doing every morning since he was a boy of thirteen. It was something I never expected my mother to do. I simply accepted the fact that only fathers did this, even though at my school girls and boys alike had to pray each morning. My mother didn't pray in the mornings at all, except on Shabbat in the synagogue, and even then she arrived at shul later than my father did and sat with the other women behind the wrought-iron mechitzah.

When I was younger, I accepted these differences in my parents' morning rituals as one of the many ways in which their roles in our family differed. Just as my father was the one we asked for our allowance, and my mother was the one we asked if we could go to a friend's house, my father was the one who talked to God, and my mother was the one who kept the house running so that he could have the time to do so.

The year after my bat mitzvah, one after another the boys in my grade turned thirteen, the age at which a boy becomes responsible for his own actions, the age of bar mitzvah.

I had witnessed my older brother's bar mitzvah and the enormous preparation that went into it. The party itself was much more lavish than my own, but that is not what bothered me. I spent a few months preparing the speech for my bat mitzvah, which paled in comparison to the year Jonathan had spent in preparation for his bar mitzvah. After all, not only did he have to deliver a *d'var torah*, he also had to read an entire portion from the Torah scroll without any punctuation or vowels, all with the correct musical notes, as well as lead the prayer service and read the Haftarah, a reading from the Prophets, also according to the correct musical notes. The thought of performing this enormous one-person show was frightening. When my brother prepared for his bar mitzvah, I knew that my parents would not expect this of me, and I was more relieved that I would not be called upon to perform in this manner than jealous of his more involved initiation ritual.

Once I saw my male peers reaching the age of bar mitzvah, reading from the Torah and leading the service, I awoke to the inequity of the religious laws. All the boys in my class managed to pull it off, even those who received much poorer grades than I did in the religious subjects in school. I began to feel that I had been cheated by not even being allowed to try. This was a rite of passage that all boys went through to prepare them for the challenges of adulthood as responsible and active members of our religious community, but my female peers and I were not expected to live up to these challenges. Chanting from the Torah was not a skill that an Orthodox Jewish girl needed to learn—when would she use it? Women did not get close enough to touch the Torah, let alone read from it.

As the boys in my class became of bar mitzvah age, they began to show up for school *tefillot* in the mornings with their tefillin, which are worn during morning prayers on weekdays. Since the boys had been three years old, they always wore their tzitzit and *kippot*, while the girls did not. These differences felt merely sociological, like boys having short hair and girls wearing skirts and dresses. It was a dress code disparity that didn't hold great religious significance for us; it seemed natural because it had been introduced at such a young age. But when the boys who had for years been wearing their *kippot* and tzitzit showed up in seventh grade with their new blue velvet bags containing their shining leather tefillin, I was bothered terribly. They had something tangible to show for their new status as adults in our religious community. I had nothing. Coming of age for my male peers meant taking on more mitzvot, from which we girls were excluded. There were no new rituals or synagogue skills to mark our Jewish adulthood.

I watched from the other side of the mechitzah as the boys in my class wrapped the leather tefillin straps around their forearms and placed them like crowns on their heads. The boxes, which contain the sacred verses of the Shema, are placed between their eyes and on their biceps as a reminder of how this proclamation of God's oneness should always be on their minds and integrated into their actions. I longed for some tangible ritual to draw me closer to God at this turning point in my life as a Jew, but there was nothing. At the close of my first year as a newly initiated responsible member of the Jewish people, I was beginning to taste the alienation that would plague me as a religiously observant Jewish woman.

In order to feel like an insider in my own tradition, as a young woman I would need to remain an outsider in the synagogue and with respect to a number of mitzvot that were central to Jewish religious practice.

I first put on tefillin ten years after my bat mitzvah. I was married and living in Washington, D.C., worlds away from the close-knit Orthodox community in which I had grown up.

One evening on the phone, I told my mother that I planned to have a second bat mitzvah at Fabrangen, an informal and completely egalitarian prayer community, the *havurah* in which I had become active. It would be on Shabbat, and I would read from the Torah. I had not yet confessed to my mother that I had been regularly participating in egalitarian services. The geographic distance between us made me brave.

My mother's disappointment was evident in her silence, and then in the tension in her voice. "Joining an egalitarian havurah isn't a good answer to your religious questions," she said. "You're settling for quick and easy solutions, and that will get you nowhere. You'll be sorry later. The people in this havurah of yours aren't committed to halakhah. They'll never provide a solid Jewish community for you."

I told her that I agreed with much of what she was claiming. In fact, I would later leave this havurah for the very reason that she mentioned. "It's true that most of them don't observe Shabbat or *kashrut* strictly," I explained, "but the *tefillah* is more sincere and uplifting than any I have experienced before. It's real prayer, not just words they're mumbling out of habit."

"You're trying to tell me that you can't find any Orthodox shul with nice *tefillot*? There are plenty of Hasidic shuls with beautiful *tefillot*. You aren't being fair."

She was right. I hadn't looked for a Hasidic shul, although I doubt that there were any in Washington, D.C., but that wasn't the point. My mother was trying to tell me that she knew that my choice of prayer community was not just about finding spiritual *tefillah*. It was also about egalitarianism, and she was correct.

I tried to explain to my mother: I wanted to be part of a Judaism that was both egalitarian and committed to halakhah, tradition, and mitzvot, or at least in a serious dialogue with the tradition. In other words, ideally I wanted to be part of a community struggling with the integration of modernity into a living Judaism, without casting off all laws that seemed inconvenient, irrelevant, distasteful, or difficult—and one that also viewed greater women's participation in ritual as increasing the community's capacity for holiness, not watering it down.

"If and when I have daughters," I told my mother, "I want them to do all the mitzvot, including the ones they aren't obligated to perform."

"Like what?" my mother asked.

"Like tefillin," I immediately answered, as though it were obvious. *Of course my daughters would pray with tefillin*, I thought. Yet in that moment I realized: How could I expect a daughter of mine to put on tefillin if I didn't do so myself? I would have to be a role model for her. I would have to commit to putting on tefillin every morning, and I would have to start before my children were born.

The next morning, Jacob presented me with my first pair of tefillin. They had belonged to his great-uncle. They were old and worn; the black paint was chipping from the leather, and they were significantly larger than the ones that contain the scrolls of the size that most *sofrim*, religious scribes, write today.

Jacob showed me how to put on my new tefillin. Standing behind me, he demonstrated how to wrap the straps that attach to one of the boxes around my arm and put the other box on my head, letting the straps from that box hang down over my chest. He told me at which point in putting on the tefillin I should say the various *b'rachot*. My hands trembled as I wrapped the straps; my voice shook as I recited the words.

Wearing tefillin for the first time felt so strange. I had seen only men do it, and even though I knew intellectually that I was permitted according to halakhah to wear these ritual objects, I still felt as if I were breaking a taboo. Some rabbis maintain that a woman should not perform this mitzvah because she does not have a *guf naki*, a clean body. That idea resonated in my head, along with the strong visual image of men and boys praying in tefillin. I had never seen a woman in tefillin, yet I felt reborn as a religious Jewish feminist. The two worlds of my childhood, the modern and the Orthodox, actually met fully within me. For the first time in a long time, I did not feel torn apart.

As I recited the biblical verse that refers to tefillin while wearing them, I felt a strong connection to generations past. Our Torah, our most ancient religious Jewish document, tells us to wear tefillin. Although we do not know exactly when the verse was first interpreted to describe the ritual objects we use today, I knew that Jews have been wearing tefillin similar to mine for thousands of years!

Wearing the tefillin was distracting at first, as I imagine it is at the beginning for any person who starts performing this mitzvah, including bar mitzvah boys. I was so aware of their presence on my arm and head that I had trouble meditating on the prayers themselves; I was too busy thinking about the tefillin and why I was wearing them. It was also difficult to get used to the actual physical sensation. I have come to see this heightened awareness of the tefillin as one of the reasons for wearing them. When the novelty of wearing the tefillin wore off, they helped me focus on my prayers and the words I was saying. Prayer has become a more physical act that requires my whole self, my entire being, body and spirit.

Other aspects of Jewish prayer have a similar effect—synchronized bowing, standing, sitting, swaying, covering our eyes, stepping forward and backward—but none of these movements is as regular or tangible as tefillin. They are "signs," as they are called in the Shema, physical reminders of our love for God and the mitzvot.

Wearing tefillin has also helped me to take *tefillah* more seriously. Prayer now includes the concrete physical act of wrapping the tefillin and the commitment to perform this act every day. Prayer can feel so amorphous and subjective. It would be easier to tell myself on busy mornings, "Well, I'll just pray on the bus or as I walk the kids to school." My prayer has had to become more serious and deliberate. My commitment to wearing tefillin when I pray has forced me to set aside much-needed time and space each morning to spend with God—no excuses accepted.

When I finished my morning prayers that first day of wearing tefillin, Jacob showed me how to rewrap the straps around the boxes and put them away in their bag. Reversing precisely the steps of putting them on, we unwind the straps from around the fingers, take off the head tefillin and put them away, unwind the straps from around the arm and put the arm tefillin away. Everything about these objects is ritualized; they are to be treated with such care and attention to detail that one cannot help but be aware of their holiness.

It was obvious to me, as I put the tefillin back in their bag, that discouraging women from wearing tefillin is only one of the ways the Rabbis surrounded these ritual objects with rules and regulations. There is a specific time to wear them, a prescribed way to put them on and take them off, and a particular group who should wear them. Guarding their holiness also means restricting and structuring their use.

Yet I believe that I bring a new holiness to the mitzvah of tefillin when I don them to pray. By wearing tefillin I am, perhaps, chipping away at some of the restrictions intended to intensify their holiness. However, my adoption of this mitzvah works toward the same goal the Rabbis had in mind. My decision to lay tefillin every morning, and to take this as a serious religious obligation, is a testament to the beauty and spiritual power of this mitzvah, so charged with spiritual and historical meaning. Now that, thank God, most contemporary Jews (even within Orthodoxy) would agree that a woman's body is no more physically unclean than a man's, a woman taking on this mitzvah no longer desecrates the tefillin; instead, she affirms their sanctity.

This is a male tradition; male scholars interpreted this biblical verse with only men in mind. Why choose to make this mitzvah my own? Why not create a new ritual, a female reinterpretation of this commandment?

This is the mitzvah we were given in the Torah. It is our tradition, practiced by Jews through the Crusades, the Inquisition, pogroms, and the Holocaust. It is a profound practice, beautiful and powerful. Because I saw my father pray this way each morning, this image is ingrained in my mind: a person absorbed in prayer, swaying meditatively in deep concentration, wearing a tallit and tefillin. It is possible to draw the image anew for our children and ourselves, making the body of a woman in that mental picture interchangeable with that of a man. I have to step into that picture in order for it to become flexible for my children.

The tradition about who should wear tefillin can evolve in a changing world without detracting from the spiritual power of the tefillin themselves. The adoption of this mitzvah by more serious observant Jews enhances their significance. Since I began wearing tefillin, I feel as if my prayers are lifted to a higher plane, coming from a deeper place. I feel bound to God as I bind God's words to my arm and head with these holy straps, wind them around my finger like a wedding ring, and recite the verses from Hosea: *I will betroth you to Me forever; I will betroth you to Me with righteousness, justice, kindness, and mercy. I will betroth you to Me with fidelity, and you will know God.*

As a child, putting on tefillin would have felt almost as transgressive as eating pork. I did not know the intricacies of the laws relating to women wearing tefillin; I just knew that women did not wear them. No one *told* me that my body was unclean; the words were not necessary. I was a girl and would someday become a woman. Somehow my skin and my entire body were different from that of my brothers.

The first time that I pressed the holy leather of Jacob's great-uncle's tefillin next to my skin, I knew I had taken back a mitzvah that had been stolen from me, that was rightfully mine. Smiling to myself, I imagined the man whose tefillin I was inheriting somewhere in another realm, shaking his head and sighing, "Oy! What is this world coming to? Women putting on tefillin! Next thing you know, men will be changing diapers!"

Once I began laying tefillin, Jacob kept encouraging me to take on the mitzvah of tzitzit, which would mean wearing a tallit while praying in the mornings, and a *tallit katan* underneath my shirt while it is light outside. It is one of his own favorite mitzvot. He could not understand why I would take on laying tefillin every day yet not wear tzitzit. "Tzitzit are so much easier," he would tell me over and over again. "You just put them on, and then you're done."

It made sense rationally, but it felt like a bigger emotional step for me. The tzitzit would be with me, on me, all day long. Unlike tefillin, the tallit is worn even on Shabbat. If I took on the obligation to perform this mitzvah, I would have to wear my tallit in shul on Shabbat, even in Orthodox synagogues (where I often pray) and even at my parents' and my in-laws' synagogues when I was visiting. It would mean coming out of the closet as a "radical" religious Jewish feminist. I would be making a statement every time I prayed in any Orthodox shul.

If I was going to have to defend myself at every turn, I needed to first feel absolutely certain that I was on the right path.

One morning, that feeling of certainty came over me as I was praying the morning service, reciting the Shema. The third paragraph in that prayer (a passage from the biblical book of Numbers), which Jews (or, according to Orthodox halakhah, Jewish men) are obligated to recite three times each day, contains God's commandment to wear fringes, tzitzit, on the corners of our garments. Once a day during the daylight hours, when we recite this prayer and say the word "tzitzit" (which appears three times in the prayer), the traditional practice is to kiss the fringes on the *tallit katan* or *gadol*.

Although a woman is not halakhically required to recite the Shema, traditionally boys and girls, men and women, are expected to recite this paragraph as part of our daily morning prayers. Somehow, as I child, it never seemed strange to me to recite God's commandment to us to wear tzitzit even though it was clear that my female peers and I were not considered obligated to wear them—and even more, that we *shouldn't* wear them.

On that particular morning, as I recited the Shema, the words jumped out at me. The contradiction aroused me from years of empty recitation. For twenty-two years I had been reciting this prayer without truly meaning what I was saying, and I knew that I would never again recite that paragraph during morning prayers without wearing tzitzit and kissing the fringes while I said the word "tzitzit," just as I had seen the men and boys around me doing since my childhood.

I believe that I am commanded by God to wear tzitzit. The traditional rationale behind a woman's exemption from this mitzvah is that it is a time-bound commandment. The commandment to wear tzitzit only applies during daylight hours, when they can be seen by natural light (although there is no prohibition against wearing them at night), and women are exempt from most positive commandments connected with a particular time of day or year. However, I cannot find a reason that women as a class today should be exempt from performing this mitzvah, which sanctifies our bodies and the clothing with which we cover our nakedness. It is a constant reminder of what is expected of us as Jewish people bound by the mitzvot. As the verse in Numbers 15:39 tells us, the mitzvah of tzitzit is to remind us of all of God's mitzvot so that we will perform them, not sway after our hearts and eyes, and therefore be holy. The essence of the mitzvah has no relation to time. It seems as though women are missing out on the power of performing this mitzvah because of a technicality. I imagine that God is, as it were, waiting for Jewish women to reclaim this mitzvah, to say, "It is ours, too! How dare you take it away from us!"

For a woman to perform this mitzvah, as well as the others from which she is exempt, the drive must flow from within her. There are many women who feel comfortable in the ritual role that halakhah has thus far carved out for them. I do hope that masses of women will eventually see the beauty in these mitzvot and set aside their exemption, as they have historically done with other positive timebound mitzvot, such as *shofar* (hearing the blowing of the ram's horn on Rosh Hashanah) and sukkah (sitting in a temporary hut on Sukkot). Until then, the smaller number of us who feel a deep connection to the mitzvot of tefillin and tzitzit should be able to grow in our religious practice, free of discouragement from others.

The reason given by the Rema to discourage women from taking upon themselves this mitzvah is *yoharah*, pride or arrogance.[1] This characteristic is generally mentioned in halakhic literature in relation to excessive piety in the performance of mitzvot. For example, a groom who insists that he can on his wedding night concentrate while reciting the Shema, despite his exemption from doing so, is considered guilty of *yoharah*.

Why should performing this particular mitzvah be considered arrogant, while hearing the *shofar* or sitting in the sukkah is not? It is interesting that the majority opinion in halakhah does not take issue with women performing other mitzvot from which they are exempt. It is only tefillin and tzitzit, holy objects or garments, that cause the problem. Perhaps the discomfort of the Rema, and various other *poskim* after the talmudic period, with a woman performing these two mitzvot reflects a view of women as inferior, less holy in some ways, and not worthy of placing a sacred garment or ritual object on their bodies. As an observant woman, I find these mitzvot especially meaningful, because they help me to see my body as worthy of bearing sanctity—an idea that many women, including myself, may find difficult to internalize after years of absorbing implicit messages to the contrary.

Women, too, need to be reminded of the mitzvot. Tzitzit are a visual reminder of God's will and God's presence in our lives at each and every moment of the day, and I know that I need such a reminder. Even when I am spending the entire day sitting and studying Torah, it is easy, for example, to forget to pray the afternoon prayer service before sundown. When I am spending the day with my young, demanding children, it is even easier to forget to perform certain mitzvot, especially those that must be performed at a certain time. That is one of the rationales for exempting women from timebound mitzvot, but it also is a strong argument *for* women wearing tzitzit. The mitzvah of tzitzit is not an act that comes and goes as the hands of the clock turn. It serves as a reminder to perform other mitzvot.

My tzitzit remind me all day of what I would like to be. They remind me that my body should be sanctified and that I was created in the image of God. Despite the criticism and even occasional berating I receive, despite the fact that it sets me apart from almost every other religious (and nonreligious) Jewish woman,[2] I wear tzitzit to remind me of my responsibilities.

There is no explicit reason given in the Talmud for women's exemption from positive timebound commandments, but theories abound in the writings of medieval and modern religious thinkers. Probably the most common view (although there is no textual basis for it in traditional rabbinic sources) is that the exemption is given because women are busy raising children, so their time is left flexible to devote to the erratic schedule of child rearing, an equally important task.[3]

Rabbi Samson Raphael Hirsch, writing in nineteenth-century Germany, suggests that women are spiritually superior to men (both innately and due to their more cloistered existence away from the temptations and distractions of the world outside the home), and therefore do not need these mitzvot.[4] Others, like thirteenth-century Rabbi Jacob Anatoli, say that a woman should serve her husband, so the Rabbis didn't want to obligate her in mitzvot that might take her away from her God-given role.[5] Rabbi David ben Joseph Abudraham of the fourteenth century posits a similar explanation, although he does not declare that women *should* be subservient to their husbands, stating only that women *are*, as a point of fact, and that the Rabbis did not want to create a situation where women's husbands would be asking them to do one thing for them while the women would also have to, for example, lay tefillin. In order to preserve peace in the home (*shalom bayit*), the Rabbis exempted women from some of the mitzvot that must be performed at a specific time.[6]

Another popular explanation suggested by the contemporary Rabbis Emanuel Rackman and Norman Lamm[7], among others, is that women are innately more aware of the sanctity of time due to their bodily cycle. They do not need these timebound mitzvot, which are designed in part to make us aware of time and its cyclical nature and to sanctify it. They add that if and when a woman marries and keeps the laws of *niddah* (in which the couple abstains from sexual relations while the woman is menstruating and for seven days after she stops bleeding) and mikveh, that will serve as a substitute for the timebound mitzvot.

Another theory is that the category of positive timebound mitzvot is descriptive and not prescriptive, because there are many positive timebound mitzvot that a woman *is* required to perform. In other words, the category of positive timebound mitzvot came *after* the fact that women were not performing these mitzvot, but women do not perform them for a number of other reasons. The category, then, more or less describes many mitzvot from which women are exempt, but it is not an all-encompassing principle. (The Gemara itself points this out in BT *Kiddushin* 33b.) Rabbi Saul Berman, another contemporary Modern Orthodox rabbi and one of the proponents of this theory, prefers to use the categories of public mitzvot and private mitzvot, and writes that women are exempt from these mitzvot perhaps because they are public rituals and women may be innately more private beings, or perhaps because the Rabbis were sending the message that women *should be* more private than men.[8]

None of these theories includes all of the mitzvot from which women are exempt. For instance, women's exemption from wearing tzitzit is not explained by any of these theories. If it is a public versus private issue, tzitzit are not a public ritual, so why are women exempt from wearing them? If the Rabbis were worried about children, wearing tzitzit does not interfere with the hectic life of a parent. The mitzvah does not require any time commitment whatsoever. Nor do tzitzit remind us of the cyclical nature of time.

These theories also do not reflect the historical reality of the time in which the exemption arose. A woman in talmudic times lived with her husband's family and would most likely have had a number of other women around to care for her children while she performed a mitzvah. Moreover, her husband would have been equally busy with household maintenance work, or the couple would have had servants to perform household and childcare duties, in which case both husband and wife would have been free to perform mitzvot.[9]

As for the idea that women do not need these mitzvot because we are on a higher spiritual level than men and don't require so many reminders during the day of the mitzvot and God's majesty, this theory simply does not ring true for me. Women *do* have many positive obligations that must be performed within a certain period of time (even though they are not technically classified as positive timebound mitzvot), such as Shabbat candlelighting and Grace After Meals (which must be recited within a certain period of time after eating a meal). Thus, the notion that we are in some way above performing positive mitzvot linked to particular times does not make sense. In addition, because the Rabbis of the Talmud so often portray women as distracting men from spirituality (not leading them toward it), it is intellectually dishonest to claim that the Sages exempted women from these mitzvot because women are spiritually superior.

Many of the apparent sociological underpinnings for women's exemptions are no longer applicable. Fathers often have substantial parenting responsibilities today. If women are exempt from timebound mitzvot because of their parenting responsibilities, men who are caring for their children should also be exempt. Women are also clearly active in the public sphere today, challenging our exemption from what Berman calls the public mitzvot.

Furthermore, keeping the laws of niddah and mikveh does not take the place of mitzvot like tefillin, *shofar,* or sukkah. I don't understand how one could be said to substitute in any way for the other; they are such different experiences. Praying with tefillin each morning adds an element to my spiritual life that is not fulfilled through the mitzvot associated with menstruation. All of these are important mitzvot in my life, but they fulfill very different functions.

Our lives are radically different from women's lives during the time of the Talmud. Women today, like men, are active in a world that is very much governed by the clock. Even with menstruation as a reminder of the cycle of the moon, we live our daily lives by clock time, not lunar time. Whether we are working outside the home or as "stay-at-home parents," there are schedules to keep that can often seem to take over our lives. Women as well as men need to stop and remind ourselves that there is a Higher Power more important than the clock, that time itself is in the hands of God.

Most important, perhaps, the theories that the mitzvot of niddah and mikveh should substitute for the positive timebound mitzvot and that the exemption was granted to allow time to devote to child rearing do not apply to postmenopausal women, women without children, and women whose children are grown. This is not a minority of women, and halakhah must address them. Even allowing for the higher percentage of women's lives that was devoted to childbearing and rearing in the ancient world, it would still be strange for halakhah to have been designed with only those women in mind.

The perspective that I find most convincing is suggested by Professor Judith Hauptman in her book, *Rereading the Rabbis: A Woman's Voice*. She defines the category of positive timebound mitzvot as mitzvot that will come your way no matter what the circumstances of your life. Hauptman posits that women were exempt from performing this category of mitzvot, which she calls "the highest form of ritual act,"[10] in order to restrict their performance to men, the heads of household.

The mishnah (an individual unit in the work known as the Mishnah) where this exemption first appears is found among other *mishnayot* that deal with acquiring a wife and with the hierarchy of society in mishnaic times. In these *mishnayot* we find that slaves, like women, were also exempt from certain mitzvot. From the context of this mishnah, it seems clear that women's exemption stemmed from their lower social status. There is no doubt that men were of higher social standing than women in the time of the Mishnah, when this exemption first appears in halakhic literature; therefore, it is easy to understand why the Rabbis would have placed women on a lower rung on the ladder of religious worship. Dr. Noam Zohar puts forth a similar argument in his article, "Women Then and Religious Status:

Deciphering a Chapter in Mishnah": "Women were excluded from certain rituals and commandments not because of some inherent incapacity, but because of social stratification. Like slaves, they are partly barred from direct access to God by the interposition of 'another master.'"[11]

Whatever the original reason for this exemption, it is interesting to note that many mitzvot in this positive timebound category are performed by women today with no objection from contemporary rabbis. In fact, women are encouraged to perform them.

For example, it has become the practice in most Orthodox communities to have a special *shofar* blowing for women who missed hearing the blasts in synagogue because of a conflict with their responsibilities at home. Although women are not required by the letter of the law to hear the *shofar*, they are strongly encouraged to perform this mitzvah nevertheless. The practice is so strong that, until I learned the halakhah on this matter from the original sources, I had always assumed that women are required to hear the *shofar*.

Tefillin and tzitzit are treated differently. Both tefillin and tzitzit are mitzvot that fit into this category of positive timebound mitzvot. Tefillin are traditionally worn only during the morning prayers (although during talmudic times, tefillin were worn all day and classified as timebound because they were not worn at night or on Shabbat and holidays), and tzitzit are required to be worn only during daylight hours. Women are obligated to wear neither tefillin nor tzitzit, nor are they encouraged to take these mitzvot upon themselves if they feel able and willing. "*Mochin b'yadan*"—we protest their actions, the Rema writes about women wearing tefillin. As I have mentioned, he based his opinion not on the Babylonian Talmud but rather on a contradictory passage from the Jerusalem Talmud (the less authoritative of the two), and on the writings of the Tosafot, who raise the issue of *guf naki*, bodily cleanliness.

It is unclear if the Tosafot thought that a woman's body was inherently less clean than a man's. Two teachings about *guf naki* appear in the Talmud (in *Shabbat* 49a and 130a) in relation to tefillin: one should not pass gas or sleep (lest one pass gas or ejaculate unconsciously) while wearing tefillin. Could the Tosafot have believed that women pass gas more than men, or have less control over this bodily function than men have? Another explanation of *guf naki*[12] connects it, understandably, with menstruation, since that is the one bodily function unique to women that could be considered "unsanitary."

Another possible explanation is that women are no less clean than men, but because a woman is not obligated to wear tefillin, she should not take the risk of sullying these holy objects. Because a man is obligated, he must take the risk, even though his body is unclean and he too passes gas.[13] Perhaps, as the Magen Avraham asserts, because women are not obligated in this mitzvah, they may not be as careful as men are regarding proper cleanliness during its performance.[14]

Women are discouraged from wearing tzitzit for a different reason altogether. The biblical commandment is to wear fringes on any four-cornered garment; today people no longer wear four-cornered garments, so technically no one must wear tzitzit. However, in order to preserve this central mitzvah, men and boys customarily wear a separate four-cornered garment beneath their clothing all day long, as well as the four-cornered tallit during the morning service. As noted earlier, the Rema considered a woman who decides to take on these extra obligations guilty of *yoharah*.[15] She is, in effect, taking upon herself a mitzvah that she is doubly not required to perform: once because she is a woman, and once because (like a man) she wouldn't normally be wearing a four-cornered garment. According to this logic, she is displaying an arrogant attitude of excessive piety in her performance of mitzvot.

Women's exemption from this mitzvah emerges from the writings of rabbis living in a period when women had little autonomy or power and few rights, and most women had little or no education. It is not difficult to understand the Rabbis' fear of *yoharah* in relation to women and tzitzit, which are considered an obligation for men as well as a privilege and an honor. Perhaps it did seem incongruous then for women, who were of a lower social standing than men, to be taking on this mitzvah, which already requires the wearer to go out of his (or her) way to perform it. The Maharil (Rabbi Yaakov ben Moshe haLevi Moellin of Mainz), a fourteenth- and fifteenth-century rabbi who was the first to raise *yoharah* as an issue regarding women wearing tzitzit, mentions this reason, but he also argues there that women are not included at all in the 613 mitzvot to which Jews are obligated. He writes the following:

It also seems to me that the essence of the law of tzitzit is to remember all the commandments of God . . . And women are not included in the 613 commandments . . . They are a "people unto themselves."[16] Therefore, based on all the reasons mentioned, even though I have seen women wearing four-cornered garments with fringes, and still today there is one woman in our neighborhood [who does so], it seems to me astonishing and is considered arrogant of them, and they are called fools.[17]

The Maharil's reasoning understands women's exclusion from these mitzvot not as merely an exemption but almost as a prohibition. It is an unusual approach within halakhic literature. Most opinions hold that women do receive a reward for performing even the mitzvot from which they are exempt,[18] which would not make sense if women were, in fact, a "people unto themselves" in relation to the mitzvot. The more mainstream opinion is that women are included in the 613 mitzvot, but exempt from some of them for whatever unknown reason.

The Maharil's position is troubling, not only for its basic sexism but also because of the extent to which it excludes women from the fundamental observances and obligations of Jewish life. When he groups *yoharah* with foolishness in relation to women and mitzvot, distancing himself from women, relating to them as the "other" by calling them a "people unto themselves," the misogynist attitudes of his time color his approach. As Aviva Cayam writes, in her article, "Fringe Benefits: Women and Tzitzit": "The social environment, common practice, and tone of the times all factor into the rabbinic determination of arrogant religious behavior."[19]

The Talmud relates the story of Kimchit, a woman so righteous that she didn't let even the beams in her house "see" a strand of her hair.[20] Why, we might ask, when a woman wants to take upon herself additional mitzvot, is she guilty of *yoharah*? It is (apparently) appropriate, even praiseworthy, for a woman to take upon herself extra stringencies when it comes to modesty, but when it comes to prayer, ritual, and touching holy objects, a woman who wants to go beyond the limits of her obligations is considered unseemly, even arrogant.

We need to read these sources with a critical eye as we make contemporary decisions about women and mitzvot. Surprisingly (or perhaps not), the Rabbis themselves leave us room to disagree with them.

Even with the strong language of *mochin b'yadan*, no rabbi actually forbids a woman to do these mitzvot. If the Rabbis had wanted to forbid their performance for all women and all times, they could have done so. However, discouraging is not forbidding; even protesting is not forbidding. I would like to believe that the Rabbis were saying, in effect: "We will try to prevent you, but in the end, it is your decision. If you must, go ahead."

Perhaps the Rabbis could even envision a future in which women would take these mitzvot upon themselves. The Maharil did mention Rabbanit Bruna, the woman in his community who wore tzitzit. And the sages in the Talmud did relate the story of Michal; the compiler of the Gemara could have left her out. Perhaps even then they could foresee a time when more women would follow in Michal's path, a time when women taking on previously "male" mitzvot would be considered a positive development.

Whether or not the Orthodox rabbinical establishment wants to recognize it, we have already reached that time today with regard to some of the mitzvot. Many women have already taken upon themselves the obligations of Torah study and formal prayer, as well as hearing the *shofar*, waving the *lulav* (the "four species" used on the holiday of Sukkot), and dwelling in a sukkah. Perhaps the Rabbis of old had an unconscious sense that women's full inclusion, in its time, would be part of *tikkun olam*, repairing our broken world.

The summer after I took upon myself the mitzvot of tzitzit and tefillin, my daughter Michal was conceived. Was being blessed with a daughter a sign from God that I was on the right track, that I am indeed a proper role model for a religious Jewish girl?

My mother is visiting us in Israel for two weeks during our first year of living here. She volunteers to dress Michal for *gan*. I have an intuition, when they come into the kitchen for breakfast, that my mother did not put tzitzit on Michal, but I am not sure.

"Mom," I say, "did you remember to put on Michal's tzitzit?"

"She didn't want to wear them," my mother answers. "She told me quite emphatically that she did not want to wear them. It was her own decision."

Just the other day, my mother and I had been discussing the topic of Michal's tzitzit.

"It's not fair to make her an outcast like this," my mother had argued. "It's your own agenda, not hers."

I agreed with my mother that it would not be fair to force Michal to wear tzitzit if she expressed a strong discomfort with it, but so far she hadn't, I explained.

It seems too much of a coincidence that today, all of a sudden, Michal has decided that she does not want to wear her tzitzit—only a few days after my mother and I had that discussion.

"Who brought it up, you or Michal?" I ask.

"What does it matter?" is my mother's reply, as she walks over to the stovetop to light the flame under the kettle. "She just doesn't want to wear them."

Her disapproval is not simply criticism. She worries about her granddaughter, just like she worried—and still worries—about me.

Michal has started first grade. It is exciting and rewarding to see my first child growing up, although these emotions are peppered with simultaneous feelings of sorrow and nostalgia. I remember Michal as a pudgy, precocious baby and feel a twinge of sadness that I will never be able to bring back those times.

As she has grown older, Michal has worn her *tallit katan* less and less often. Now that she is more aware of her surroundings, socially involved, and self-conscious, she is embarrassed to be different. Yet she also knows how important it is to me and Jacob that she wear her *tallit katan*. Sometimes she does wear it, though now always with the fringes tucked in. She even had me shorten the strings on one pair so that they wouldn't hang down lower than the hemline of her dresses. "I don't want people to see that I am wearing tzitzit," she has admitted to me. "They will laugh at me."

Understandably, on the first day of first grade, Michal did not wear her *tallit katan,* and I did not force the issue. On the third day, when I asked her if the children say a *brachah* on their tzitzit during *tefillot* in her school, she told me that they do, and that there are some boys who wear a *tallit katan* underneath their clothing and some boys who wear a child-size tallit over their clothing for *tefillot.* I asked her if she would like to do either one, and I was pleasantly surprised to hear that she wanted me to buy her a tallit.

Excitedly, I ran out the next day to find a child-size tallit that she would like enough to wear, and I was delighted to discover a beautiful, colorful one, with flowers, pomegranates, and a lovely picture of the Old City of Jerusalem.

Michal loved it when I showed it to her, and she wore it the next day, Shabbat, in the children's *tefillot* at shul. However, on Sunday (a regular school day and workday in Israel), when I told her that I was putting it in her school bag, she said that she had decided to wear it only on Shabbat.

I was disappointed, but I didn't let Michal know. I could see the conflict on her face as she hesitated, half smiling and half frowning, when she told me her decision. She did not want to let me down, yet she also did not want to be different. Like any child, she wants to be accepted by her peers.

"But why did you tell me that you wanted me to buy you a tallit?" I asked, trying to hide my annoyance.

"I thought I wanted to, but I changed my mind. I'm allowed to change my mind. Right?" she asked, quoting back to me my own refrain. "People are allowed to change their minds," I often tell my children. This is not the first time they have used my own wisdom against me.

I told her that in her school, which is made up of a mix of religious and secular children, there are many children from various types of families. They are all different from one another, and so they will respect her family custom. Her teacher, I added, said that she could wear the tallit in class, so she needn't be afraid or embarrassed.

My reassuring did not help. She refused to be the only girl wearing a tallit. As if to appease me, she said she would wear her *tallit katan* that day and say the *brachah* on those tzitzit. I asked her if she would wear the *tallit gadol* if there were another girl wearing one in her class, and she said yes. I left it at that.

Later that day, I telephoned the parents of a girl in her class who I thought would be open to the idea of their daughter wearing a tallit. Coincidentally, the father said that their daughter had recently asked them to buy her a tallit for school. She was the *hazanit* (prayer leader) and noticed that when boys lead *tefillot* they wear a tallit but that she was not offered one. The parents had decided to buy their daughter a tallit. I was thrilled.

Today, Michal switches back and forth between enthusiastically wearing and not wearing her *tallit katan* and *tallit gadol*. After nearly two months of not wearing her *tallit katan* underneath her clothing to her new school, she woke up early one morning, dressed herself, and came into our bedroom.

"Look," she said proudly, pulling up her shirt. "I'm wearing my tzitzit today!" She said this with a big smile, and since then she has been wearing her *tallit katan* and kippah every day, even to school.

I truly feel for Michal. It is not easy to be my daughter. I sympathize with her, for I remember what it was like to have to choose between the path that would surely disappoint my parents and the path that felt most true to my nature. I hope that she will choose the path that is right for her and not base her decision upon what she knows will please me most. I can't help but hope that what will make her most happy will also be what will make *me* most happy. If not, I will make my peace with this as with many of our differences as mother and daughter, separate human beings.

Some halakhic opinions hold that women should not wear tzitzit because these are "men's garments." Deuteronomy 22:5 says, "There should not be a man's instruments on a woman, and a man should not wear a woman's dress." Some interpretations say that a man's "instruments" means instruments of war.[21] Others simply say that all men's clothing is forbidden, which is the plain sense of the verse.

The *Targum Yonatan,* a commentary on the Bible whose author lived in the land of Israel sometime in the early centuries C.E., says that this refers to tefillin and tzitzit.[22] Although this is a minority view, and the *Targum Yonatan* is not a halakhic source, some modern *poskim* take this interpretation into account when asked if a woman can wear tzitzit, perhaps because tzitzit are actually garments and are usually made for men. If one accepts the interpretation of the *Targum Yonatan,* there could be a halakhic problem with women wearing tzitzit that are bought in a regular store.

In order to cover my bases, I commissioned a seamstress friend of mine, who lives here in Jerusalem, to design and sew special tzitzit just for Michal and me. With lace trimming and flowers, these could not be mistaken for a man's undergarment. These tzitzit are also much more comfortable, since the usual *tallit katan* is made with a man's clothing and body shape in mind. She has even made for Michal a pair of pink satin tzitzit. Two of Michal's girlfriends have already started wearing a *tallit katan* because they saw Michal doing so. Maybe she'll start a trend among her girlfriends.

When we moved to Israel, I decided that I needed a new tallit, one especially for Shabbat. I wanted a purely white one—white stripes on a white background—to help me feel the purity of Shabbat and set this day of the week apart from the others. The tradition of wearing white on Shabbat and using a white tablecloth on the Shabbat table originates in the kabbalistic idea that on Shabbat we are given an additional soul, a more pure soul. I like the idea of wearing a purely white tallit to help me incorporate this idea into my Shabbat prayers. Shabbat is a sanctified day on which we are not supposed to think about mundane matters like money or work. It is a day during which we are supposed to be on a different spiritual level, closer to Godliness, like angels.

I go to Yad LaKashish, "Lifeline for the Old," a wonderful shop in Jerusalem that sells crafts made by the elderly. I had bought my first tallit there on a trip to Israel. I remember how I had entered that shop five years ago filled with excitement and a bit of fear. I was excited to be buying my first tallit; I had never purchased a ritual object for myself, and choosing my own tallit thrilled me. A tallit is a very personal item. Like all clothing, it tells you something about its wearer, and, like any frequently worn article of clothing, it takes on the shape of the body it clothes. I needed to choose my tallit carefully.

The one I chose had a white woolen background with soft blue-gray stripes and draped across my shoulders nearly to the floor. There were some unique and quite special *tallitot* there, with stripes of all different colors, some woven and some hand-painted, some made of silk or a thick cotton weave, but I wanted something that looked traditional, not conspicuous or flashy. As a woman wearing a tallit, I would stand out enough; why bring more attention to myself? But I also wanted something special, that would not necessarily be associated with the *tallitot* our grandfathers wore.

The shop had *tallitot* of many different shapes and sizes: some were more like scarves than shawls, and some were even fitted to the contours of human shoulders to prevent the tallit from slipping off the wearer. I chose the traditional shape and size. I wanted something in which I could wrap myself, even though I am often annoyed by constantly having to put my fallen tallit back on, especially with children pulling at me and needing to be held. Pulling the tallit back over my shoulders has sentimental meaning for me. It reminds me of when I was a small child and my father had to pull his tallit back on when he picked me up in shul. And as a friend said to me, "Each time I pull my tallit back up over my shoulders, I am pulling myself back into the act of prayer."

My kids are at the ages when they require constant physical attention, so I have had to find creative ways to keep my tallit on. Tallit clips don't last long. I've resorted to tying the tallit around my shoulders like a shawl, or tucking it into the straps of my baby sling or front carrier.

When I first went to Yad LaKashish, I suspected that the saleswoman might react negatively if I told her that the tallit was for me. But when she asked me, I told her the truth. She did not even try to hide her disbelief.

"But you're *datiyah*," she said, using the Hebrew word for a religiously observant woman, and eyeing my hair covering and shin-length skirt, much like the clothing she herself was wearing.

"Yes, I am," I replied, looking her right in the eye, half friendly, half daring.

"I don't understand. Only the *Reformim* do that."

I explained that halakhah permits women to take on these mitzvot, albeit with reservations, even though we are not obligated to perform them. She did not know this. I also told her that I consider taking on these extra obligations to be a strengthening and broadening of my commitment to Jewish practice and tradition, not a diluting of the mitzvot or an attempt to undermine the entire system. I even quoted to her the opinion of the late Rabbi Israel Gustman, who came from Lithuania to Israel and was the head of Yeshivat Netzakh Yisrael in Jerusalem. He says that women who believe they can perform the positive timebound mitzvot should, because they have no good excuse not to![23]

When I left the store, the woman was still perplexed; I could tell from the patronizing way she was smiling at me. I hoped that our meeting at least expanded her thinking. Perhaps I had opened her up to reexamining Jewish gender roles and the possibility of women performing more mitzvot. At very least, I showed her that women like me exist who are both religiously observant and willing to explore new options as Jewish women. I hope that on the occasions when she sees a woman buy a tallit, she won't necessarily assume, "She just wants to do the mitzvot she isn't obligated to perform but isn't interested in the ones she *is* required to perform!"

I return to this same shop to purchase my new Shabbat tallit, but to my disappointment, they have no completely white *tallitot*. I have my heart set on buying my Shabbat tallit that day, and I am determined to find one, even if it means going to Meah Shearim.

Meah Shearim is an ultra-Orthodox, or *haredi*, neighborhood in Jerusalem known, among other things, for its male residents throwing stones at people who drive through the neighborhood's narrow streets on Shabbat. There is an obtrusive sign hanging over the main street at the entrance to the neighborhood that reads: ALL JEWISH WOMEN AND GIRLS MUST DRESS MODESTLY. I went to this place five years ago with Jacob to buy tzitzit for both of us: my first set and some new ones for Jacob. The bearded, black-hatted man in the store, with *peyot* (side curls) and a long black coat, asked us in Hebrew for whom we were buying them. Jacob said, "For me."

"Which kind?"

"The mesh ones," Jacob answered.

"You know those aren't really so kosher," the man said, stroking his thick, unkempt, red beard.

"My rabbi says they're fine," Jacob said. "Do you have them or not?"

The man took out a box from beneath the counter and held it out to Jacob. "Help yourself. We have all sizes."

Jacob made his selection.

"Will that be all?" the storekeeper asked.

Jacob looked at me.

"No," I said. "We also want a few more pairs for a bar mitzvah boy—about my size," I said, lying and feeling like a coward for doing so. I did not want to get into an argument with this man, especially when I knew that I had no chance of winning. He would never be convinced of the validity of my position, no matter what halakhic sources I quoted to him. Despite our common commitment to Torah, mitzvot, and Jewish law, our worlds were very different.

I left Meah Shearim that day with mixed feelings. On the bus home, I felt like calling out to all of the passengers, "Look! I have my own pairs of tzitzit!" I sat impatiently in my seat, counting the stops until mine, when I could go back to the friend's house where we were staying and try on my purchase. I wanted to say the *brachah* on the tzitzit for the first time and press the fringes against my lips. I wanted to make this mitzvah my own. But I was disheartened that I had had to act surreptitiously to enable myself to perform a mitzvah, one that I believed was not only my right but my personal duty to perform. If I was so sure that I was doing the right thing, why did I feel so bad?

However, not once did I think: *Why couldn't I have been born a man?* Easier is not necessarily better. Perhaps my appreciation of these mitzvot is even greater because I do not take them for granted. Because I have chosen to make these mitzvot my own, I sometimes believe that they are more precious to me than to men who grew up performing them, much as I imagine a convert to Judaism feels about all of the mitzvot.

There is a legal principle in Jewish law that one who is not obligated to perform a mitzvah but does it anyway receives a lesser reward than one who is obligated and performs it.[24] As odd as it might seem, I understand this rationale. Because I have voluntarily chosen these mitzvot, it may be easier for me to perform them. It was my decision. On the other hand, even with my strong motivation to take on these mitzvot, performing them is not an easy task, neither practically nor emotionally. Shouldn't this earn me an equal heavenly reward?

When I go to Meah Shearim to buy my Shabbat tallit, I remember the time I bought my tzitzit there. I decide to again use my story about buying for a bar mitzvah boy "about my size," but this time I have fewer reservations about my dishonesty. I have Michal and Adin with me, and they are cranky about the whole excursion. The streets are so narrow and crowded; it is hot, and they are tired. I want to buy my tallit and leave; I am not in the mood to be lectured about a woman's role or modesty. I find just what I am looking for in a small shop filled with religious objects, and I buy it while a friend waits outside with my children. Then we leave Meah Shearim as quickly as possible.

The trip to this neighborhood, where I feel so alienated and out of place, is worth it in the end. When I put on my new white tallit that Shabbat in a halakhically progressive yet traditional shul, I feel comforted wrapped in the soft wool. I feel as if I am being hugged by God. I am living in Jerusalem, my favorite city, where I feel most spiritually alive. I am in a supportive environment; there are even a handful of other women who are wearing *tallitot*. The alienation I felt while buying the tallit is now replaced by a feeling of support and belonging.

When the time for the Torah service arrives, the women break off for our own Torah reading, where we will have *aliyot* (the honor of being called up to the Torah) and take turns reading from the Torah scroll. I am asked to come up to the Torah for an *aliyah*, and when I say the *brachah* in Hebrew—"Blessed are You, Lord, our God, Ruler of the Universe, Who chose us from among all the nations and gave us the Torah. Blessed are You, Lord, the Giver of the Torah"—I wrap my new tallit tightly around myself and close my eyes. I am so grateful for the peace that Shabbat brings to my life, for a community where I am accepted with all of my differences, and for the opportunity to sanctify my life and connect to the Divine through mitzvot. At this moment, I am whole.

I am not the first woman in my family to have worn tefillin. My father is the youngest of three siblings. The oldest is his sister, Essie, who is mentally ill and lives in a group home in Virginia. His brother, Norman, lives in Haifa, a port city in the north of Israel. Every time I visited Israel, I made the trip up to Haifa to visit Norman and his family. So naturally, when we moved here permanently, we took Michal and Adin up to Haifa for Shabbat to see their great-uncle and great-aunt.

I am torn. My uncle and aunt are *dati*; they have belonged to the same Orthodox shul in Haifa for more than thirty years, and although their own outlook is Modern Orthodox and open, there is no doubt that most of the members of their congregation would not take well to my wearing a tallit in their shul. I do not want to make my aunt and uncle uncomfortable or put them in an awkward position because of my personal religious choices, but I also know that I will feel inconsistent, a coward, not living up to my commitments, if I don't wear my tal-lit. I pack it and decide to put off my decision until after I discuss it with them.

After we arrive and settle in, my Aunt Sandy sets out some tea and cake for us to eat while we catch up on the past year since our last visit. They want to know if I am still involved in religious feminism. Then my aunt says, quite matter-of-factly, "You know, Essie did the same thing. She wore tefillin, too."

I had no idea! Essie moved out of my grandparents' house when my father was still a small child, so he has few memories of her. In the 1940s she moved to Israel to live on a kibbutz. In 1948 she drove an ambulance in the Israeli War of Independence. I knew very little about her life in Israel, except that she was married to a man on a kibbutz and they had two daughters who now live in Virginia. Eventually, my aunt and her Israeli husband divorced, and Essie came back to the United States with her two daughters. I don't know the details, and I don't know if that is because my parents wanted to shelter me from the diffi-culties of her life or if they simply do not know much about it them-selves.

In any case, I am curious to hear more about Essie from my aunt and uncle. It seems that she was always searching and never quite sat-isfied. She did many interesting and daring things in her life that I admire and identify with—moving to Israel, volunteering in the War of Independence—but tragically much of her dissatisfaction seems to have been due to her mental illness, which was not diagnosed until later in her life. For a period, she experimented with wearing tefillin, my uncle tells me. She was frustrated with her role as a woman in Judaism. In the end, she rejected most of Jewish tradition, although when I last saw her—a woman in her seventies—at my grandmother's funeral five years ago, she was very much interested in talking about Judaism and Israel.

It is strange to think that I have something so intimate and partic-ular in common with my Aunt Essie, whom I remember mostly as the aunt who said disturbing things when she used to call our house in the evening during my childhood. I was scared of her then, and now I am finding out that she might not be as different from me as I thought.

I wonder: *Am I taking on these mitzvot only because I carry the same genes that make my aunt so unstable? Is my lack of satisfaction with my lot unhealthy? Am I, too, searching for something unattainable? Am I too extreme?* I know that my ideas and actions are not mainstream, but I've never considered that they might be out of the realm of sanity.

I remember a conversation I had with a relative before I left for Israel. "Everyone thinks you're crazy" is exactly how she phrased it. "Everyone" in this case meant the members of her suburban New York Orthodox community. I was not surprised to hear that her friends do not support my struggle. To my sometimes ungenerous mind, where she lives is a bastion of complacency, a huge pocket of supporters of the status quo, and I make trouble. I rock the boat.

Now, when I think about my aunt's journey, I wonder: *Is there some deep-rooted instability that has set me on this path that I see as a fight for justice?*

At the same time, I gain a new respect for Essie and a new perspective on her life. The narrow picture I had of her as my "crazy aunt" now opens up to begin revealing the courageous woman she must have been. She is now a sister in my struggle. Suddenly her alienation becomes so acute to me that I feel her pain. I shiver when I think of how alone she must have felt, and thank God that my loneliness is more on an ideological level than an emotional one. I am supported by family and friends who may not do as I do, but who for the most part validate my actions as a legitimate way to express Judaism. And, most important, although I sometimes question my own motivations and my path, most of the time I trust my faculties and my ability to reason.

Should I try to reach out to my aunt? Should I try to help her access within her that young, idealistic woman she once was? It may hurt her more to remember. Maybe her decision to wear tefillin was an attempt to find God in her painful life, or perhaps it was really a rebellion against the system in which she grew up. It must have felt so stifling to her, even more than it did to me. Imagine growing up as an undiagnosed schizophrenic in the Orthodox Jewish community in Brooklyn, where there is already so little tolerance for those who are different. It is interesting to me that she chose, at least for a short period, to alienate herself even more by wearing tefillin.

What is not surprising is that she packed up and left, even if it meant facing extreme hardships in British-mandated Palestine, not yet a Jewish state. She must have been in search of a place where she could be happy and at peace. I am saddened by the fact that she did not find that peace here in Israel. Although there are times when I feel lost even here in my own country, in many ways I feel that I have come home.

My questions and rebellions, my quest for something different, do not unsettle me in a fundamental way. Although I sometimes feel alone and misunderstood, and I wonder to myself if I am making the right choices, the inner peace that I often feel was never Essie's experience.

Sometimes when I see other, more "normal" religious women sitting on the bus reciting the morning prayers, *Shacharit*, with their hair completely covered and their long sleeves and skirts, or sitting in shul without *tallitot*, I envy their comfort, their willingness to see things in neat categories, their ability to submit to a system of rules, the way they appear to fit in. On those occasions, I wish I could believe that, as a woman, I am indeed so essentially different from men. My life would be so much simpler if I could accept the traditional distinctions that women are naturally more nurturing and men more self-absorbed, that women see the bigger picture and men see the details, that women are more private and men more public. If I believed that women are not obligated in certain mitzvot because they are inherently male mitzvot, not at all suited for a woman's spiritual needs, my religious life would be much simpler.

If I could surrender to these sometimes tempting ideas, I wouldn't have to think so much about each religious act I perform, every hour I take away from being with my children so that I can study Torah, and question my own motivations as others are constantly doing for me. I wouldn't have to wonder: Am I one of those "holier-than-thou" women that the Rabbis are talking about? Am I doing this for the sake of God, or for the sake of feminism? For my own spiritual development or to prove a point? Do I really believe that this is one way to bring us closer to the perfection of the world, or am I merely doing this for an ego boost, a moment in the spotlight, to attract attention? Am I doing this out of love or anger? Purity or bitterness of heart?

As much as it would be easier at times to believe that women simply do not need the mitzvot I've taken on because we are already so connected to God, so aware of time and in tune with our spiritual centers, I cannot. There are too many exceptions for this generalization to be applicable. Perhaps because I know myself to be an exception to so many of the rules about "feminine" characteristics, I feel their untruth in my core. I need these mitzvot as much as the average man does. I don't see the world as essentially divided between women and men; I see each person as an individual with his or her own talents, weaknesses, and spiritual needs.

Yet I cannot honestly claim that my motivations are related only to my private spiritual needs. (If that were so, I would wear my tefillin only at home, as I know some other women do, and shy away from making any public statements on the issue.) My religious commitments are connected to my desire for social change. Like those who started the Modern Orthodox movement, I embrace developments in society that are seen as secular by others, but which I believe to be no less than divine revelations that advance the Jewish concept of being created in the image of God. These ideas—feminism, democracy, the fight against racism—should be integrated as fully as possible into Judaism, much like the abolition of slavery and the requirement of monogamy were in the past.

Change will always be more gradual in religious communities than in secular ones, because religious communities tend to be more conservative and more attached to tradition. There is a legitimate fear that with change comes loss of tradition, leaving a shaky foundation. I sympathize with this fear. Judaism is precious to me; I too want to preserve it. In order for change to be organic and binding, it should not happen too quickly. The community needs to be educated and engaged with new ideas.

In expounding upon ritual animal sacrifices, Maimonides writes the following:

> It is impossible, according to the nature of humans, to suddenly discontinue everything to which they have become accustomed . . . The general mode of worship among all people, and to which the Israelites were also accustomed, consisted of sacrificing animals. It was in accordance with the wisdom and plan of God to not command us to give up all these rituals of service; for to obey such a commandment would have been contrary to the nature of humans, who generally adhere to that to which they are accustomed.[25]

He goes on to explain that in order to reach a higher goal, the replacement of idol worship with monotheism, God first introduced worship through the Tabernacle and Temple sacrifices. The Israelites would not have been able to accept cerebral prayer, involving no physical act, at that stage in history. Yet as society progresses, we are able to make progress in our religious expression. I could argue that this reasoning should apply to our understanding of gender as well. Just as we were able to move from offering sacrifices to reciting words of prayer, we should be able to move from a religious order that too often excludes women to one that gives women equal opportunities for religious experience and leadership.[26]

Judaism is dynamic, not a stagnant religion with fixed rules. God created humans, we learn, so that we might act toward perfecting the world. Religious change must be part of that progress. If we let Judaism stagnate or worse yet regress, we are thwarting God's plan. In the halakhic realm, we are more than God's partners. No divine voices or prophets will send us messages or indicate a clear path. The interpretation of texts and the responsible development of halakhah is in our hands alone.

Maimonides presents God's final purpose for the world as monotheism and the values of Torah. This includes, of course, the notion that all people were created in God's image. Our laws and practices must reflect this ideal fully for women and men. Maimonides also reminds us that intermediate practices do not represent God's final vision for us. Insisting that God's eternal plan is for women's role in Jewish ritual and life to remain the same throughout history ignores the developments we have already seen—and our responsibility to continue repairing not only "the outside world" but the Jewish world as well.

The decision to cover my head embodies all of the tensions of my religious life.[27] Modern sensibility holds that requiring women to cover their *hair* is oppressive; a religious sensibility maintains that wearing a *head* covering can be humbling and uplifting, reminding us that there is a higher power in the world.[28] I have chosen to embrace the mitzvah of head covering in a way with which I am comfortable: I do not cover my *hair*, I cover my *head*.[29]

The requirement of hair covering for women was originally about modesty. The Mishnah in *Ketubot* (7:6) says that a woman who goes with her head uncovered is to be divorced without receiving her *ketubah* money, and her act is categorized as violating *dat yehudit*, the accepted practice of modest Jewish women. The Gemara on this mishnah in *Ketubot* 72a–b, in order to prove that head covering is a Torah law, cites Numbers 5:18, which deals with the *sotah*, a woman accused of adultery. During one of the steps of the *sotah* ritual, the purpose of which is to shame and frighten the woman and perform a test to see if she is indeed an adulteress, the priest uncovers her hair. The Gemara then declares that, although according to Torah law a work basket worn on the head is enough of a covering, according to *dat yehudit* this is not enough. The conclusion in the Gemara is that a work basket is indeed enough according to *dat yehudit*, when walking from courtyard to courtyard by way of an alley (which can be interpreted as semi-public space), and that in one's own private courtyard (and obviously at home) no head covering is required at all.[30] According to Torah law (or *dat Moshe*), the Gemara seems to be saying that a work basket is enough even in public places.

Another passage in the Gemara, in *B'rachot* 24a, brings the opinion of Rav Sheshet that a woman's hair is *ervah*—literally "nakedness," although in halakhic literature the term refers to things that would be considered immodest to expose in public. The source in *Ketubot* requires a head covering for reasons of modesty, or propriety, but does not declare hair *ervah*—an important distinction, since the *Ketubot* source could allow for some of one's hair to be covered at some times, while the *B'rachot* source would seemingly require that all hair be covered at all times. It seems that while the mishnah in *Ketubot* speaks only about married women, the discussions in the Gemara, in both *Ketubot* and *B'rachot*, refer to both married and unmarried women,[31] and, indeed, according to a number of authoritative sources, such as the *Shulchan Arukh* and Maimonides,[32] hair covering for women in the marketplace (which is interpreted to mean a public space) is a requirement for all women, unmarried women included.[33]

By the thirteenth century, it seems that unmarried women began to keep their hair uncovered in the home, which is why *poskim* then allow for men to recite the Shema (the assumption here is that the man is praying the Shema at home, which was the general practice then) in the presence of an unmarried woman with her hair uncovered.[34] By the

eighteenth century in Europe, unmarried women left their hair exposed
even in public,[35] and *poskim* tried to reconcile Maimonides and the
Shulchan Arukh with the practice they saw around them by saying that
what is forbidden for unmarried women is for their hair to be *loose,*
while for married women a hair covering is required.[36]

According to the position that *ervah* and *dat yehudit* are not relative terms but rather objective prescriptions as to what modest dress is
and always should be,[37] the act of these single women who started to
leave their hair uncovered would be considered a violation of Jewish
law. However, according to the position that both *ervah* and *dat yehudit* are relative terms, subject to change as society's expectations for
appropriate dress change,[38] they are acting within halakhah. I follow
the latter position, and because of the Gemara passage in *Ketubot* that
declares head covering a Torah law for married women, I follow what
I see as the Torah law. I consider Rav Sheshet's position and the *dat
yehudit* practice (as it is clarified in the Gemara in *Ketubot*) as relative
to the customs of the times. What the Gemara calls Torah law—that is,
the requirement to wear a head covering similar to a work basket in
public places—I maintain for my own practice, and try to find meaning
in it that speaks to me in my own time and place.

I am aware that there are *poskim* who seem to apply the *ervah*
source even to what the Gemara in *Ketubot* calls Torah law, declaring
that the hair of any woman today is not *ervah*, and therefore the
requirement for women to keep their hair covered at all is irrelevant
today, for married and unmarried women alike.[39] Although I could rely
on the opinions of these rabbis, I choose to wear a *head* covering. Not
only would I feel intellectually dishonest in saying that the Gemara in
Ketubot does not consider some form of head covering to be required
by Torah law, but I also see this requirement as an opportunity to bring
more meaning into my life. Because I do not find the idea of *head* covering to be inherently oppressive, and because men too have the practice of covering their heads, I feel whole—both as a feminist and as a
religious Jew—when I cover my head.

I cannot wholeheartedly agree with those *poskim* who say that
there is no relevance today in the practice of married women covering
their heads. It seems to me that on the level of Torah law (i.e., the
requirement to wear a head covering of some sort), the practice of head

covering for married women does still have social significance. Much of observant Jewish society has made a collective decision that wearing a head covering of some sort—at least part of the time, and whether it covers the head alone or all of the hair—is still relevant for married women today. This practice is increasing, even among women whose mothers did not cover their hair.[40] This is not so much for reasons of modesty—to keep a sexual body part covered (i.e., *ervah*), or to avoid sexual impropriety (i.e., *dat yehudit*)—as it is a sign of being married and therefore no longer "available."[41] This is a different type of expression of modesty, one with which I am comfortable. A head covering on a religious woman in the society in which I live signals that she is off-limits to men other than her husband.[42]

Wearing a symbol that to the men around me indicates that I am proudly involved in a monogamous relationship, that I am absolutely not interested in their sexual advances, appeals to my feminist sensibilities. With a hat on my head, especially here in Jerusalem where a woman wearing a hat signals "married and religious," I feel liberated as a woman; I am sending a message that flirtation is out of the question. If a man wants to relate to me, we know the rules in advance. This, to me, is different than saying that it is sexually improper for a woman to go out without a head covering, which is the plain meaning of the Gemara in *Ketubot*. A married woman uncovering her head is not performing a promiscuous act (since today it would not be perceived this way, even in Orthodox circles other than *haredi* ones). However, by covering her head she signals her status. These are different understandings (though both related to married women's sexuality), with different implications.

Some argue that because men don't wear a similar garment to signify their married status, this is a sexist practice. Jacob and I both wear wedding rings, so, logic would say, we should also both wear head coverings that symbolize our married state. However, a symbol only has social meaning if it will be understood by others. Jacob wears a kippah, but even if he intended his kippah to symbolize that he is married (in addition to its other functions), others would not perceive this. I feel fortunate that I can wear such a clear symbol that I am married, and I know that my husband wishes he could, too. Once, while Jacob was on a business trip, a woman asked him out on a date. When he showed her his wedding ring, she apologized. He wears his wedding ring as a public symbol of his marriage, hoping to avoid such awkward situations.

In addition to its symbolic value, wearing a head covering has other meanings for me that are parallel to a kippah for observant men. According to traditional Jewish practice, in custom if not law,[43] individuals (men and women) should keep their heads covered while praying, reciting blessings, and studying Torah. Many women (even those who do not normally cover their heads outside of the home) have inherited the practice of covering their heads while lighting Shabbat candles on Friday evenings and while reciting the blessing when immersing in the mikveh. The implicit idea behind this practice is that when one is invoking God's name, "standing before" God, or studying God's Torah, one should keep one's head covered as a sign of respect and awe. This too is out of a sense of modesty, though a different kind, reminding us of our humble place in the universe.

Today, unmarried and married women who do not normally wear a head covering do not generally cover their heads even while praying, reciting most blessings, and studying Torah, although many halakhic sources hold that they should.[44] Some women make a point of wearing a kippah when praying, studying Torah, and reciting blessings, but this is rare, even—or especially—in the Orthodox world.

There is a widespread custom—one that my mother followed while I was growing up and still does today—for married women who do not usually cover their heads to wear hats to synagogue. This is most likely originally based on the idea that people should cover their heads while praying, as well as loosely on the sources that say that a woman's hair "that she is accustomed to covering" should be covered if she is in the presence of a man, even her husband, who is reciting the Shema.[45] It has largely become a way for men who are looking for a potential wife in shul (or for others looking on their behalf) to distinguish single women from married women, since it would be very rare to see an unmarried woman wearing a hat in synagogue. Evidence of a change in meaning is the seeming inconsistency of those married women who wear hats to synagogue. These women generally do not wear a head covering when praying or when reciting a blessing outside the synagogue, and the hats that they do wear to shul do not necessarily cover all of their hair, so that men—if looking to the other side of the mechitzah while reciting the

Shema—can still see more than a handbreath of their hair, one traditional measure of the amount that may be exposed.

I believe that any woman today who would wear a kippah if she were a man (a good test of this is if she would expect her husband or sons, real or imagined, to do so) should wear some kind of head covering, at least when she prays, recites blessings, and studies Torah. Hair is no longer considered *ervah* in our society, but there is still ample reason for women to cover their heads. The Gemara tells us that such a practice is required by Torah law; we have the additional weighty custom of covering one's head during prayer, blessings, and Torah study; and for married women there is the sociological fact that if one lives in a community with other observant Jews, a woman wearing a hat is signifying that she is married.

An additional benefit to wearing a hat, one that also applies to wearing a kippah, is that it serves as a kind of religious dress code. This gives the wearer the chance to present herself to others as a religiously observant Jew and to remind herself of this fact. It also serves as a way to bring the idea of sanctity into the way we dress. If our religious mindset should permeate every aspect of our lives, then it should also affect the choices we make when selecting articles of clothing to place on our bodies. For me, wearing a hat adds meaning to the everyday mundane act of dressing.

I cover my head, keeping in mind (and heart) all of these conflicts and complexities. It is a personal decision, and a not purely rational one, yet it locates me in the chain of Jewish tradition.

This mitzvah can become oppressive if approached differently. In the Talmud we read a list of "the curses of Eve."[46] Rav Dimi mentions the final three: (1) she (woman) is wrapped in her clothing as though in mourning; (2) she is separated from others; and (3) she is locked in prison. Rashi explains these, respectively: (1) It is shameful for her to go out with her head uncovered; (2) she is forbidden to all men except her husband, while he may marry many women;[47] and (3) *kol k'vudah bat melech p'nima*, "the king's daughter is all glorious within."[48] (This quote, from Psalms 45:14, is used by many in the Orthodox community who advocate traditional gender roles as a catch-phrase to show that women should remain in the private sphere.) It is apparent from his grouping of hair covering with other oppressive restrictions (curses, in fact) that for Rashi the connotations of this mitzvah are negative. He is offering not a critique but a statement of fact. In the same vein, in *Ketubot* 72a–b we learn that a woman who goes outside with her head uncovered may be divorced without her ketubah money.

If I understood this mitzvah in accordance with the views of Rav Dimi and/or Rashi, or even the mishnah in *Ketubot,* I would not be able to observe it. I intentionally do not cover all of my hair, because exposing my hair in public is today not perceived as a shameful act nor as a brazen sexual act. In addition, a man today cannot, according to many revered *poskim*, divorce his wife against her will because she does not cover her head in public.[49] These distinctions are important in my conceptualization of this mitzvah, for it would be problematic for me to perpetuate a system that advocates this kind of double standard and cruel misogyny. However, that is not the way this mitzvah is perceived today in the communities with which I associate myself. These communities have imbued it with new meanings, and it is these contemporary (yet traditional) meanings that I embrace.

The practice of head covering is too rich for me to simply cast off without trying to make it work. If the original function or significance of a mitzvah no longer has meaning—or if it has negative meaning—in our time and place, we can often find new meanings that uplift our lives in different ways. For me, head covering is an expression of two forms of modesty: humility before God and sexual modesty as a married woman who is not looking to attract other men.

When I see a woman without a head covering, I can't help feeling that something is missing, especially when she is with her husband or son who is wearing a kippah. It is as if there were a void where a mitzvah should be. We have been prevented from observing many beautiful mitzvot (those reserved for men) in the past, and we are losing others now because of their oppressive associations. Head covering is one example of the latter, and immersing in the mikveh is another. Reclaiming them and imbuing them with meanings that speak to our spiritual needs can be empowering when it comes from women themselves rather than being imposed by a male legal system that too often has only men's spiritual needs in mind, even while speaking about women's mitzvot and bodies.

I strive to find beauty in the mitzvot, even when it means assigning new meanings to them. When I find that the halakhah as it stands is in direct and irreparable conflict with sensibilities and values to which I am committed (values that can usually also be found in the Jewish tradition), I try to find a window for change within the halakhic system— by searching for a minority opinion that supports my position, by studying the traditional sources and coming to my own conclusion based on these sources, or by asserting that when a Torah value is in conflict with a rabbinically innovated practice, the Torah value should be paramount.

My desire to take on the mitzvot from which the Rabbis exempted women is not an attempt to overthrow Jewish law but to embrace the mitzvot and work to make the halakhic system more inclusive, to make it embrace me. Out of a love of Torah, I insist on my right to experience it fully. Out of this same love, I work to create a community in which timeless Torah values, such as fighting for the rights of the oppressed and loving one's neighbor as oneself, will be considered more important than ephemeral sociological and cultural influences. My vision is an expression of hope for what Judaism is at its core and can become.

CHAPTER FOUR

◆

God: Believing

And you shall love the Lord, your God, with all of your heart,
and all of your soul, and all of your might.
— Deuteronomy 6:5

ON FRIDAY AFTERNOONS, before Shabbat, my mother would take my siblings and me to the local branch of the public library, where we would return the books we had taken out the week before and take out new books. I was a ravenous reader, and I loved scanning the titles on the shelves to plan my reading for the coming week. One such Friday when I was thirteen, while searching for new titles, I saw the twinkle in one girl's hungry, mischievous eyes smiling up at me from the cover of a slim book. I read the title: *The Diary of Anne Frank.* Without even reading the blurb on the book's jacket—my usual next step in selecting my reading materials—I knew that I must read it; I had to find out about this girl. I started it right there in the library, sitting on the floor between the bookshelves, and continued reading until I finished the book after lights-out that night. I cried myself to sleep, unable to believe that she was dead, that anyone could snuff out her light.

I was convinced that if I had lived in Amsterdam fifty years earlier, we would have been the best of friends. I too had aspirations to be a published writer some day, and I had begun keeping a diary. I was drawn to her inquisitiveness, her spunk, her dreams, her rebellious streak. In one day, I had made a friend and lost her.

Anne's story awakened me to the reality of the Holocaust. Had I been born in Europe two generations earlier, her fate would have been my own. I had heard older survivors tell me their stories, but here was a girl my own age speaking to me from her hiding place. The fact that she had not survived allowed me to relate to her story all the more. If she had lived, she would have been yet another survivor in her sixties relating the story of a miraculous escape. But Anne was frozen in time; she will be forever a teenager. She will always be the friend that I lost among the six million.

After reading Anne's diary, I could not get enough of Holocaust literature. I read Elie Wiesel's *Night*, an autobiographical novel based on his experiences as a child in Auschwitz. The night I finished this book—which ends with the march in the snow that he, his father, and his fellow concentration camp prisoners were forced to take, barefoot, from Auschwitz to Buchenwald—I could not sleep. I tossed and turned with the terror and extreme darkness of the book hanging over me. Finally, I went into my brother Jonathan's room and woke him. I couldn't bear to be awake and alone with that book haunting me.

After reading these true stories, I lost the faith that I had in a just world with a just God watching over us. Without such a God, life looked much more frightening. My eyes were opened to the realities of a world with evil. In the absence of the God of my childhood, the God who was described to me in Jewish day school, the God who punishes the wicked and rewards the righteous, the God who cares about what we eat and wear and say, what would fill that void? Could I find meaning amid the chaos that I suddenly felt engulfing me, or would my life remain as empty as it felt when I read Anne Frank's last entry in her diary?

I did not know if there was a God, but I did know that even if there was, this was not a God that I trusted. I lost all faith in what I had been taught in school about what was right and what was wrong. The entire system of Jewish law simply lost its relevance for me. Although I had already begun questioning my status as a woman in Judaism, I had never questioned the idea that the Torah was given by God. Now I was no longer certain there was a God at all, and even if there was, it was not one from which I cared to take orders. Before, I had rashly faulted the Rabbis with misinterpreting our holy texts. Now I no longer believed that these texts were sacred at all. In the simplistic, black-and-white manner of an adolescent, I decided that the whole religion must be a farce, and I wasn't going to be duped. I wanted to discover good and evil for myself rather than have rabbis who lived almost 2,000 years ago tell me what I should and shouldn't do in the name of God. Without a strong belief in God, other doubts began to stir within me.

The first time I turned off a light on Shabbat, I was thirteen years old. It was late on a Friday night, and I was in bed reading. I had neglected to set my "Shabbes clock," the timer we attached to our lights so the lights could go on and off without our having to flick a switch (which would violate Shabbat restrictions against being *makeh b'patish*, literally "hitting with a hammer" or completing an act of creation by closing electrical circuits, and doing activities similar to lighting or extinguishing a fire).

I finished reading and wanted to go to sleep, but my bedside lamp was still on and shining brightly in my eyes. On any other night of the week, I would have reached up and turned it off without a thought, but since it was Friday night, I lay there, wondering what to do. I hadn't set the timer because I now thought it was silly. Could I really find the courage to go against the rules I had been taught were from God? But if I no longer believed in a God who cared about whether or not we turned lights on and off on Shabbat, why shouldn't I?

As I reached up to flick the switch, my hand trembled and my heart raced. I didn't believe that lightning would literally strike, but it was difficult to erase that image from my mind.

Click.

I slept fine that night. I felt liberated, as if I were finally discovering who I was. It was a step away from observant Judaism that would eventually lead me back again. I needed to find my way back to Judaism afresh. Although I never would have used these words then, I needed to discover my own path to God.

The summer between my junior and senior years of high school, I was a counselor at a small Jewish summer camp in New Hampshire. I had heard that the camp was looking for counselors from Orthodox day schools to be role models for their campers, who came mostly from nonobservant Jewish families and whose parents sent them to a Jewish camp to learn more about their religion. I liked the idea of getting away for the summer, especially outside New York. I was feeling suffocated by the New York Modern Orthodox scene, where I felt I had to fit into a mold of the good Jewish girl, and I thought New Hampshire would be a welcome change.

Since the age of thirteen, I had been breaking Jewish law behind my parents' backs—turning on lights on Shabbat, eating fowl with dairy, and writing on Shabbat. This camp was not Orthodox, which was probably what attracted me most. It was a traditional camp, with two daily services: an Orthodox minyan with a Mechitzah, where only men participated fully, and an egalitarian minyan without a Mechitzah, where men and women participated equally. Both my parents and the camp directors, of course, assumed that I would *daven* in the Orthodox minyan, but I was fascinated by egalitarianism. My reaction to so much of what I found troubling in Jewish law had been to throw it all away, but here was a different approach, one that rejected only the sexism of the traditional service and kept the rest. This service included all the things that I knew from shul back home, but women could lead the service, read from the Torah, carry the Torah, and open and close the *aron kodesh*, the Holy Ark, where the Torahs are kept. Coming from an Orthodox environment, I perceived this as nothing short of a revolution.

My first Shabbat at camp, I went to the egalitarian minyan and surprisingly felt quickly at home. I listened as a woman led the service in a strong soprano voice, which I had never heard in synagogue. It felt strange but very appropriate. Why shouldn't a woman lead the group in prayer? She's Jewish, too; she's obligated to pray herself, so why shouldn't she lead? Her voice brought me a new sense of the sanctity of the words of the prayers. As I listened, all the reasons I had learned about why a woman can't be the prayer leader fell away: she's not obligated in communal prayer, she's not counted in the minyan, her voice is *ervah*, she's not supposed to be a public person. I remember a pure and simple sense of the rightness of hearing her voice. It not only seemed just; I also imagined that this was what God would want—a divine picture of prayer on earth.

After I had been going to this minyan for several weeks, the *gabbai* (the person in charge of organizing the service and assigning the roles) asked me if I would like to come up to the Torah for an *aliyah*. He asked my full Hebrew name, as well as my father's and mother's. (In

Orthodox shuls, only the father's name is used when calling a man up to the Torah.) I was nervous, but I couldn't refuse this invitation. It would be a long time before I would have a chance like this again—certainly not at home or in school, and certainly not at the Orthodox all-women's yeshiva where I was registered to study in Israel for a year after high school. I could barely concentrate on the reading as I anticipated my turn to go up to the Torah. I silently practiced over and over again the two *b'rachot*, the blessings I would need to recite while standing up there: one before the reading and one after. Then they called my name.

"*Ta'amod!*" the *gabbai* called out, using the third-person feminine singular future form of the verb "to stand." I was accustomed to hearing only the masculine form used in this context. But he was speaking about *me*, calling *me* up to the Torah. "*Haviva Rena bat Daniel Z'ev v'Rachel, chamishit!*" That was my name he was calling. I stood and started to make my way up to the *bimah*, the raised platform on which the reading is done.

My body trembled as I walked that short distance. My legs felt like Jell-O. When I reached the *bimah*, the reader showed me the place in the scroll where he would begin reading after I said the blessing, and the *gabbai* handed me a tallit. To my surprise, I knew exactly what to do. I took the tallit and with its fringes touched the spot on the parchment where the reader would begin, and then kissed the tallit where it had touched the parchment. I took the handles of the Torah scroll and held one in each hand, squeezed them tightly, and closed my eyes.

"*Baruch atah Adonai, Eloheinu melech ha-olam, asher bachar banu mikol ha'amim v'natan lanu et torato; baruch atah Adonai, noten ha-Torah.*" Blessed are You, God, Ruler of the Universe, who chose us from among the nations and gave to us the Torah; blessed are You, God, the giver of the Torah.

I recited the blessing as though I had been saying these words aloud all of my life. Although I had heard them recited countless times, and had said them quietly during morning services (this *brachah* is a regular part of the individual daily prayers), I had never said them aloud, and certainly not in public in the context of the Torah service. As a girl and then a woman in the Orthodox community, I would never have had occasion to do so, because I had never been allowed to have an *aliyah* to the Torah. I had never seen the inside of a Torah scroll. I had never even been this close to a Torah scroll before.

As the reader chanted, keeping his place with a tiny silver pointer in the shape of a hand, I was not paying attention to the meaning of the words. I was too distracted by the enormity of the moment. There I was, standing up at the Torah, touching the handle of the scroll, watching the black letters dance before me on the yellowing parchment. I was struck with the antiquity of these words that were also in some way mine—as much mine that day as they were the Jews' who first heard them thousands of years earlier. As I stood there, I felt worthy of having recited the words of the blessing. *God did give the Torah to me, too. It is my Torah.*

Until that moment, the Torah had not been fully mine. No one had ever invited me to touch a scroll, look at it, or read from it. It was something distant, words in a book—a copy, but not the real thing. Once I was invited up to the Torah, it came alive for me in a way that it never had before. This sacred scroll, this parchment that I dare not touch with my bare hands, this was the living Torah! Encountering it was part of the way back to the living God.

When I was sixteen years old, I was diagnosed with a genetic, degenerative, muscular disease called fascioscapulohumeral muscular dystrophy, or FSH for short. In my case, as in most cases, it affects only the upper body muscles: of the face, shoulders, and upper arms. In rare cases, it also can affect the lower body muscles, such as the legs, so that the victim of the disease becomes wheelchair bound.

As far back as I can remember, I could not pucker my lips, whistle, hold air in my cheeks, drink from a straw, or blow up a balloon. Neither I nor my parents made much of it; it was accepted as an idiosyncrasy of mine and written off as a result of the fact that I was born six weeks early, weighed only three pounds and three ounces, and spent a month in an incubator before I could come home.

One summer, when I was sixteen and in Israel volunteering on a kibbutz, picking fruit, I realized that I could not lift my arms high enough to pick the fruit on the upper branches of the trees. I could not lift my arms past the height of my chest.

When I returned from Israel, I told my parents about my arms. I did not want to tell them over the phone and worry them; they might have assumed that it was worse than it was. When I finally told them, they were quite concerned, and thus began my countless trips to doctors. I saw neurologists and muscular experts and had test after painful test: an EKG (electrocardiogram), an EMG (electromyogram), and biopsies, all to no avail. None of the doctors or tests could diagnose the cause of my problem.

One day, my cousin, a pediatric neurologist, suggested that I see a colleague of his who, he was certain, would be able to tell me what was wrong. As soon as he looked at me, this doctor gave a name to my condition: FSH. I felt such relief knowing what I had, but at the same time it was frightening to know. Now it was real.

I have a degenerative, genetic disease for which there is no cure. It is not a fatal illness, and in many cases the afflicted person is never seriously debilitated, but there is always a chance that I could become wheelchair bound in the future. I live each day knowing that some day my life may become physically much more difficult. I do not take my mobility for granted.

On the day that my handicap was given a name, and I was told that I could not assume that I would always be physically independent, the reckless teenager in me was lost forever. The feeling of absolute immortality with which I was privileged as a healthy suburban kid, growing up in a democratic country in a time of peace and plenty, was gone. Anne Frank had shattered my innocent view of the world as a just and orderly place, but I had still felt myself beyond the reaches of indiscriminate tragic forces that strike the lives of *others*. Now misfortune had struck *me*, but a different kind of misfortune: left in abeyance, always there, hanging over my head—a strong possibility, but not quite here.

We all know that tragedy can strike at any moment; in that respect I am no different from anyone else. Since the day that I was diagnosed with FSH, I have chosen to live my life with that conscious knowledge rather than putting it inside a mental drawer, locking it away until it forces itself out into the open again. I live my life now as though I am running a race, and my opponent is my mortality, my vulnerability. I have so much that I want to accomplish—raising a family, educating myself, contributing something meaningful to this world—and who knows how much time I have been allotted?

My parents tell me to slow down, to take it easy, not to push myself so hard. That is their job; I am their daughter, and they will always feel the need to protect me, from others and from myself. We all want to be able to ward off the inevitable mortality that lurks, waiting for us all, even for our children. It is difficult to admit that we can protect them only to a point and that the rest is beyond our control. My parents tell me to slow down, but in a sense it's the same thing that I do when I insist on pushing myself to the limit. We are both fighting back against mortality. Their hope is to ward it off and buy more time. Mine is to accomplish all that I can before it catches up with me, to beat it in a race against the clock.

Since becoming a parent, I have learned to slow down, to take on less. It's impossible not to with three small children. Everything gets accomplished more slowly. Much of my time is no longer my own. I race less, and try to appreciate each moment more. I've become more relaxed about my time since the kids were born, but I'm also more aware of its passing.

It is my first Sukkot living in Israel, and I am in the sukkah praying *Shacharit*. Sukkot is the seven-day period when Jews are commanded by the Torah to leave the security of our permanent houses and sit in *sukkot*, temporary huts, under the stars, in order to remember that our people lived in such huts during their journey from Egypt to the Land of Israel. It is a time to reflect on the fragility of our own lives, to feel the vulnerability, even as we are aware of God's protection.

I am thrilled to see so many *sukkot* all over the city: on porches, in backyards, in courtyards, even in the street. Growing up in the Diaspora, I saw *sukkot* only outside a smattering of homes in our neighborhood. Seeing so many reminds me that here I am no longer a minority. Sometimes the smallest thing, like noting that there's no newspaper here on Saturday, reminds me that I live in a Jewish country.

It is hot out here, although it is only nine o'clock in the morning and I am protected by the shade of the branches that are the roof of the sukkah. Draped over my shoulders is my woolen tallit; the heat feels even more intense. I receive some shocked and derisive looks from passersby as they hear me singing and look into my sukkah to see only me, a woman, wrapped in a tallit. Yet I would rather be hot and the object of people's scorn than remove, in my own sukkah, the prayer shawl that has become a necessary part of my morning *tefillah*. Without it, I'd feel almost naked.

I am singing *Hallel*, a set of Psalms praising God that is sung on holidays of particular joy. As I chant in Hebrew "Thank God, who is good, whose lovingkindness is everlasting," I shake the Four Species— which consists of a *lulav* (palm frond), willow and myrtle branches, and an *etrog* (a lemonlike fruit)—in the six directions of the universe. Adin, who has just turned one, is sitting on the ground below me, playing contentedly with a pot holder and some plastic silverware we left in the sukkah after dinner last night. When I look at my son, I deeply and sincerely feel God's lovingkindness.

At this time a year ago, I spent Sukkot in the hospital with Adin. He was two weeks old, and those two weeks of his life could have been his only ones.

We had driven out to Long Island from the Bronx, where we were living, to spend the holiday with Jacob's parents, but we decided to stop at Jacob's grandmother's apartment to visit her and introduce her to her new great-grandson. The visit was lovely. Although frail and shaking from Parkinson's disease, Lilly (who would die only two months after we moved to Israel), held her new great-grandson, tears of joy in her eyes. As I nursed baby Adin, she reminisced about her own breastfeeding experiences with her three sons, one of whom had died from Hodgkin's disease in his twenties. She spoke of this son, Arthur (one of the people for whom we had named Adin), with a love and tenderness that seemed a result of having lost him at such a young age. Because of his untimely death, he would always remain her baby.

I remember noting the way in which Lilly was able to speak of her dead son without breaking down. She mourned him; there was no doubt about that. But she seemed somehow able to accept the fact of his death as fate. She was not overwrought with grief. After all, he had died about twenty years before. She was sad, but had no anger that I could detect.

Lilly was not a religious woman. Jacob's father, her son, had found Orthodox Judaism on his own while serving in the United States Army. He is a *ba'al t'shuvah*, one who "returns" to Judaism, a somewhat ironic term since it usually refers to people who had no religious upbringing.

After his religious transformation, Lilly tolerated his religious demands on her: she observed Shabbat when she stayed in his home, and she acted in his presence and the presence of his friends as if she lived a religiously observant life.

Listening to her speak of Arthur's death, I wondered how Lilly reconciled herself with the injustice of his being taken from her and the world at such a young age. Without a religious framework, I wondered, from where did she draw her strength and support? Lilly was an uncomplicated woman, with no pretenses and surprisingly few needs or demands in life. It was precisely her simplicity and lack of need to examine things further that baffled me. She did not pursue a life of the spirit. What helped her through this incredible loss?

Lilly would eventually spend her last months living in a nursing home, where she sat and watched television, ate only when someone stood over her and shamed her into it, and waited to die. With little will to live and no fighting spirit left to speak of, she seemed to keep going in spite of herself. She sat and waited to die much like she now seemed to accept Arthur's death—passively. She accepted what life offered her with no protest and no search for a deeper meaning. It was merely what was.

We left Lilly's apartment and went on to Jacob's parents' house, a seven-minute drive from where his grandmother was living. A couple of minutes after we got into the car and were on our way, Michal announced from the back seat: "I have to make!"

We had just asked her at Lilly's apartment if she needed to use the bathroom, and we were annoyed at what we thought was just an attempt to capture our attention. With the new addition to the family, she was probably feeling deprived of attention. The next five minutes were chaotic, with Michal crying, and Jacob and me trying to coach her in the skill of "holding it in." When we parked in front of Jacob's parents' house, Jacob jumped out and ran with Michal into the house, while I got out of the car and opened the door to the back seat to get Adin. I remember noting that he had been crying at the beginning of the ride and was now quiet. I expected to find him sleeping soundly in his infant car seat.

When I opened the car door and leaned over to scoop Adin out, my world suddenly stopped. I felt like I was in a tank of water. Everything looked bloated and blurry, out of focus, surreal. Adin, my precious two-week-old baby who had done nothing but eat, sleep, cry, and digest and excrete his food, was sitting in his seat, lifeless and blue in the face, with his cheeks puffed out like balloons, his lips swollen and purple, and his head hanging to the side as if he had been strangled. I did not think that he had any life left in him. I thought I had lost him forever.

I fumbled clumsily with the car seat straps, trying desperately to get him loose. My fingers felt like useless appendages. *That damn button! It's stuck again!* I pushed with my fingers using all my strength, and after what seemed like hours, I succeeded in opening the safety lock. I flung the straps off Adin and grabbed him out of the seat. I turned him upside down and shook him; blood spurted from his mouth and nose. With my baby hanging upside down from my hands, I ran inside the house, screaming, "Jacob! Jacob! He's not breathing. I don't know how to make him start breathing!"

Jacob was with Michal in the bathroom, and he came out to see what was wrong. I practically threw Adin into his arms and stood with my hands over my face in shock. Jacob put Adin on the dining room rug and began breathing into his tiny mouth. Adin was lying there, still and limp and bloody, not the color of the living. I had the thought that Jacob was breathing air into a corpse. I felt utterly helpless.

I noticed Michal coming toward me. She had her pants around her ankles, and she was crying. "What's wrong with Adin? What's wrong with my baby?" Quickly, I grabbed her into my arms and took her to the living room, where I held her close, repeating like a mantra, "Everything will be all right, Michal. Don't cry." I did not believe this in the least. It is what I wanted to believe, and it is what I wanted her to hear. I didn't want her to feel my shock and pain.

I don't know exactly how long I sat there rocking Michal in my arms, but after what must have been less than a minute, I heard Jacob call from the other room: "He's breathing! He's breathing!" I ran in with Michal, and just as I saw Jacob—his shirt covered with spots of blood, holding a breathing and almost pink baby on his chest—I heard sirens coming down the block. Within seconds, two police officers and two ambulance medics were in my in-laws' dining room, and before I knew it I was in the back of an ambulance watching Michal, in my mother-in-law's arms, shrinking into the distance.

The end of this story is happy. We spent the next week in the hospital with Adin, and they observed him and did every test possible. They found nothing wrong and gave us no answers. We left the hospital with Adin hooked up to an apnea monitor with an alarm that would sound if he stopped breathing again.

Those few minutes during which I thought I had lost my baby were the worst moments of my life. What was happening to me did not seem real; yet I knew it was, and I felt totally powerless. Tragedy was striking, and all I could do was let it happen. I felt a complete lack of control, painfully similar to how I had felt when I was mugged a few years before at gunpoint. It was as if someone were grabbing Adin away from me and I had no power to fight back.

That Sukkot I did not sit in a sukkah. There was no sukkah at the hospital, and I refused to leave Adin's side. Perhaps I did not need to sit in a sukkah that year. I had experienced the essence of Sukkot when I saw my baby devoid of life, when I held Michal in my arms so as not to lose her, too, when I sat in that hospital room praying that my baby would be okay. I felt viscerally the vulnerability of the Jews who wandered through the desert, not knowing where they would end up, at the mercy of God and nature. My life was a fragile sukkah, and it did not tumble down—this time.

I look down at Adin now as I sing God's praises. If we hadn't discovered him at that moment, it would have been too late. Our precious gift from God would have been taken from us. We came within a few seconds of mourning our newborn baby, who, after being with us now for only one year, is an irreplaceable part of our lives. His name, so fitting for him, means gentle, kind, delicate, and precious. He is so sweet and loving, but he is also tough. He's been through so much in his short life. He's already experienced the thinness of the barrier between life and death.

If we had lost Adin, would I still be standing here in this sukkah singing God's praises? What would my life have looked like had Adin not made it back to the world of the living? Would Jacob and I have been able to sustain our marriage? Would we have had the courage to go ahead with our plans to move to Israel? Would I have had confidence in myself as a parent with Michal? To have another child? Would I have abandoned Judaism again out of anger at God? Would I have been able to sustain a belief in a divine force in the world, or would I have returned to my teenage belief that all is chaos?

There is room for such doubts in Judaism. On Sukkot we read the book of *Kohelet* (Ecclesiastes), traditionally ascribed to King Solomon, who many believe was prone to depression. This refrain echoes throughout that mysterious and deep poem: "*Havel havalim. Hakol havel.* Futility of futilities. All is futile."

"The sum of the matter, when all has been considered: Fear God and keep the mitzvot, for that is the whole of humanity. For all of humanity's deeds God will judge, all that disappears, whether good or bad." This is how the book of *Kohelet* ends, although many scholars believe that this ending was tacked on later by the Rabbis to Solomon's text. With or without the ending, it is a fitting reading for the holiday of Sukkot, the time we set aside to experience our vulnerability.

How do I stand here in the sukkah praising God when I know that I could easily be standing here today without Adin at my feet? In a moment, my sukkah could fall in, tragedy could befall me, my life could be over or changed forever. Why do I sing *Hallel*?

In the end, I ask myself, what do I have but my life, to live in the best way I can? I will never know all the answers. I will never know why there is seeming injustice in the world, but I will always be accountable for my own actions.

According to Rabbi Isaac Luria, the great Jewish mystic who lived in Safed in the sixteenth century, when God created the world the first step was *tzimtzum*, the withdrawal of the *Ein Sof*, God as infinity, leaving in its center a vacuum. Into this vacuum a ray of light was channeled through vessels. Some of these vessels could not contain the power of the light, so they shattered and released the light in the form of sparks, along with shards of the broken vessels, into material existence. Most of the light was returned to its divine source, but some remained in this world. As human beings with free choice, we can fix this brokenness. By acting ethically and spiritually, by living a life of holiness and devotion to God, we can liberate these sparks and restore them to divinity. This is called *tikkun*, the repairing of the cosmos.[1]

If I don't strive to use my life in meaningful ways, there will be a cosmic loss in the universe. My potential will have been wasted, and an opportunity for *tikkun*—no matter how minor in the great scheme of things—will have been lost forever.

That is why I praise God beneath this makeshift ceiling of branches and bamboo. It is as temporary as my life, but while it is here it does have a purpose. I thank God for whatever life I have been granted, and I praise God in order to find what is good and holy in myself.

This moment, at least, has been infused with the sacred because it has been fully lived.

From the time that Michal was three years old until the age of six, when she started first grade, she went to *ganim* run by the Reform movement here in Israel. Most of the children in these *ganim* were from somewhat religiously traditional homes, but some were not. Some were even self-proclaimed atheists. For good and for bad, Michal was exposed to some ideas that she would not have heard in an Orthodox *gan*. She and the other girls wore *kippot* during *tefillah* just like the boys did, which I saw as totally positive. However, she also heard opinions about God and religion that she would not likely have heard in a more traditional setting, about which I was more ambivalent.

One night Adin, Michal, and I had just finished singing the Shema, and I was sitting in the rocking chair nursing Meira. I usually sit with the kids as they fall asleep; with three young children vying for my attention, after school activities, play dates, and an otherwise hectic schedule, this is often our only quiet time together. During this time they tend to engage me in conversation about what is on their minds.

"Do you believe in God?" Michal asked me last night from the top of the bunk bed she shares with Adin.

"Yes," I answered. "Why do you ask?"

"Well, Danielle told me that she doesn't believe in God."

"Why not?" I asked.

"Her *ima* says that there is no God and that there was a ball of fire that burst and that's how the world was created."

"But isn't it possible that God created that ball of fire that burst and became the world?" I asked.

Michal sat up in bed, looked at me, thought about my question, and then asked, "Why do you believe in God?"

"Well, we can't know for sure, can we? But I prefer to believe in God because it gives me hope that the world can be a better place. The idea of God gives us the chance to make our lives more special. God wants us to be better people, so when we believe in God we try to be better people. Isn't that a good idea?"

"Yeah . . ." Michal agreed.

I looked down at Meira sucking at my breast. I held her tiny hand in mine and brought it up to my face, feeling her soft skin like rose petals against my cheek. *She is so perfect, her presence so miraculous*, I thought. "When I gave birth to you and Adin and Meira, that made me believe in God even more. You guys grew into people inside me. It seems like God must have had something to do with that. It's amazing. Don't you think so?"

"Hmmm. I guess so." Michal lay down on her pillow. "I'm going to tell that to Danielle tomorrow," she said and began to drift off to sleep.

I wonder if Michal and my other children will wrestle with the idea of God as I did and still do. I assume they will, and that will not upset me. How can one be absolutely certain that there is a God, especially knowing that people suffer every day? I choose to believe in God because it is better than living in a world with no God. Like many others, I have rejected the image of God from my childhood: the old man who sits in a chair in the heavens and judges us all, punishing the wicked and rewarding the righteous. However, I do believe in a force that adds meaning to our lives, that uplifts what could be a mundane existence, commanding us to make our lives holy and helping us bring the sacred into the world. The God that I experience has to be summoned by human beings. We need to work with God to create sacred space in our lives, to repair the world and make it a holy place.

CHAPTER FIVE

◆

Halakhah: Law

*For some people, the observable changes in halakhah
during the course of history will support the negation of its
eternal validity. For others, its adaptability to changing
conditions will guarantee its continued preservation.*
— Jacob Katz
Divine Law in Human Hands

AS AN ADOLESCENT, I often saw my parents as either hypocrites or slaves to the *yetzer hara,* the evil inclination. What we learned in Jewish day school and overnight camp did not mesh with the philosophy of Judaism that we lived at home. Our practices at home were more liberal than what I learned outside our home, and I assumed that my parents' approach was wrong. Especially at summer camp, I learned that certain family practices (such as swimming at beaches and swimming pools where men and women swim together) were unequivocally "against the Torah," and that is what I believed. The Jewish law that I learned in school and at camp was simplified so that we children could understand it. I did not appreciate then the true complexity of and diversity within the halakhic system—a complexity that my parents' religious lifestyle represented, to a large degree.

When we learned about tzitzit, we were told that all Jewish men and boys above the age of three should wear a *tallit katan.* My father, however, did not wear a *tallit katan* beneath his clothing, although he did wear a *tallit gadol* when he prayed each morning. All the boys in my class were required to wear a *tallit katan* underneath their clothing, and my father didn't even own one!

I was not aware then of the history of the mitzvah of tzitzit. Since the commandment is to wear the tassels on one's four-cornered garments, if one is not wearing a four-cornered garment it is not necessary to fulfill this commandment. The general practice in the Orthodox community is for men to wear a *tallit katan* in order to fulfill this important mitzvah, which is commanded explicitly in the Torah. However, if a man does not wear a *tallit katan*, it is not a transgression in the way, for example, that not keeping Shabbat would be. At school, I learned simply that all males should wear tzitzit; the intricacies of the law were not explained to me. In my eyes, my father was blatantly sinning.

Similarly, I learned that every Jewish man and boy should wear a kippah on his head at all times. My father never wore his kippah to work at the law firm where he is now a partner. My teachers did not explain that wearing a kippah is a *minhag*, a custom, and not strictly law, and that the custom has obligatory force only when reciting a blessing and praying.[1]

Married women must wear a head covering while in public, I learned in school, but my mother wore a hat only when she was in shul. No one explained that there are many opinions on how a married woman must cover her hair—ranging from those who say that a woman's hair is not considered *ervah* in today's society and doesn't have to be covered at all, to those who say that every strand of a married woman's hair must be hidden at all times (even in the privacy of her bedroom). My mother, who did what her mother did, was following the opinion (even if she did not realize it) that hair today is not *ervah*, and that the proper practice of married women covering their hair is relative to contemporary social norms of modesty.

The disparity between what I learned in school and at camp and what I saw at home confused rather than broadened my perspective, because no one explained to me the legitimacy of alternative and multiple approaches to observance. What I was presented with at school and camp, I believed, was authentic Judaism, whereas my parents' religious lifestyle was a reflection mostly of their weakness.

The variety that I encountered as a child ultimately encouraged me to develop a more accepting attitude toward pluralism in the Jewish world. I understand now that my parents' practice was a result not of weakness but of their own struggle with the balance between tradition and modernity. They often followed more lenient halakhic positions that allowed them to more easily assimilate into the modern world. Their choice was in some ways a risky one, as parents passing on a religious tradition to their children. A more intellectualized and more nuanced religious approach is sometimes harder to grasp. A simplistic outlook is easier to rationalize away, but it is also easier to hold onto as practice.

Yet I believe that had I been shown nothing but a black-and-white model, I would not be religiously observant today. In my case, the simplistic portrayal of the Jewish legal system that I learned in school backfired. Rather than making our religion easier to grasp, it frustrated me. As I discovered life's complexities, the model I had learned no longer worked. Without the alternative of my parents' model to turn to, once I passed adolescence and let go of the grudges and anger, I might well have abandoned the religious lifestyle entirely. I am grateful to them for providing a textured model of religious observance, alongside the approach I heard at the educational institutions to which they chose to send me. The stricter, more closed model may appear to be safer, but many children (and adults) react negatively to a model that they feel is not intellectually honest, and rebel against it. Freedom and openness can be effective aspects of passing on a religious way of life.

I don't think we need to present children with simplistic models of Judaism. My children and I often discuss varying religious observances, and they have been able to apprehend, at their own levels, the concepts of pluralism and individual choice. They were surprised to discover that not all Jews keep Shabbat, and that even those who do don't necessarily keep it the way that we do. But now that they know, they often quote this idea back to me—for instance, when they see Jews driving cars on Shabbat. I have explained to Michal that although most women do not wear a tallit in shul, some do, and that a woman may choose whether or not she wants to wear one; Michal did not have any trouble understanding what I was trying to convey. I have even told her that some people think that women should not wear a tallit.

"But that isn't fair!" she said, her hands on her hips. "Right, *Ima*? Right, girls can do everything boys can do? Right, if they want to they can play baseball and Power Rangers? And boys can play with dolls and wear jewelry?"

Of course, this was not the first time that the topic of gender had arisen. When, to my dismay, Adin and Michal began labeling certain toys and games as either "for boys" or "for girls," I told them that boys and girls can play all the same games and with all of the same toys. I told them that the only difference between them at this age is the way that they go to the bathroom.

Michal was reciting my own teachings back to me. Unwittingly, she was also pointing out to me a tension between my pluralism and my feminism. A true pluralist, I often feel, should be able to present all practices as morally equivalent, as long as they are within certain ethical guidelines and no one is being forced to comply with these practices. However, as a feminist and a pluralist, I struggle with this perspective. On one hand, I believe that women should be given the choice to pursue all endeavors and not be hampered by their gender, biology permitting. On the other hand, I respect the beliefs of others who do not agree with me, as long as the women in that society or community comply and are not being restricted against their will—and, of course, as long as these beliefs are not forced upon me. I do not advocate forcing my opinions on the women in such a culture, although I advocate dialogue with them so they can see that other options exist. ("Choice" is a complicated matter, in light of cultural conditioning and societal approval.) I explained to Michal that not everyone believes that men and women can do all of the same things, and that although this may seem unfair to us, they do not see it that way.

"Although we do not agree with them, we have to respect their beliefs," I told her. "As long as they do not try to tell us what to do, we should not tell them what to do, but we can talk to each other and explain why we do and think what we do."

The concepts of personal choice and different beliefs and observances are not beyond the comprehension of most children, and I am disturbed by the assumption of many adults (who themselves believe in these concepts as ideals) that it would be best to present things to children more monolithically. My parents lived their lives open to these ideas. They exposed us to Conservative Judaism through our relatives and our friends when I was a child. In school, the norm was Orthodox observance, despite the fact that the student body was composed of children from Conservative and Reform homes as well as Orthodox homes. These differences were not acknowledged and certainly never condoned. Even I, who came from an Orthodox home, was made to feel alienated when the halakhah we studied in school did not coincide with the way we practiced at home. I can only imagine how my non-Orthodox peers felt.

We have chosen to send Michal (our only child old enough for elementary school) to a pluralistic school that is intentionally composed of an equal number of religious and secular children. One of the purposes of this mix is to foster understanding, respect, and friendship between these two often polarized groups. It is a principle of the school to respect the various practices in each child's home and to foster this value of mutual respect among the children. Michal tells me, nonjudgmentally, that although she and her religious peers pray in the mornings, the secular children in her class go to a separate classroom for a different activity. When I ask her what activity, she shrugs her shoulders and says, switching into Hebrew (a habit she has when speaking about her activities in school), "*Hem m'chabdim otanu* [they respect us]." As her mother I am, of course, charmed that Michal considers "respecting" an activity. I am even more glad to hear that she is already assimilating this concept of mutual respect.

My gratitude to my parents for presenting me with a complex model of Jewish observance, and my appreciation of the delicate balance they were attempting to maintain, still leaves me with questions. I wonder why, for instance, my father chose not to wear a *tallit katan*, or a kippah to work. Even if there was halakhic backing for his practices, why did he choose to do fewer mitzvot rather than more? When I ask him, he says that it was the accepted practice among his peers not to wear a kippah in the "outside world." Although they were not ashamed to be religious Jews, they did not want to "advertise" it either. They were afraid of anti-Semitism and wanted to blend in with the rest of society.

"I wanted to be judged on my merits," he explains. "Even as a kid I wore a baseball hat instead of a kippah. In my generation, we didn't want to stand out. This was before pluralism and multiculturalism became the fashion."

As a child, he felt embarrassed to wear a *tallit katan*, and he found it physically uncomfortable. They itched, he says, and even if he tucked the tzitzit in they would often come out of his pants. When he lived in a dormitory at law school, it would have been "out of the question" to wear them. He may not have been ashamed to be a religious Jew, but certain ancient practices did embarrass him. He also admits that he never liked wearing a *tallit katan*.

My mother tells me that her decision not to cover her hair when she married was not a decision at all. She never felt the need to choose. "Even the wives of the rabbis in the Modern Orthodox world did not cover their hair. It just wasn't something my peers considered."

"Did no religious women cover their hair back then?" I ask, incredulously.

"No, of course some did, but they were all more right-wing than us. Covering your hair was something that belonged in Boro Park [a right-wing Orthodox neighborhood]. My father's mother did wear a *sheitl* [a wig]," she continues, "but it was so ugly. My mother's mother wore one back in Europe, but she left it there. We associated covering hair with the 'old country.'"

In my parents' generation, Modern Orthodox Jews did not want to stand out. They felt conflicted about holding on to those traditional practices that would draw attention to them, and head coverings for both men and women in the "outside world" fell out of practice. My parents and their peers were also obviously ashamed of some of these practices that seemed so backward and out of place in the modern world. For my father, wearing a *tallit katan* and a kippah, and for my mother, wearing a *sheitl*, *tichl* (head scarf), or hat (outside the synagogue) would have been akin to declaring a desire to return to the *shtetlach* (small villages) of Eastern Europe.

In deciding not to adhere to these traditions, my parents and their peers were choosing to present themselves as modern people; to an observer, they look no different than any other upper-middle-class New Yorkers, Jewish or non-Jewish. That is how they want to be perceived: as modern, enlightened thinkers, not as Jews tied to ancient and seemingly archaic practices. Although it has become acceptable to wear a kippah or a hat on the streets of New York City, my parents admit that they are set in their ways and still feel uncomfortable "advertising" their Jewish identity.

I wish that my parents had articulated to me their own conflicts, ambivalences, and thoughts regarding their religious observances. Instead, because I did not really understand their perspective, the seeming incongruity of their lifestyle was magnified in my eyes to an irrational degree, leaving me angry, confused, and disillusioned with my parents and the community they had helped to build. Although the nuanced religious lifestyle with which they raised us was an important practical model, I wish I had had the vocabulary with which to understand it.

I don't fault my parents for seeking a comfort zone rather than a higher level of religious commitment, nor do I fault them for raising me in a nonegalitarian religious environment. There was little if any consciousness at the time of gender issues within Orthodoxy. Although the women's movement was in full swing and did affect the liberal movements of Judaism, there was no comparable movement in the more traditional Jewish world when I was growing up in the 1970s and '80s.

Covering my head and wearing a *tallit katan* are vital mitzvot that express Judaism as something that I take with me wherever I go. I want Judaism to permeate my entire life, as I believe the mitzvot are meant to do. I am not ashamed of my religion, either; my head covering is out there for everyone to see. The goal of my parents and their peers was to have tradition and modernity coexist; my goal is to harmonize them, so that each enhances the other.

One of the most significant areas of Jewish law that my parents observed less strictly than what I was taught in school was kashrut. Traditionally, not only nonkosher meat itself is forbidden, but anything cooked in a pot or oven that was used to cook nonkosher food is also off-limits. The same applies for meat and dairy: not only may one not mix meat and milk, one must also have separate cookware and flatware for dairy and meat meals. My parents kept the latter half of this rule strictly at home. In our house we even had separate sinks for meat and milk utensils. Outside our house, however, we ate food in nonkosher restaurants, although the food itself was not in the categories that are forbidden by Jewish law.

My parents' laxity in this area was based more on practical considerations than on theoretical ones. Neither of them grew up eating out anywhere but in kosher restaurants (although they rarely ate in restaurants at all as children), but when they were in Europe for their honeymoon, there was little to eat that was strictly kosher, and they started eating kosher-by-ingredient foods in nonkosher restaurants. They tremendously enjoyed eating out, especially when traveling. For special evenings in the city, my parents would arrange to meet friends at a fancy nonkosher restaurant and eat fish. This was before there were so many quality kosher restaurants in Manhattan, and they didn't want to give up the pleasure of dining out. Most of their friends did this as well; it was generally accepted in their community. My father also often took clients out for business, and he felt that he had to wine and dine them. It would have been awkward for him to order only a salad.

I sensed, from the negative comments that my father sometimes made about ultra-Orthodox Jews, that he thought the rabbinical strictures regarding kashrut, like those that affect how Jews dress, were overly restrictive, creating unnecessary barriers between Jews and non-Jews, religious and nonreligious Jews. I also sensed that my father, a man who appreciates a gourmet dinner and a fine wine, believed that these laws were too ascetic, turning Judaism into a religion of self-sacrifice and self-punishment, which is something he associated with Christianity rather than Judaism.

We did not often violate the rabbinic laws of kashrut as a family. My mother was more ambivalent than my father about their practice of "eating out"; this was not a practice of which she was proud, and she did not necessarily want to pass it on to her children. When we did go out for dinner, which was not often, it was usually to one of the few kosher establishments available to us: Chopsie's Pizza or McDavid's in Washington Heights, the home of Yeshiva University; or Shmulke Bernstein's on Essex Street on the Lower East Side, another half hour or so south of "the Heights." But once a year, the night before Passover, when our kitchen had become *Pesahdik* (kosher for Passover) and all kosher restaurants were closed in preparation for the holiday, we would go to the local Friendly's, where my siblings and I would order a "Fishamajig," our favorite pre-Passover treat.

A Fishamajig, a Friendly's innovation, is a fried fish sandwich with melted cheese and tartar sauce between two slices of a Kaiser roll, and I loved it. I relished the greasy breaded fish, and I salivated over the gooey yellow cheese, food coloring and all. To bite into the sandwich and let the tangy tartar sauce ooze out of the corners of my mouth was gastronomic heaven. This was a particularly special treat because it was something we did along with the rest of America. We actually saw other children eating Fishamajigs at Friendly's on television commercials! With a Hebrew name, special dietary restrictions, and strict limitations on what I could do on Friday night and Saturday, I never really felt part of American culture.

I see now that this is the point. At least one of the purposes of the *mitzvot lo ta'aseh*, the "negative" or restricting commandments, is to set Jews apart, to make us different and therefore holy. When each aspect of our lives is touched by Jewish law, we are constantly being reminded of our need to mirror Godliness. We are not *supposed* to blend in with everyone else. When we restrict our actions, we make our experience of living a completely conscious one, in which we are constantly thinking about how we act, always working towards making our lives more meaningful. Abstaining from nonkosher foods means not eating everything available to us, developing a consciousness about what foods we put into the bodies that are a gift from God. Refraining on Shabbat from activities that are related to work and the act of creating gives us time to reflect upon our lives instead of getting caught up in a constant rush of goal-oriented activity.

As a child, I grudgingly appreciated that there was something special about being different, but I did not absorb the value of making sacrifices on a day-to-day level in order to achieve a broader and longer-lasting goal. Sometimes I just wanted to be like everyone else.

However, every Passover, the fact that I so much looked forward to eating a Fishamajig was a theological problem for me. It was cooked in a nonkosher restaurant with nonkosher utensils, and the kashrut of the cheese and cooked fish could not be guaranteed. Despite how much I loved the taste of this sumptuous fast-food dish, I thought that I was committing a sin every time I ate one. As my bat mitzvah approached, I became much more concerned about sinning. After all, it was now I who would be accountable to God, not my parents. When girls reach twelve, and boys thirteen, they are responsible for their own transgressions and also reap the rewards of their own good deeds. The spring before my twelfth birthday, as Passover approached, I decided to stop eating Fishamajigs.

As usual, about a month before Passover, my mother announced to the family that we were beginning to clean for the holiday. No more food was allowed outside the kitchen and the dining room. We would each be responsible for cleaning our own rooms, schoolbags, and jackets. The entire house, from garage to attic, underwent a thorough spring cleaning, with the ultimate end of ridding the place of *hametz* (literally "leaven," although the custom has become to rid your house of every crumb of food and particle of dirt from the previous year). In order to accomplish this, we look in every nook and cranny, including coat pockets and beneath the cushions of the couch. Then, once the rest of the house is thoroughly cleaned, the kitchen must be completely overturned. Everything—from dishes to dish towels, from pots to pot holders—is put away in boxes and replaced by corresponding kosher-for-Passover items. My siblings and I helped to wrap the year-round utensils and pack them away in boxes to be brought down to the basement for the duration of the eight-day holiday. We unwrapped the Passover pots and pans, salt and pepper shakers, and silver *kiddush* goblets that we had packed away the year before. As we uncovered the dented tin water kettle, the fraying *matzah* cover I had embroidered in first grade, and the chipped glass frying pan my grandmother used to fry her *matzah brei* every year, the tastes and rituals and songs of the holiday returned to consciousness like long-lost friends.

Before the special holiday foods, of course, was the pre-Passover treat of the annual Fishamajig at Friendly's. This year I was determined not to give in to my *yetzer hara*. When the waitress, in her tight peach top, miniskirt, and white ruffled apron, came to take our orders, I waited my turn and then announced self-righteously, in a loud, clear voice: "I'll have a cold tuna sandwich on rye."

My younger siblings, Noah and Rebecca, were too young to appreciate the significance of what I was doing, but my parents and Jonathan looked at me with surprise. I *always* ordered a Fishamajig. What was wrong with me?

"Here's Miss Holier-Than-Thou," Jonathan said when the waitress left. "She can't eat a Fishamajig because it isn't kosher enough for her. She has to get a *c..o..l..d*"—he drew out the word for a few beats for emphasis—"tuna sandwich. She doesn't want any of the cooties from the hamburgers to rub off on her."

"That will be enough, Jonathan," my mother said, looking over at me with a reassuring smile. She had more of an inclination toward strict Orthodoxy than my father did. I've always assumed that if it weren't for my father, she wouldn't eat in nonkosher restaurants at all, and maybe she would have sent us to more right-wing Jewish schools.

"We'll have tuna sandwiches, too," my mother told the waitress, indicating my father and herself with her hand.

When the waitress brought out our orders, I eyed my siblings' Fishamajigs and French fries. They looked delicious, and for a moment I regretted my decision, especially when the waitress put my tuna sandwich in front of me. It looked so plain, so ordinary. We had tuna all the time, even at home. But I knew that I could not turn back now, and I reminded myself that I would be sorry if I gave in to my stomach. *Isn't God more important than some greasy fish?* I asked myself. As a child of eleven years, I understood the rabbinic law my siblings were breaking to be coming directly from God. There were French fries on my plate next to my sandwich—clearly also cooked with nonkosher utensils—and I knew that I would have to give up those as well, so I offered them to my siblings, who were delighted.

It was the best tuna salad sandwich I'd ever tasted, and it wasn't the overly generous amount of mayonnaise, the soggy iceberg lettuce, or even the out-of-season pink tomatoes that made me savor every morsel. It was the reward I was earning each time I swallowed. *Surely I will merit a place in the World to Come,* I thought with each bite.

In my freshman year of high school, we studied the talmudic Tractate *Hullin,* which deals with, among other things, the laws prohibiting eating dairy and meat together.

In the Torah, the commandment appears three times, "Do not cook a kid in its mother's milk."[2] In the Mishnah, there is a discussion about how to interpret these verses. [3] All agree that, according to Torah law, one is forbidden to eat with milk only the meat of animals that suckle their young, but there is a disagreement as to what the rabbinical law is in this regard.[4] The majority opinion broadens the prohibition to include fowl, so that people would not become confused and transgress the original Torah prohibition—this is called putting a "fence around the Torah."

The Mishnah, however, also includes the minority opinion of Rabbi Yossi HaG'lili, who says that only the flesh of a species that produces milk is prohibited; according to him, fowl should not be included in the prohibition. Although Rabbi Yossi's opinion is not accepted as law, like many other minority opinions it is preserved in the Mishnah. When I studied this mishnah in Talmud class in high school, I was surprised to learn that such a basic element of traditional Jewish practice today, refraining from eating milk with any meat, including fowl, is disputed in the Mishnah itself. I had not realized that the Sages actually disagreed on such an elemental aspect of Jewish law.

Although our school opened up to us the dialectical world of the Mishnah and the Gemara upon which our halakhic system is based, it did not include in the curriculum a class that integrated what we learned in Talmud class with our current practice. I sat in class, amazed at the diversity in our ancient legal texts, and I wanted to know how that translated into the rigidity of the Orthodox Judaism presented by my teachers. When I raised my hand in class and asked my teacher this question, he shooed me away with his hand. "Those questions are not for this class," he said. "We don't have time for theology."

Since no one would give me a reason to follow the interpretation of this prohibition as it was accepted by the mainstream, I decided to follow the interpretation that made the most sense to me. One Saturday night when my parents were out, Jonathan was in the city, and I was minding Noah and Rebecca, who were watching television in my parents' bedroom, I took some leftover turkey from Friday night's dinner from the refrigerator and melted some cheese on it in the toaster oven.

I don't remember if I even liked the taste of the dairy-fowl combination. It was the act itself that was important to me. It was not enough for me to simply doubt. I could not live only in the world of ideas. It was not enough for me to think that I considered Rabbi Yossi's opinion valid; I had to act upon my convictions. I had to make concrete, tangible, and real this new complexity that I had discovered in the Judaism that was such an integral part of my life.

My rebellion was a cautious one. I was careful not to make anything in my parents' kitchen nonkosher. When I melted the cheese, I did it on a disposable foil pan and then put the temperature of the toaster oven on broil so as to render it kosher again with the high temperature. Although I thought I had decided that the rabbinic law was nonsense, I apparently wasn't so certain.

I wonder if it would have made a difference to me if my teacher had answered my question by explaining the necessity of following communal norms in order to be part of a larger social group. I can now make the argument: in any legal system, a decision must be made as to what is within the system and what is outside it. In this particular case, the law was decided against Rabbi Yossi HaG'lili. In order for the community to remain intact, for common practices to define identity, a system of law must set norms and standards; the alternative is anarchy. Each member of a community cannot individually choose which opinion to follow if "community" is to have any meaning.

There are no mechanisms to formally enforce Jewish law. In this respect, Jewish practice has become a personal matter. However, communities require norms that define what is and is not "kosher." There will always be room to maneuver within those definitions, but the purpose of the law is to draw boundaries. According to current Jewish law, the opinion of Rabbi Yossi HaG'lili is outside those boundaries.

Our tradition preserves these rejected opinions, demonstrating the diversity of ideas involved in making a halakhic decision and maintaining their validity, perhaps for later generations to resurrect and utilize in their own halakhic decision making. This is stated explicitly in the Mishnah itself: "Why do we preserve the words of the minority along with the majority, being that the law is like the majority? In case the opinion of the minority should find favor in the court's eyes and they should want to rule like the minority."[5] The Mishnah stipulates, however, that "the court cannot overturn the ruling of a previous court unless it is greater in wisdom and number . . . Said Rabbi Judah: If so, why do we preserve the words of the minority along with the majority seemingly for no practical purpose? So that if a person should say, 'This is how I was taught,' we can say, 'You were taught the words of so and so.'" At very least, the authors of rejected opinions are still our honored teachers.

Halakhic development takes place on a communal rather than an individual level. For a community to resurrect Rabbi Yossi HaG'lili's opinion would be different from an individual making a personal decision to eat fowl with milk. In fact, the Gemara reports, in the time of Rabbi Yossi HaG'lili, in his town they did follow his opinion. However, with such a strong and unilateral tradition of not following Rabbi Yossi's opinion, even a community—much less an individual—would be hard-pressed to prove the validity of resurrecting his opinion.

As an adult wrestling with the issue of how to effect change within a slowly progressing system of halakhah, I appreciate the complexity of this issue and the delicate manner with which one must approach any such project. In order to have an impact on the community and therefore upon future generations of halakhically minded religious Jews, one must be in touch with the community in order to sense when an innovation will likely be woven into the fabric of communal practice. Such innovations will only be accepted if they are both pushed forward at the grassroots level and rooted in classical Jewish sources. That is where the preservation of a wide range of opinions comes into play.

Even if my teacher had explained to me the tensions between desiring individual autonomy while trying to remain within a community and a long history of tradition, my guess is that I would have eaten that turkey-and-cheese melt anyway. As a rebellious teenager wanting only to express my individuality, community and tradition were not just low on my list of priorities, they were my enemies. At fifteen, to conform was to stifle my essence. I wanted only to be myself without sacrificing anything for anyone, whether living today or thousands of years ago. Now I recognize that my Jewish identity and my need to be part of the Jewish community and tradition is actually part of the essence that I was so afraid of losing.

What fascinates me when I look back on this act is that I did not go out and eat a cheeseburger at McDonald's. In some ways, eating turkey and cheese was even more of a rebellious statement, because I was taking the system and turning it against itself. I was using the system in order to reject it, as if I were saying, "I can beat you at your own game!" Yet there was a part of me that did want to remain connected with my tradition, that still needed to find some kind of acceptance in the community in which I was raised. I could allow myself to rebel, but only with the opinion of Rabbi Yossi HaG'lili to validate my rebellion.

I am in New York, my first time back since our *aliyah*, our emigration to Israel, at the first International Conference for Orthodoxy and Feminism. The turnout is tremendous. At most, 400 women were expected. 1,000 showed up.

A young woman approaches me. She wants to talk. She pulls me aside and tells me about her goals and aspirations. She wants to become a *poseket*; she wants to be able to answer questions relating specifically to the area of *taharat hamishpachah*, family purity, and is willing to put in the necessary time studying to reach that level of knowledge.

"Can I ask you a personal question?" she says in a lower voice.

"Sure," I answer.

"How do you do all that you're doing with two small children?"

I tell her that it isn't easy and that I have resigned myself to the fact that it will take me longer to reach the level of learning to which I aspire than it would a person with fewer responsibilities. I may never even reach that goal, I consider aloud, because I can never achieve the kind of single-minded focus that I could before I had children, but that is a decision I have made willingly. My children enrich my life in ways that text study cannot, and I do not want to sacrifice that satisfaction for the sake of my studies. I learn so much from the experience of parenting that cannot be learned from a text. Raising children is also a form of Torah. Doing so much isn't easy, I say, but it's manageable if you're willing to make some compromises.

"I'm asking," she continues, "because I got married almost a year ago, and my *heter* [dispensation] is running out." The *heter* she is referring to is permission by a rabbi to use birth control. Apparently, he gave her only one year.

I am somewhat taken aback by what she has told me. I am aware of the fact that there are those, even in the more modern sector of the Orthodox community, who ask for a *p'sak* (a personal ruling by a rabbi who specializes in answering questions of Jewish law that must be followed once received) on areas of halakhah as personal as the use of birth control. Yet the fact that this woman did so puts her original question into a completely new light in my eyes. She is asking me about balancing serious study with childrearing, because she knows that in a few months she will be opening herself to the possibility of conceiving, and she is apprehensive about becoming a mother. I had thought that she was asking in order to come to a decision on her own about when to have children, when in reality the decision has in effect been made for her. She came to me not to ask advice but rather to find out what her life is going to look like a year from now, a fait accompli if she and her husband are fertile and there are no complications.

Understanding this now, I add, "You should never have children if you don't want them, if you don't feel ready. It's a huge responsibility that should not be taken lightly. It will change your life, without a doubt, and unless you're open to that change, unless you want that change, you shouldn't do it. If you don't feel you're willing yet to give up many of your own needs, you shouldn't become a parent. If you're not ready, you will feel trapped. Besides, children can sense resentment in a parent."

She looks at me with her green eyes wide open, and I hope that the seriousness of what I am saying reaches her. I feel ambivalent about nearly telling her directly to disregard a *p'sak* she received from a rabbi whom she respects, especially at a conference on Orthodoxy and feminism, which I have come to because of my commitment to both halakhah and feminism. Here is a woman so committed to the law that she is willing to trust that this rabbi, a scholar of Jewish law, knows what is best for her in light of both the halakhah and the facts of her particular case. Since she has consciously decided to place this important decision in the hands of her rabbi, who am I to criticize her decision? On the other hand, how can I condone handing over the responsibility for deciding such important issues regarding one's personal life? Will the rabbi be raising these children?

I wonder why it is that I am so resistant to the concept of asking a rabbi for a *p'sak*. I was born and raised in the United States, a democratic country, but so were many of my more traditional peers. My attitude, I am sure, is in part due to my parents' approach. They never went to a rabbi to ask for a *p'sak*. My father believed that it was idolatry, that people who did this were worshipping their rabbi like an idol. For my parents, Judaism was a religion of autonomous decisions strongly steeped in religious tradition. What was not convincing to them, what did not appeal or speak to them, was not necessary as long as it was not flagrantly unacceptable in their community. Normative halakhah had an enormous influence over their lives, but it was not the final word. The final decision was always theirs.

This is an approach to halakhah that I have taken with me into adulthood. I feel acutely the tension between my need for autonomy and my desire to submit to the authority of a system of law in order to be part of a larger community and tradition. My parents showed me through their example that one can make personal decisions about halakhah while still remaining committed to the system as a whole, without having to put one's life completely into the hands of others. My parents asked rabbis and scholars for advice, but they never asked for a *p'sak*. My parents were never willing to hand over the responsibility for their life decisions to another person, and neither am I.

Yet what is different about my parents' approach and mine is that they never strayed from their own community's norms of practice. They always had communal support for their religious decisions. My father was not the only one of his peers who did not wear a kippah to work. In fact, most of his peers did not. He never asked a rabbi for a *p'sak* on the issue, but he did do what those around him were doing. On the other hand, when I wear a tallit or tefillin, I am going against the normative practice of even most of those whom I identify as in my community. They do not, for the most part, condemn what I am doing, for it is not forbidden; nevertheless, most women in my community choose not to wear a tallit and tefillin themselves.

I take the practice of every mitzvah seriously, and I believe that I must personally integrate mitzvot into my life and make the decisions about how each and every one will play out. Without this approach to religion, it loses much of its transformative power for me. Submitting to a divine force that in some ways will never be understandable to us as limited human beings is an important and humbling religious experience, but to submit and hand over all religious decision making to another human being *is* almost akin to idolatry. It is a difficult distinction to make, when rabbis are the teachers of our tradition and are attempting to represent God's will. However, human beings can only *interpret* the Torah; we can never directly know God's will. We must, in the end, make our own decisions about what God wants from us. Halakhah should be used as a guide for that decision making process, especially on a communal level, but we must acknowledge the fact that halakhah itself is not the word of God. The alternative has been proven to be quite dangerous, leading to physical violence and even the assassination of an Israeli prime minister.

Those who have spent time studying, who know the issues involved in adhering to halakhah and also have insight into the personal religious realm, should serve as guides for us in our religious development, much as one might solicit the advice of a stock analyst when considering an investment or a social worker when exploring options for an elderly parent. Where a religious guide differs from these examples, however, is that halakhah touches every aspect of one's life. Both of the above examples are also religious decisions about which one may potentially wish to consult with a religious guide whom one can trust. If you find such a guide, you should consider yourself fortunate, but to allow another human being to make a final decision for you is another story entirely. It is akin to idol worship because it absolutizes the authority of a single individual. We have no prophets today, and no one individual can speak in God's name.

The night before my older brother, Jonathan, left for college at Brandeis University—a secular university founded by Jews when there were quotas for Jews in American universities—I was sitting at the top of the plush, carpeted staircase, my ear between the wooden banister rods, listening to the discussion going on downstairs in the kitchen. I could picture the scene: my mother, father, and brother sitting around the Formica table in the breakfast room; my stocky, brown-haired, brown-eyed brother looking like he would rather be anywhere but there; my short, bespectacled father nervously biting on the earpiece of his glasses or smoothing his thinning, graying hair over his receding hairline; my petite mother clutching a mug of tea and nervously nibbling on Nestle's chocolate bits straight from the bag.

"We are very proud of you, Jonathan," my father was saying, and I knew that he was. Jonathan did not excel academically at the local elementary Jewish day school. He was a fine student in English and history, but his math and science grades were poor, and my parents, like most upper-middle-class Jewish parents, expected their children to excel in all areas. Originally, they sent him to a small, all-boys' yeshiva high school because they thought it would be a more nurturing environment for him, since he was also, in addition to his poor math and science grades, not particularly outgoing. It was not until he convinced my parents to switch him into a large coeducational liberal Orthodox Jewish high school in tenth grade, where he was encouraged to develop his talents rather than dwell on his deficiencies, that he blossomed into the intellectual that he is today. When Jonathan was accepted into Brandeis, my parents were thrilled, especially my father.

My father always told us that he was not especially studious, although when he put his mind to it, he did very well in school. My impression of him in his youth is as a carefree yet directed young man who could somewhat effortlessly accomplish what he put his mind to, both socially and academically, even with a small physical handicap: his half-closed left eye. I know that he played basketball and had an active social life at school and at a variety of summer camps. He met my mother when they were counselors at a Jewish summer camp when they were both in their late teens.

This image I have of my father is quite the opposite of how I remember Jonathan as a child. He was chubby and quiet, with a talent for art and an active imagination. He had friends but was not particularly social or popular. He did like to perform in plays, however, and came out of his shell through theater. He was not athletic and would rather spend his free time drawing or playing imaginative games. Jonathan and I would stay up at night after our parents thought we were asleep, weaving elaborate stories that we acted out with our stuffed animals. We created an entire make-believe world with regular characters that we brought to life each night after dark. My brother was not the idealized son of a father who imagined Sundays in the park tossing a baseball around, and that, coupled with Jonathan's poor grades in math and science as a kid, must have been a disappointment for my father.

"Brandeis is a good school, and we want you to excel there and explore," continued my father. "I never had that opportunity, and we want you to have it." My father went to college at Yeshiva University, the only university outside Israel that combines the study of sacred Jewish texts in a religious environment with secular study. The school's founders believed in the principle of *Torah Umaddah*, Torah and Science, which was also the motto of the Modern Orthodox movement. My father, however, felt that YU had failed in its mission to offer both Jewish and secular subjects side by side at a serious institution of learning. He told us often about the poor quality of the education he received at YU, especially in the secular subjects.

My father continued to speak to my brother in the kitchen: "I never opened Plato, Aristotle, or Homer until I got to law school. I want you to read all of them and more." What saved my father, he tells us, was his three-year stint at Yale Law School. It was there that he was introduced to all the books he says he should have read in college. He considers most of his four years at YU a waste of time and would not send any of his four children there, despite the risks of sending a young adult into an atmosphere that could easily tempt him or her away from Jewish values.

"But," my father added (I had been anticipating a catch), "I'm not paying all this money to have you throw away everything that Mommy and I believe in and have spent the past eighteen years trying to demonstrate to you is the best way to live." My parents had apparently noticed Jonathan's lackluster attitude toward Jewish ritual and law. Jonathan had never exactly been a Talmud scholar. In fact, it was I who studied Talmud with my father on Friday nights, and it was I who won the "Mishnah Bee" in second grade. Jonathan would eventually become a doctoral candidate in Jewish history at Brandeis, but he was never interested in the intricacies of Jewish law, and he never seemed to feel particularly bound by them, either.

"Mommy and I discussed this at length, and we've decided that in order for us to be able to send you off tomorrow, you must promise us three things," I heard my father say. Now, this was getting interesting. I moved down a few steps.

"First, you have to promise that you will lay your tefillin every morning." I could picture Jonathan's face drop. He put on his tefillin in school during prayers each morning because he had to, but on Sundays I knew he never did. My mother would ask him when he came downstairs for breakfast, "Did you *daven*? Did you put on your tefillin?" and Jonathan would nod his head. I knew he wasn't lying directly, because I asked him once; his answer was, "Yeah, I put them on, and then I take them right off."

"The other things we want you to promise are that you will keep kosher and observe Shabbat—and that means not only the *lo ta'asehs* [the prohibitions]. We also want you to promise that you will go to shul on Shabbat night and morning, not go out on Friday night, and not sleep until noon, as I'm sure a lot of the other students in your dormitory will be doing."

Not going out on Friday night would be a huge annoyance to my brother, who I was sure was looking forward to finally being free from restrictions like these, but waking up to go to shul on Saturday morning would, I knew, be simply impossible for him. He had only managed to do it until then because my parents dragged him out of bed. Similarly, even if he promised to put on tefillin every morning at college, I knew he would never keep that promise. He would have to be motivated to perform this inconvenient ritual. He would have to wake up earlier and set aside time to pray, which I knew he would never do. He couldn't wait to be free of what he saw as the burden of laying tefillin.

I'm quite sure that my parents knew this as well. They were neither oblivious nor stupid. They knew what went on at college, and they knew that most teenagers and young adults go through a period of questioning and searching and often rebelling. So why did they ask him to make a promise he would never keep? Perhaps it was to absolve themselves of future responsibility. They were sending him off to be an adult, and they had done all that they could to encourage him to continue in the traditions they had passed on to him. They brought him up in a traditional home, and they even made him promise to continue the most basic of these traditions while away, but they could not physically force him to keep these laws for the rest of his life. This was a final effort to remind him of what they thought was important and right.

Sitting on that staircase then, I did not know enough about parenting in general or my parents in particular to understand the desperation in their demands. I was horrified by the ultimatum they were offering Jonathan. How dare they try to control him that way, from back home in Westchester when he would be so far away in Waltham, Massachusetts! My heart went out to my brother, not only because I felt sorry for him but also because I knew that this would be my plight as well in three years' time.

By now I was sitting at the bottom of the steps, and I wondered what Jonathan would answer. He couldn't promise them what they wanted to hear, because he wouldn't keep such a promise, but he also couldn't refuse. They had offered him an ultimatum; they had trapped him. He would have to promise, which meant that he would have to lie. I sat and waited.

"I can't believe what I'm hearing!" Jonathan exploded. "What am I? A first grader?" I could tell that he was pacing now. As he had become a teenager, he had become much more outspoken, especially

with my parents. Throughout high school, he and my parents argued a
lot. It was as a result of his arguing that he was allowed to switch high
schools. "Do I have to promise you I'll brush my teeth before I go to
sleep? Give me a break." So he had opted for a third possibility: trying
to convince them to reconsider.

"That's not a bad idea," my mother finally piped in. "You've never
been very good at remembering that, either."

"Hardy har har," Jonathan said in his Ralph Cramden voice. "It's
so funny, I forgot to laugh."

"Listen, Jonathan," continued my mother, surely taking chocolate
bit after bit out of the yellow and brown plastic bag. "It may seem
unfair to you, but we couldn't think of any other way."

"This is the most ridiculous thing I've ever heard!" he tried again.
His voice cracked. He was obviously on the verge of tears.

"Is it really?" That was my father again. Maybe he did think that
by promising to do these things, Jonathan would be shamed into living
the life of an observant Jew while at college. More likely, Jonathan
would break the promise and then feel a tremendous amount of guilt
about doing so. Was that my parents' objective?

"How can I make this promise to you? Let's say I can't keep it."
Jonathan's voice was softer now, tired, as if in defeat. I could picture
him with head lowered, arms sagging at his sides.

"Oh, you can keep it," I heard my mother say. "It shouldn't be so
much to ask. You've been Orthodox all your life. You'll just have to get
up off your rear end and pull yourself together. No more lazing around.
That's part of being an adult." My mother often seizes the opportunity
to lecture us on the art of being an organized, tidy, and responsible
adult. "Do you think it's always so easy for Daddy to wake up earlier
so that he has enough time to *daven*?"

My adolescent self was amazed at what seemed like a double standard in my mother's outlook. She was telling my brother that he had to
pray and put on tefillin every morning, even though it would never have
occurred to her to do the same herself. It would, of course, have been
an even bigger leap for her than it would eventually be for me. Because
I grew up with an expectation of certain kinds of egalitarianism—no
matter how misleading that expectation was—the reality of the inequal-
ity between men and women when it came to Jewish ritual was jarring

to me. I did not take it for granted, but my mother did. She was raised in a world with much clearer gender roles; the idea that there are certain mitzvot that only men perform flowed naturally from her gendered worldview. *This is what religious Jewish men do*, she undoubtedly believed, without thinking these words consciously, *and I want to send off a proper religious Jewish man*.

What surprised me was that my parents could not acknowledge out loud the reality that my brother Jonathan did not want to keep the laws of kashrut and Shabbat and put on tefillin every morning. If their son actually intended to abandon the beliefs and practices and age-old traditions of his people, they did not want to talk about it. Was this because they thought that by talking about alternatives to their commitments, they would be condoning them? Perhaps they believed it most important to present at this stage in Jonathan's life an unambiguous message about what they thought was acceptable.

With all my father's talk of openness to the world, when it came to the religious observance of his children, the expectations were different. He was much more tolerant of the behavior of others than he was of the behavior of his own children. His standards were higher. Both he and my mother expected us to follow in their footsteps—to make similar, if not the same, decisions as they did when choosing a religious path. As a parent, I struggle with this issue myself. How do I pass on my religious values to my children? I don't want to be overly didactic, because that approach would probably have the opposite result from what I intend, but I want them to understand how important these values are to me and to our people. How can I convey that without rigidly enforcing behavior in my home?

Sometimes I wonder if wanting to pass on my ideals about religion to my children is a noble cause at all. What I want most for my children is for them to be happy, healthy (both physically and emotionally), moral, self-confident, self-loving human beings capable of loving others and appreciating the good in them. Their relationship with Judaism, Torah, and God should not be biased by my own. I should honor their right to choose their own paths. Yet I want so much to see them continue as links in the chain of the Jewish tradition. If they turn away from Judaism completely, it is hard to imagine that I would not be disappointed, even devastated. Is this fair?

Trying to negotiate this tension is not a simple matter. But I cannot present everything as equal. I cannot pretend—nor do I want to—that I don't care if they abandon religious Judaism altogether, but what I can try to do is instill in my children a love of Torah and Judaism, no matter what form it takes—even a completely nontraditional or an ultra-Orthodox way of life. I don't want them to see Jewish practice as a burden. I want them to see it as a gift that enhances their lives.

I would be fooling myself if I refused to admit that I would like to see my children adopt the values to which I am committed. I am a pluralist but not without strong opinions. I would love to see a daughter of mine praying with tefillin. I would love to hear a son of mine tell me that he refuses to say the *brachah* in the morning thanking God for not having created him a woman. If that same daughter chose to live as a Buddhist in Tibet, could I be happy for her? If that same son decided to live as a *haredi* Jew in Boro Park, could I be happy for him? Although some lifestyles may be fine for others, will I be just as openminded with my own children and the choices they make? Perhaps the most difficult thing about parenting is being able to let go of the desire to mold our children. They are not clay in our hands. They are human beings whose needs may be very different from our own.

I hope that I will have the strength and clearheadedness to be a role model to my children of someone who has carved out her own way and found her own spiritual route, while trying to maintain a respect for others, a sense of communal responsibility, and a tie to my past. If I succeed in transmitting to my children these values and a solid religious education, they will have the tools to negotiate their own religious paths, and whether they decide to lay tefillin, eat only kosher food, or keep Shabbat will be an informed, serious, personal decision.

My parents' approach has changed over time. My younger brother, Noah, is engaged to be married to a woman from a Reform background. My parents tell me that they like Maya, his fiancée, very much, and they think that the two are a good match: mutually supportive, attentive to each other's needs, and complementary in their strengths and weaknesses as well as in their personalities and likes and dislikes. However, they can't hide the fact that they are, in one respect, disappointed—not so much because Maya is not from an Orthodox background (although that would make things much easier and more comfortable, they admit), but because they sense that Noah and Maya do not intend to live an Orthodox lifestyle. "Could you talk to them?" they asked me during their last visit to Israel. "Just let them know you are available if they have questions, like about going to the mikveh and things like that."

I assured my parents that I would be happy to offer my services if Noah and Maya want my help, but I will not force anything on them. I will just let them know that I am available.

What impresses me about my parents' attitude is the humble, almost ginger, manner in which they are approaching this issue. It is clear what their ideal vision for their son's lifestyle is, but they are not confronting him as aggressively as they once would have done. They are respecting his space and treating him like an adult. Most important, they realize that what matters most is that Noah is happy. They do not want to minimize that or sour it for him. They try to steer him in the direction they see as most desirable, but they do this quietly and don't let it dominate their relationship with him and his wife-to-be. I admire the way that they have ordered their priorities, and I recognize how much they have grown as parents in the past two decades. Parenting, it seems, is a lifelong learning experience. That is both its beauty and its challenge.

The phone rings. It is 7:00 A.M., and I am putting away my tefillin after my morning prayers. Jacob is away on one of his frequent business trips, Michal and Adin are still asleep, and Meira, who is six weeks old, is swinging in her infant swing in the kitchen. I zip up my tefillin bag and pick up the phone.

"Hello," says the voice on the other end, which I recognize as that of Daniel, one of my best friends since childhood. We grew up together in the same community, went to the same schools until college, lived near each other in Washington, D.C. (where he still lives), and we remain close friends even though we live in different countries and time zones. It's midnight where he is, and I realize that this is the first time I've heard his voice since before Meira was born. We communicate mostly by e-mail, so his congratulations had come over the Internet.

"I was up late, so I decided to call and wish you *mazal tov*," he says. "I finally took my orals and passed them, so now I have time for things like phone calls to Israel. Now all I have to do is concentrate on writing my dissertation."

"That's great news," I say. I started a doctorate at Bar-Ilan University the previous year, and I know that writing a dissertation is no small task. Daniel has no children, so for him, I imagine, the idea of finishing a doctoral dissertation does not seem quite as far off as it does for me.

I can't help hoping that one day soon Daniel will decide to have children. He would make a good father, I think. He enjoys and appreciates children. He is a schoolteacher and an administrator and loves what he does for a living, but for him, having children is a complicated matter.

Several years earlier, after I had moved back to New York from Washington, I met Daniel one day for coffee. He was in graduate school at the time, getting a degree in education. Daniel has a gift for teaching, and he spent a few years after college teaching Jewish history at the elementary school that he and I both attended as kids. At the time we met for coffee, he was studying for a Master's degree in education so that he could return to the Jewish day school system with even more to offer, in administration and curriculum development as well as teaching.

Late the night before, when I was already in bed, Daniel had called to say that he would be in New York the next day. "Can we get together for a couple of hours?" he asked me.

It was not a convenient time for me. It meant that I would have to leave school—the women's yeshiva where I was studying Talmud and Jewish law full-time—early and meet him before picking up Michal, then one year old, from preschool. I would have preferred to meet him later and have him over for dinner, but I heard in his voice how important this was.

"I really need to talk to you," he said. We arranged a time and place for our meeting. I hung up and turned over in bed to go to sleep, wondering what was so serious that we couldn't speak about it over dinner at my apartment. I was mildly worried, but knowing Daniel, it could be any number of issues, so I set aside my inclination toward analysis and went to sleep.

We met at four o'clock the next day at a kosher coffee shop in Riverdale, a heavily Jewish middle-class neighborhood in the Bronx where I had been living for a few months since our move back to New York. I hadn't seen Daniel in months, and he looked wonderful, the best I had ever seen him look. He had lost at least twenty pounds, and he had new wire-rimmed glasses that made him look both intellectual and hip. He was wearing all black: a pair of black jeans and a black turtleneck, and his hair was cut short, with a little length on top so that you could see his hair's natural curl.

"You look great!" I exclaimed. "When did you lose so much weight?" Since he was a teenager, Daniel had been trying to lose weight. He tried liquid diets and Weight Watchers and appetite suppressant pills, but nothing seemed to work. There were times that I noticed him eating in a way that seemed almost obsessive; it was painful to watch. It was as if he were trying to fill an emptiness in his life as he downed an entire pot of macaroni and cheese.

"I've been really watching what I eat lately. I have a very small, light breakfast and lunch, and then I eat a regular dinner, but not very heavy. I'm also staying away from fat." He said this now as if it were so simple. It was just a matter of reducing his food intake. Whatever had been causing him to eat obsessively was now gone. He was "cured."

I had a feeling that his drastic weight loss was related to what we had come here to discuss. He was no longer trying to fill that hole in his life. It had been filled, and he had brought me here today, to this coffee shop on Johnson Avenue, to tell me by what.

We sat down at our table. Daniel looked nervous, anxious to sit down and begin our conversation. "Are you ready to order now?" the waitress asked.

We both ordered coffee—I without caffeine, he with—and I wondered if he would start talking about whatever topic had brought us here, or if he would wait for our drinks so as not to be disturbed by the waitress. I was becoming more curious by the minute. I had a few ideas about what he might say, but none stood out as the most probable, so I gave up on guessing and waited.

"I wanted to meet you today so that I could tell you something in person," he began. Apparently he was not going to wait. I looked into his face and recognized a familiar nervous smirk that had a habit of spreading across his mouth whenever he was embarrassed or anxious.

"Yes?"

"I'm gay," he said. There were a few moments of silence, and then he said: "Are you surprised?"

"Give me a minute to process this," I said. The truth was, I wasn't surprised—once I heard him say the words. I had never *assumed* that he was gay before, but now that I knew, it made a lot of sense. Suddenly, so many scattered pieces fit together into a neat puzzle.

Daniel had been involved with at least five women since high school, some more seriously than others. He and I had never been involved romantically. I had met a few of his girlfriends. He had brought a couple of them home to his parents' house—which was a block away from my parents' house—for Shabbat or Passover. There was always something strange about the way he related to women who were supposed to be his girlfriends. Something was not quite right—a certain tension and discomfort, coming mainly from Daniel, although I sometimes sensed that the women also felt uncomfortable. I don't think I ever saw him touch a girlfriend in public, and I used to wonder if that was some kind of barrier he erected around himself to guard against intimacy. He was the kind of guy who seemed awkward in his body. His tendency to be overweight, to pad himself with that excess fat, was part of that, I thought. Now it all became so clear to me. He had been guarding against sexual intimacy because he was not interested in women, and he felt he could not act upon the sexual urges that he had for men, so he made himself asexual.

Sitting in that coffee shop, I also began to understand the pain behind Daniel's extreme cynicism and anger regarding anything involving Jewish religious practice and belief. In junior high school, when I began my own rebellion and questioning, Daniel too began to rebel. Unlike me, however, he never returned, and his issues with the religion in which we both grew up seemed so personal, even more so than my own. He would scowl every time we talked about religion. He seemed personally wounded, or scarred, by his Orthodox upbringing, no matter how "modern" it was. His fascination with Jewish history always seemed to me like a mission to prove that the religion was based on lies and illusions. Now this all made so much sense to me. Of course—he was gay!

"Well, are you surprised?" he asked again.

"No, not really," I answered, shaking my head.

"Did you know already?"

"No, not really," I said again.

"I've been wanting to tell you for a long time, but I couldn't figure out how. So then I finally decided to just do it. Like this."

"How long have you known?" I asked, wondering how long "a long time" is.

"Oh, since junior high school, at least," he answered. Now I *was* surprised. Daniel was twenty-six years old! I'd known him since we were kids, and he hadn't even hinted to me that he was gay.

"You've known since then? How could you keep it inside so long?"

"Well, I don't know if you know that I've been seeing psychologists since I was a kid." Daniel was never a "happy" child; at some point he was depressed enough for his parents to send him to a child psychologist. "So I discovered it then, but I have been trying to fight it all those years, to repress it—to change. I had so many different psychologists, and they all tried to help me. A short time ago, I guess a short time before you moved back to New York, I decided to stop fighting it and just be myself. It's useless. I can't change, and trying only makes me miserable. I'm finally happy for the first time I can remember."

If his physical appearance was any indication of the health of his psyche, I knew that he was telling me an indisputable truth. "Well, that's great, Daniel. I'm truly happy for you." And I was.

For the next half hour or so, we talked about his new social life and how much better he felt now that he was at peace with his true self, but then came the inevitable questions.

"Are you planning to tell your parents soon? Your sister and brother? Are you going to come out to everyone?"

"I don't know, Haviva. That's one of the things I wanted your advice on. What do you think? You know my parents."

I certainly could guess that they would be devastated and scared. They would be angry, and would take it all very personally. They would definitely give him a hard time. However, I also thought that they should know, in order for them to have a genuine relationship with their son and in order for Daniel to be happy. I thought that by telling his parents, he would be honoring them with his honesty. He would be performing the mitzvah of respecting one's father and mother.

"I think you should tell them and everyone else," I said. "Clearly, you'll be better off the less you have to hide and continue your charade. It must drive you crazy every time someone asks about setting you up with a woman. I've heard your mother pressuring you to get married. How can you bear it?"

Daniel did tell his parents—one year later in his psychologist's office—and he called to tell me how they took the news. His mother cried. She admitted her disappointment, sadness, and even anger and said that she did not want to know any details of Daniel's social life. "I wish you hadn't told us at all," she said. She even told him that he should try to change his sexual preference. His father, on the other hand, reacted in a very rational way. He kept a serious and somber face and didn't shed a tear. "He has tried to change, and it didn't work," he said. "It seems that this is the way he is, for good. The psychologist says so. All we can do now is accept that fact and help Daniel in any way that we can. We may not approve of his lifestyle, but he is our son."

Daniel's mother has gradually changed her attitude. She seems to have come to terms somewhat with her son's homosexuality. She is not supportive of his lifestyle, but she has at least acknowledged it. At first she refused to meet his partner, Steve, but he has since been on family vacations, and last year, for the first time, he went home with Daniel for the Passover seder. Daniel says that his mother will never feel comfortable with the fact that her son is gay. She will probably always see it as at best a disappointment and at worst a tragedy that has befallen her family. Homosexuality still disgusts her, and she does not see any way to reconcile a gay life with Judaism. Still, like many parents of gay men and lesbians, she has come a long way from that day in the psychologist's office.

"So what's it like with three kids?" Daniel now asks me in our phone conversation across the ocean, and I am brought back from my memories of that New York day to my Israeli apartment.

"Harder than two," I answer, "but of course, she's worth it. She's really adorable—not an easy baby, but wonderful, even when she's crying. Are you guys still thinking about adopting?"

"Yes. We talk about it a lot, but I'm not sure what we'd do about the Jewish thing. I'd like to have that resolved before we bring any kids into the picture. Steve is interested in converting. We go to shul often on Friday night, and he's going to classes. We've even gone to see a rabbi, but I feel funny about it. I've been so ambivalent about my own Jewishness that it seems strange to ask Steve to become Jewish. Why would he want to become part of a religion that calls what we have a sin? Why do I even care if he's Jewish or not? Sometimes it's such a mystery to me that I want to raise my children Jewish at all. Why do I? Am I a glutton for punishment?"

I have no answers for his questions. Life as an actively religious Jewish gay person is bound to be a struggle. Daniel's homosexuality made him feel alienated for a while from everything Jewish. As I was being made to feel that my gender somehow made me less holy, Daniel was being told that his sexual desires made him the antithesis of holy. What an overwhelmingly humiliating and harmful way it must have been to grow up!

Yet he has not abandoned Judaism entirely. Ironically, since he has accepted that he is gay and has come out of the closet, he has begun a journey back to Jewish religious practice. He is searching for a way to find spiritual and cultural expression in the religion and way of life that he always saw as oppressive. He does not live a completely religiously observant lifestyle, nor does he feel personally bound by halakhah, but he does observe Shabbat and most holidays, and he is very much tied into the Jewish community and Jewish culture. He is now the principal of a Reform Jewish day school. His partner, Steve, did eventually convert, and they own a house together. They recently made their kitchen kosher. There may be more surprises to come.

"It is important to me to be involved in a Jewish school," he says. "Ideally, I would like to be an administrator at a Modern Orthodox day school, but I want to be out while I'm doing it. Those kids need to know about being gay, and they need to know that it's okay. Otherwise some may go through the torture that I did. It's like you insisting that you wear your tallit and tefillin in public. It's a protest of sorts, a refusal to let them tell us what we are and how to be—a refusal to conform, repress our true selves. Just as important, it's a way to reach out to others who have the same feelings and are afraid to affirm them. My being in a leadership position and at the same time openly gay will provide a role model for the gay kids who pass through the school. It will also sensitize heterosexual kids at a young age and hopefully prevent them from becoming bigots."

It's a shame that Daniel cannot reach children in Orthodox Jewish day schools; an Orthodox educational institution will not, at this time in history, hire an openly gay person. The Orthodox mainstream does not want to provide gay Jewish role models for their children. Although he is reaching Jewish kids in the liberal Jewish day school where he works, Daniel will not be able to realize his dream of going back to the "scene of the crime." That is one of the big differences between my struggles and his. Although my religious lifestyle choices are clearly not approved of by a large portion of the Orthodox community, I can still connect with people in that world. "Feminism" may be a dirty word in most of the Orthodox community, but not in all of it—and it is certainly not as dirty a word as "homosexuality."

I have no solution for Daniel. I can only tell him why *I* stick with Judaism, why *I* continue to struggle. I don't want to lecture him on the topic. We talk some more, about lighter issues, mutual friends, and then we say goodbye. I have to get the kids dressed and off to *gan*.

"I'll send you an e-mail soon," I say. Then I hang up the phone and sigh. As despair-ridden as I sometimes feel on my journey as a religious feminist, at least I have some hope; at least I have seen changes in attitudes about women's roles and opportunities in religious life in my own lifetime. A woman with my ideas and dreams would have been in Daniel's place only a generation or two before me: frustrated, angry, and in many ways alone. While the specific issues he faces are not strictly my own, they are very much echoed in my own journey, as I immerse myself in Jewish tradition even as who I am and what I do appears to challenge it.

> *If a man has intercourse with a male in the same manner as with a woman, both of them have committed a* to'evah. *They shall be put to death.*
> —Leviticus 20:13

I am heterosexual and already have built into my psyche a certain bias against gay and lesbian sex. I cannot relate to it or imagine someone else desiring it. Since the majority of human beings are straight and since heterosexuality seems more "natural" because only sex between a man and a woman can produce offspring, part of me, I must admit, is inclined toward the idea that homosexuality is a perversion. I can even make that notion fit theologically with my view of Torah and mitzvot.

It is clear that the Torah views human beings as having a strong *yetzer hara*. After God destroys the world with the flood, God promises never to curse the land or destroy the entire human race again: "For the inclination of humanity's heart is evil from its youth."[6] One of our tasks on earth is to fight our *yetzer hara* and overcome it, and thus become holy. In fact, the verse prohibiting homosexuality is part of a long list prefaced with the general commandment: *Kedoshim tih'yu* or "you shall be holy."[7]

I can entertain an elaborate theology of holiness that asserts that no matter how strong one's *yetzer hara*, it still must be conquered; that is our challenge. I can almost even believe such a theology as I argue for it. Something about it, however, screams out to me, *Injustice!* For if a man is a lover of men, isn't that the *neshama*, the soul that God has given him? Why would God create up to ten percent of the earth's population with a sexual desire that can be healthy and loving for two consenting adults, that can breed supportive romantic relationships that last a lifetime—and then forbid that mutual love, calling it a sin? There is something about forbidding homosexuality that is different from the other prohibitions on the list. This verse unsettles me in a way that none of the others surrounding it do.

Forbidding the other acts, which include incest, adultery, and intercourse during menstruation, does not negate the emotional core of a person, or hamper his or her ability to have healthy relationships and a healthy self-image. People who observe these prohibitions can still have an active and satisfying sex life, just not with particular individuals or at a particular time. Jewish law generally tends to channel desires in a healthy and constructive way through mitzvot. But there is no mitzvah through which a homosexual can channel his or her sexual desires. There is no way in which a gay man or a lesbian can sanctify a romantic relationship in accordance with halakhah as it stands today.

In the case of incest, we do not consider a man who acts upon a sexual desire for his daughter, for example, as a psychologically healthy human being. Recent studies have shown that homosexuality, on the other hand, is not a mental illness. All of my personal interaction with gays and lesbians supports my belief that they are most healthy emotionally when they are living an openly gay life.

In light of recent scientific findings, the biblical verse in question might be reinterpreted to apply only in the social context and time period of its origin, requiring us to create a new halakhic approach to homosexuality in our own era, with a new understanding of what it means to be gay or lesbian. Such an approach is taken by Rabbi Bradley Shavit Artson from the Conservative movement in his *t'shuvah* (responsum).[8] He argues that this verse cannot be applied today because it is from a time period when "homosexuality" as an identity or a lifestyle was unknown, and therefore this is not what is described by the verse. Sex between men was part of pagan cultic practices, not part of a lasting, committed, loving relationship.

Even if Artson's reading is historically accurate (counter-*teshuvot* argue that it is not), it is difficult for us today to interpret a Torah verse so differently than the Rabbis did or to dismiss it completely—in effect, to erase its significance—because of its social context, especially where it is a prohibition that Jewish law commands us to obey even under the threat of death. Such a drastic approach would not be taken seriously by most halakhic communities and authorities today, most of whom understand change in Jewish law in less radical terms, as one new link at a time in a chain of tradition. Going directly back to and reinterpreting a biblical verse while negating all its rabbinic commentaries would be seen as breaking that chain of tradition. Such radical reinterpretation is possible in principle when there is a Sanhedrin, a formal legislative Jewish legal body, but we do not have this today. Otherwise, a *takanah*, or new enactment, could be put into effect that would nullify the applicability of the verse, but there is no consensus in this case to support this technique, which is used very sparingly and cautiously.

In order to consider a more humane view of homosexuality within halakhah, we must define the person to whom this approach would apply. It seems clear that if a person's inclinations are bisexual, the Torah's attitude would be that such a person should choose a heterosexual relationship and sanctify it in the context of *kiddushin*, or marriage, but what about those who are unalterably and completely homosexual?

Some halakhists today argue that there is no such thing as a homosexual; there is only a person who engages in homosexual acts. As long as one doesn't act upon sexual feelings toward a person of the same sex, one cannot be blamed for the feelings because these are unavoidable. In other words, a person is not defined by his or her homoerotic feelings. In fact, many people have these feelings to different degrees. What is forbidden is to engage in homosexual acts.

Many of the rabbis who espouse this position assert that a person with these feelings—even a self-defined "gay" person—can change and become "straight," with the right therapy and attitude. This assertion, however, goes against everything I know from my relationships with gays and lesbians. Most gay men and lesbians whom I know have tried a heterosexual path and would, in fact, prefer to be straight, all other things being equal. In the end, however, they define themselves as homosexual in the same way that I define myself as heterosexual. Being gay is about desires, emotions, and attractions that are at the core of a person's identity. It is more than a series of acts; it is a sense of oneself in the world and with others.

The rabbis who reject the idea of innate homosexuality categorize one who acts on homosexual desires as a *mumar* (someone who systematically rejects halakhah and the halakhic system), or more specifically, a *mumar l'teiavon* (someone who rejects a specific halakhah because he or she has a strong desire for something forbidden and wants to enjoy it).[9] As opposed to a *mumar l'hach'is*, who rejects halakhah in general or a specific halakhah because he or she disagrees with it, a *mumar l'teiavon* is one who places his or her illicit desire above the yoke of Torah. We all have God-given weaknesses that we need to work to overcome, this argument goes, and just as the community does not ostracize one who is breaking the laws of Shabbat, for instance, we should welcome gays into our communities, as long as they see that what they are doing is sinful and the result of a weakness they are striving to overcome. The goal is to change one's sexual orientation or to choose celibacy. The forbidden acts are not merely sexual intercourse between men, but any kind of homosexual sexual behavior.

One of the problems with this approach is its equation of a Sabbath violator with an actively gay person. Keeping Shabbat, although difficult for some, cannot be equated with being forced into a life of celibacy or a life without a loving partner or a family, or with entering into a marriage with a person of the wrong sex. Forcing someone to choose one of those alternatives is not in tune with other Jewish values that emphasize the importance of creating a family, educating your children, satisfying your sexual needs and the needs of your partner, and loving your neighbor as yourself. In addition, since we know that there are people who have tried to change, unsuccessfully, what kind of self-image does such a position breed in them? For those who have homo-erotic feelings but are able to live a celibate life or to perform sexually with a person by whom they are not sexually aroused, even if they are told that their desires are fine as long as they are not acted upon, this is an almost impossible attitude to internalize. They would undoubtedly continue to internalize feelings of self-loathing and see themselves as "sinful" by their nature.

In addition, it is difficult to claim that these feelings are wholly per-missible within Jewish law if acting on them would be a sin, since there is a prohibition of *hirhurei aveira*, or thoughts of sinning. An approach that draws a distinction between homosexual desires and actions, claiming that the former are fine while the latter are forbidden, is prob-lematic for a variety of reasons—moral, psychological, and halakhic.

An alternate way to categorize a gay man or lesbian is as an *anoos* (one who is driven to violate halakhah by forces beyond his or her con-trol). The legal consequence of the forbidden act of an *anoos* is that the act remains a sin, but the sinner is not liable for his or her actions. This definition, at least, seems more in consonance with the reality of what it means to be gay or lesbian. Whether the desire for a person of the same sex is the result of nature, nurture, or a combination of the two, all of these forces are beyond a person's control. Repressing these desires surely results in an unhealthy psyche, which can be dangerous to a person's physical and mental health, and cannot support healthy relationships.

The category of *anoos* normally applies to one who is *temporarily* compelled to violate Torah law. But what of someone who is unalter-ably and *forever* compelled to do so? Also, even for an *anoos*, who is not liable for his or her actions, a homosexual relationship is still for-bidden, *asur*. Even mutual homosexual love is a negative thing. Being considered an *anoos* with all its associations would have harmful psy-chological effects upon the homosexual man or woman—less so than the *mumar* definition, which puts the burden of sin completely on the individual's "tendencies" and lack of self-control, but harmful nevertheless.

A gay man or lesbian, as we understand these terms today, defies already existing halakhic categories. If we want to maintain that some people have unalterable homosexual desires that would be unhealthy to completely repress, allow a way for gay men and lesbians to channel their love positively, and also uphold the Torah verse that states that intercourse between men is forbidden, how can we formulate an affirmative approach to homosexuality within the halakhic tradition?

I find useful the analogy to a heterosexual couple that refuses to refrain from sex when the woman is in niddah, the time during and after her menstrual period (and beyond if she does not immerse in the mikveh, the ritual bath). According to halakhah, such a couple is punishable by *karet* (being "cut off" from the nation by God). Both this punishment and the punishment for a male homosexual act (*s'kilah*, stoning) have no practical application for us today. We have no Sanhedrin to enact capital or corporal punishments, and punishments enacted by God are out of our control. So the real issue is how the community treats such a couple. What should be the halakhic communal policy toward homosexuality?

First, we need to define the act that the Torah verse forbids as narrowly as possible: that is, as anal sex, intercourse between men. With this interpretation, we can push the analogy with heterosexual couples who continually have intercourse during niddah even further. Such couples who are part of a halakhic community most probably keep that intimate fact to themselves. Similarly, gay male couples who wish to be part of a halakhic community would keep it to themselves if they were engaging in anal sex. The goal would be for gay male couples to openly participate in a halakhic community. The ideal would be for men to refrain from anal sex; but if they do engage in it, if they do not comply with that Torah restriction, they should not publicize that fact. Nor should anyone else try to investigate what goes on in the privacy of their bedroom.

This analogy links two kinds of relationships in which a particular sexual violation is being committed in the context of an otherwise halakhically acceptable and sanctified relationship (for now hypothetically, in the case of gay relationships). A community that instituted this policy would have to create standards for a sanctified romantic love relationship between two men or two women, and these standards could be modeled upon current halakhic norms for heterosexual romantic love relationships. That is, such relationships should be, among other things, monogamous, nonabusive, and mutually supportive.

This model does not change the labeling of homosexual anal sex as a sin; it is difficult, if not impossible, to honestly read the Leviticus verse otherwise, just as it is clearly stated in the Torah that it is a sin for heterosexual couples to have sex during menstruation. These can be difficult ideas to accept, because they define what could be a loving act as sinful, but we may need to simply embrace certain religious practices (or prohibitions) that are found in the Torah despite the fact that they seem objectionable. The challenge may be to find their profound meaning. Perhaps with time, if enough people find these biblical verses problematic, an approach like Artson's would be appropriate. There is a precedent in the Talmud for narrowing the interpretation of biblical verses: for example, the way that executing the *ben sorer u-moreh* (the rebellious son discussed in Deuteronomy 21:18–22) is written out of Jewish practice in Tractate *Sanhedrin*. However, to implement this kind of novel interpretation today, as Artson does, is so rarely (if ever) done that it would require the kind of mass support that does not exist on this issue—yet.

The main difference between the approach I suggest here and the approaches I outlined earlier is that I interpret the Torah verse in the narrowest way possible, attempting to uphold the dignity of the homosexual to whatever extent possible without negating the verse itself. This approach does require that the homosexual man who wishes to remain within the halakhic community accept that one kind of sexual act between him and his partner is considered sinful, but it removes homosexual love and even physical intimacy (aside from anal sex) from the realm of sin. It requires that homosexual men who wish to avoid sinful acts refrain from having anal intercourse, but it also leaves room for the acceptance of gay couples into halakhic communities without a general assumption that they are sinners, just as there is no general assumption that married heterosexual couples in halakhic communities give in to their sexual desires during niddah. Just as a man and a woman who are married have certain restrictions upon their sex life, so too would a gay couple. Not all gay men engage in anal sex, just as some non-Jewish couples and nonobservant Jewish couples prefer not to have sex when the woman is menstruating (albeit without waiting for ritual immersion afterwards).

Most important, this model allows for a homosexual relationship to be sanctified and for a gay couple to be together openly and unashamedly in a halakhic community. It is consistent with so much of Jewish observance, which assumes that every person's healthy desires can be channeled in a holy way, abiding by certain restrictions of those desires (even when the meaning behind the restrictions seems beyond our limited understanding) and applying those desires only in constructive ways. We are all required to restrict our actions and channel our desires in ways that are in line with Jewish law and values. The requirements for a sanctified homosexual relationship have yet to be formally defined within halakhic Judaism, but if they are, it would be possible to be a proudly gay or lesbian member of an observant community.

My parents never talked to me about sex, and they rarely kissed each other in front of us. Although I knew that they were romantic with each other—we did see occasional hand-holding and pecks on the cheek—I did not think of them as sexual beings. I had no knowledge or even thoughts about their sex life then or before they were married. I did not know if they had even kissed before they were married, although I assumed that they did. Their silence made me wonder if they would disapprove of what my high school boyfriend and I were doing in the privacy of his bedroom after school.

One evening, after I had been going out with Sam for a few months, I came home at around nine o'clock. As usual, I went straight to the kitchen to get a snack and then go up to my room to finish my homework and call him. But when I entered the kitchen, I saw my parents sitting at the table, with stern, serious looks on their faces.

"Haviva, come here," my father said.

"Yes?" I said, trying to seem nonchalant, as though I noticed nothing out of the ordinary.

"Sit down. We need to talk to you," he answered. I obeyed.

"It seems that everyone except us knows where you've been spending many of your evenings after school."

"You know I've been going over to Sam's house."

"Apparently you did not tell us the whole story," my mother jumped in. "We were under the impression that at least Sam's mother was at home while you were there. You didn't tell us that you were not chaperoned."

"Chaperoned? What is this, the fifties?" I stood, unable to sit. "Why do we need someone else there? I'm sixteen years old, Mom! I don't need a baby-sitter!"

"A chaperone is not a babysitter, and you know that just as well as I do, young lady."

"Apparently not," I said. I was pacing now in the kitchen, which was adjacent to the breakfast room. "Please tell me what the difference is, because it sounds to me now as if you do think I need a babysitter. Why else would you need Sam's mother to be there?"

"Don't play dumb, Haviva." My mother was standing now, too. She put her hands on her hips and pursed her lips in the way that she does when she's both annoyed and perplexed by me. My mother and I are opposites in many ways: She wipes the kitchen counters down every night with ammonia, while I'm lucky if I do a decent cleaning once a week; she's a stickler for doing things the proper way, while I'm passionate about individual choice. "It just doesn't look right for the two of you to be alone together. What do you think people are assuming when they hear that you're alone with him in his apartment when no one else is home?"

"You tell me."

My mother talked as she made her way into the kitchen. My father was still sitting at the table. "It isn't that we don't trust you, Haviva. We know you aren't doing anything."

"We know you aren't doing anything." Now what is that supposed to mean? I wondered. Did my parents really assume that I was innocently studying with Sam after school? Was that what they expected of me? Sam and I were not having sex. We were just fooling around—what my parents would have called "necking" or "petting" when they were teenagers. Although I knew that this was something my teachers would say was forbidden, it hadn't occurred to me that my parents would agree. Though we had never discussed it, I had assumed that the fact that they sent me to a coed school and camp meant that they

approved of some premarital intimacy. *Apparently,* I thought, standing there in the kitchen, *I was wrong.*

"We're just concerned about what other people might think," my mother explained. "We're worried about your reputation."

"My reputation?" I bellowed. "Let people think what they want. Let them say what they want. I don't care. If they have nothing better to do than sit around and talk about me, I feel sorry for them. They're not my concern."

"Don't be ridiculous, Haviva. Of course you need to worry about what people are saying about you. It's your future—"

"My future?" I shouted, standing face-to-face with my mother. "You mean my marriage prospects? Don't you think it's a bit premature to be worrying about that now? Come on!"

My father, who had joined us in the kitchen and was now also pacing, spoke: "You're sixteen. Mommy was twenty-one when we got married. It's not as far away as it may seem."

There they go, judging me based on what my mother did at my age. Well, I'll never be like her, I promised myself. (Ironically, I would get married at twenty-one, and my parents would say that I was too young!)

"Well, who wants to marry someone who's so petty and judgmental?" I asked, "Not me."

"Listen, Haviva, this is not up for discussion. Mommy and I have been talking about this, and we've decided not to allow you to go over to Sam's apartment anymore after school, unless there's someone there with you. Do you understand?"

I understood quite well; that was not the question. The dilemma for me was: Do I give in or not? I had no intention of putting an end to my after-school time with my boyfriend, and if I did agree I would be lying to my parents, which was something I had avoided until then. I hadn't always told the whole truth, but I had never directly lied to them about something this important. "You can't be serious!" I said.

"As serious as ever," my father replied.

"This shouldn't be such a big deal for you, Haviva," my mother added. "So you'll go to a movie or out to eat. Or you can stay late at school together to study. We aren't forbidding you to see him"—*as though they could really do that,* I was thinking—"we're just protecting your reputation."

That night, the two worldviews of school and home merged. *My parents are just like everyone else*, I thought. *Despite all of their liberal airs*, I told myself, *they also expect me to be a good Jewish girl. They expect me not to touch a boy until I'm married.* What plagued me most, however, was that my parents seemed to have assumed that I shared their values. Suddenly it became clear: my parents did not know me at all. I was not the pure and perfect daughter they thought I was. They had trusted me, and I had let them down. In order to continue to be me, I would continue to let them down. Pleasing both them and myself were mutually exclusive, unless I could manage to hide the true me from them.

When I returned from camp in New Hampshire the following summer, I discovered that I had lost more than twenty pounds in two months. I was five feet tall and weighed only seventy-eight pounds! Camp, with its egalitarian minyan, had been a liberating experience for me. But that summer, between my junior and senior years of high school, my issues with food began. Shocked and scared, I went to a nutritionist with my mother, and we all agreed that 100 pounds was a healthy weight for me. In fact, we also agreed that unless I reached 100 pounds and proved that I could maintain that weight for a few months, I could not go to Israel the following year to study at the all-women's yeshiva for which I was already registered.

At first I had no trouble gaining weight. After about a month of eating all the fattening foods my mother cooked to help me gain weight, I hit ninety pounds, but soon I began to slip into some of my old bad habits. I stopped eating breakfast, and for lunch I would eat only a tuna platter with salad. Dinner, which I ate at home, was a full meal, but I noticed myself eating mostly vegetables and salad and only a small portion of the main course. Sometimes I bought a low-calorie snack after school—frozen yogurt or popcorn—but I found myself controlling my eating again. My mother noticed it as well.

"Have another slice of quiche," she'd say. "Do you want some ice cream for dessert?"

"No thank you," I'd answer, and a concerned look would spread across her face.

Finally, after I had plateaued at ninety pounds for about a month, she asked me why I wasn't trying to gain any more weight.

"I don't know," I answered. "I just don't seem to be able to eat more. I know I want to gain more weight, but something is blocking me."

My mother looked at me, the most disturbed I had ever seen her, and said, "Do you think you'd like to try seeing someone? Maybe that will help you figure it out."

I knew that my mother had to be quite concerned if she was suggesting seeing a psychologist, since she usually believed that some things were better left unexplored. I agreed that it would be a good idea for me to see a therapist, so we asked the nutritionist for a referral, and the next week I had my first appointment.

Dr. Miller's office was near my school, on the Upper East Side of Manhattan. It was a well-appointed office in a fancy building, with a waiting room that she and another doctor shared. I would walk over to her office twice a week after school, and while I waited for her to finish her previous appointment, I would read *The New Yorker* until another skinny teenage girl would emerge from her office, sometimes crying, sometimes not. It was always this same girl who had the appointment before mine, but we never spoke. Our eyes would meet, and we would smile or nod, but neither of us spoke about our common ailment. Perhaps we knew that to speak to each other about it would have put us into a category: *anorexics*. As long as my problem remained mine alone, it was only that: *my* eating problem. "Anorexia" was a scary word, a disease that other people had, not me.

Perhaps that was also the reason I never really opened up to Dr. Miller. She would ask me leading questions, such as, "So why do you think you're fat?" or "Why do you want to disappear?" I felt that she was trying to fit me into her mold of a classic anorexic, and I resented that. I did not think that I was fat. I hated my bony body; that's why I was there. What I wanted was for her to help me break free of the limits I was imposing but didn't understand. No matter how much I tried to convince myself that I needed to eat, to gain weight, to stop controlling my food intake so much, I just couldn't do it. I would wander around the Upper East Side during my free periods or on the way to Dr. Miller's office, looking into bakeries and coffee shops, longing for the strength to just walk in and buy some of the baked goods: the hearty, tasty muffins; the greasy, flaky croissants; the sweet, crumbly scones.

Sometimes I would even summon up the courage to buy a jumbo bran muffin and a large coffee with whole milk. I'd actually enter the store. But somehow, I would always walk out with a large coffee with skim milk and a toasted dry bagel. I felt as though I had been possessed by a spirit.

The more my parents told me to eat, the more the spirit strengthened its resolve. My mother even got into the habit of sneaking more fattening ingredients into the dishes she prepared for me. She'd put wheat germ in the vegetable kugels and quiches, and use oil to fry the vegetables—like she told me she used to do with my food when I was a baby. Strangely enough—I have been a vegetarian since I left for college—all I would eat as a baby was salami, so my parents would hide my food on the spoon beneath a slice of salami. I caught on to their tricks, however, and began spraying the white kitchen wall with food from my mouth. Now, too, I caught on to my mother's tricks and insisted on knowing all the ingredients in every dish she prepared for me.

My father finally lost his patience. It happened after a skiing trip my family took one snowy Sunday soon after my younger brother Noah's bar mitzvah. We left early in the morning and did not come home until around nine o'clock at night. After a whole day of skiing in the cold, eating only tuna fish sandwiches and granola bars, everyone was famished, and as soon as we arrived home, my mother put some leftover lasagna and eggplant parmesan from the bar mitzvah into the oven to warm.

Soon we were sitting around the table eating. I took one look at the food and reached over to take some salad. Everyone else dove into the other food, and there was silence as we chewed and swallowed; everyone's concentration was on eating. My father, however, noticed that I had only salad on my plate.

"Aren't you having any eggplant?" my father asked. He knew better than to say "eggplant parmesan," because that might remind me of all the other fattening ingredients in the dish.

"Maybe after my salad," I said, not very convincingly.

"Aren't you starving?" my mother asked, knowing that would make no difference in what I ate or didn't eat.

I shrugged my shoulders. "What is that supposed to mean?" my father asked, an alarmed look on his face.

I shrugged my shoulders again, and that is when my father lost it. He got up and stood behind me. Then he grabbed my bony wrists with his strong fist so that my fork dropped from my grasp. He took the fork into his own hand, jabbed it into a hunk of eggplant parmesan and forced it at my mouth. I sealed my lips.

"You'll eat this whether you like it or not!" he yelled. "I've had enough of your nonsense. I won't let you starve yourself to death."

That word—*death*—frightened me, because I knew that he was right. Nevertheless, all I could do was fight him. My rational mind was not in control. I tried to pull myself free, but his grip was too strong. I began to shake my head and sealed my lips even tighter.

"Stop it, Dan!" my mother said, grabbing my father around his torso and trying to pull him away from me. "Just look at what you're doing. You're hurting her!"

"She's hurting herself, Ruth. Someone has to set her straight."

"But force-feeding her won't help. You're being unreasonable. Stop!"

My father loosened his grip on me and then dropped his hands. His face dropped, too, in shame, and he left the room. Later that night, he came to my room to apologize. I knew that he was right, that I might be slowly killing myself, but I also knew that his outburst would only make it harder for me to fight the force within me. We agreed that since he seemed unable to sit back any longer and let me work this out for myself, it would be a good idea for my parents to see a psychologist as well, to help them better deal with my "problem."

My parents started to meet once a week with Dr. Stone. We never discussed their appointments or mine, but I did notice them loosening their reins on me a bit, giving me more space. I could tell that it was extremely difficult for them to watch me struggle without intervening, but their "help" had only made things worse.

I had begun to feel claustrophobic at mealtimes. I couldn't eat in public. I had to leave the school building and buy lunch at a restaurant or a coffee shop. Eating in the presence of strangers was better than with family and friends. For dinner on nights when I came home late from school because of after-school clubs or meetings, my mother would leave me leftovers from the family's dinner, and I ate alone as I read the paper or watched television. Even on the nights that I had no meetings after school, I would ask to eat my dinner in another room. Of course, my parents complied with my idiosyncrasies related to eating, as long as I continued to eat. We were no longer hoping that I would *gain* weight; we were just hoping I wouldn't *lose* any more.

One evening, my parents came home from their weekly meeting with Dr. Stone and informed me that she had suggested that we all meet together: my parents, Dr. Stone, Dr. Miller, and I. I was nervous to have my parents in a session with me, but I was willing to try anything. I was desperate. It was May, and the school year was coming to a close. If I didn't gain weight quickly, I would not be allowed to go to Israel, and even if I went to school in New York, my parents might not let me live in the dorm at Columbia University.

Dr. Stone's office was also on the Upper East Side, so I met my parents there after school. They went out to eat before the meeting. It was understood that they should not invite me to come with them; eating together was not a pleasant experience for us anymore, even in a restaurant. So I stopped off at the frozen yogurt shop near my school on the way to her office and ate a large frozen yogurt with fruit and granola as I walked. I was proud of myself that I had actually gone through with ordering the granola; for weeks I had been planning unsuccessfully to order it. I savored each spoonful on my tongue as I walked north on Madison Avenue, wondering what the evening held in store for me.

I was the last one to arrive: the guest of honor. They had been chatting, apparently, and had saved a seat for me between the doctors and my parents. The doctors sat next to each other, Dr. Stone on the swivel chair from her desk and Dr. Miller on a tweed armchair. My parents sat together on a forest green leather love seat, looking as nervous as I felt. I sat down.

"I'm glad you agreed to come," Dr. Stone began. "Your parents and I have spent a great deal of time talking about you, and I'm glad to finally meet you. You're quite an accomplished young lady."

I was surprised by Dr. Stone's remark. I did not think of myself as accomplished, especially in this particular setting. I was a failure. I couldn't even do such a basic thing as eat, and I was surprised to discover that she and my parents talked about more than my "problem" in their sessions. It was not my accomplishments that had brought us here, so while her comment surprised me, it also put me more at ease.

To Dr. Stone, I was not a walking case of anorexia. I was a whole person with talents and dreams and a life outside my illness. I was not her patient. My parents were her patients, and I was their daughter who had come to her office to help her help them, to help us all figure out together what was at the root of our problem. Suddenly, it was no longer *my* problem; it was *our* problem. We had barely started the session, and I already felt that we were making some progress.

First we talked about how it made me feel when my parents told me what to eat: the resentment, the stifling feeling of claustrophobia, the lack of control. This was nothing new; I had even talked about this with them. Then Dr. Stone asked me if there were other areas where I felt my parents had too much control over me. This was a question we hadn't explored in my sessions with Dr. Miller, and it took me a couple of minutes to respond.

"Yes, there are," I finally said. "In just about every way, I feel them trying to control me: in what I wear, how I clean up after myself, what school I go to, where I live, where I go, who I'm with." I paused for a minute, wondering if I should go on, and then decided: *Why not? The situation is drastic. If I don't find a way to break free of this force that threatens to destroy me, I could end up in the hospital with an IV stuck in my arm next year instead of in Israel or at college.*

I felt surprisingly at ease in this setting. Suddenly, after all this time of hiding, pretending, and living a double life, I wanted to hold nothing back. I went on: "I feel them controlling me about religion, too. Maybe I don't want to be just like them, just like the way they expect me to be. Maybe I don't fit the exact mold of the good Jewish yeshiva girl daughter they want. I should be free to make my own decisions."

Dr. Stone looked at my parents and waited for a reaction. I looked into my lap and did the same. I felt a tremendous relief in having unloaded that burden, but now there was no turning back. My parents would probably be devastated. I wondered: *Would they disown me? Would they lock me in a room so that I couldn't go out and defy their wishes, shame them, go against everything they believed in?* These fears were irrational, but I felt them, because I knew what their ideal expectations were, and I also knew that I could not both live up to their expectations and be true to myself. I felt so profoundly the need to make them proud that I had projected my guilt feelings onto their own needs, turning my parents in my mind into unswerving, selfish, dictatorial ogres.

Finally, after a few minutes of silence, my father spoke: "You will be free to make your own decisions soon enough, Haviva. You'll be living under our roof for a few more months. As sad and anxious as it makes us to see you leaving home, going off on your own, making your own decisions, that is exactly what you will be doing, and there's nothing that Mommy or I can do about that." My father took a breath and continued: "But while you're still living under our roof, we insist that you follow certain rules. It's our home, and we expect the common courtesy of your complying with our requests while you are still living there."

I thought back to that conversation with my brother a few years ago when he was going away to college and my parents had insisted that he promise to follow certain rules. They had tried to control him even after he left home. Apparently, something had changed between then and now, but what? *Have I raised the stakes so high that they decided to loosen their grip?* I wondered. *Have they actually gained something from all of those sessions with Dr. Stone?*

"It will be the same next year," I whined. I hated the way I sounded, but I couldn't help it. Everything was pouring out. "The rules at the yeshiva are worse. There's a curfew there, and I'll have to wear skirts all the time. If they hear that I went to the beach or went mixed swimming or was seen with a boy, they could throw me out. I probably won't even be able to ask questions about my doubts. I won't have any freedom at all. I can't be what *they* want, either. That's just not who I am."

"So who are you?" my mother asked. She was crying. "Please tell us who you are."

"I don't know," I answered, "but that's what I need to find out, and I can't do that in yeshiva. I won't be able to explore, to find out who I really am, without everyone else telling me, expecting me to be something I'm not."

Again there was silence.

"So don't go to Israel next year," my father said. "You don't have to go. You know that. We thought you wanted to go. We would never force you to. All Mommy and I want is for you to be happy."

To hear those words was like hearing the click of my prison gates opening. I felt like screaming: *No, I didn't know!* I didn't know that my parents wanted me to be happy. I thought they wanted me to make *them* happy. On a conscious level I knew that I was the one who had decided to go to Israel, but on a subconscious level I felt locked into that decision. I felt as if I had to play a role that would make my parents proud.

I could no longer play that role. This is what the spirit that was fighting to control my mind and body was trying to tell me all along: *You want to please yourself more than your parents, and you can't do both. You need to find out who you are and then be that person completely. Enough hiding and enough pretending. It's tearing you apart! You need your parents to know the true you, whoever that is, whether they are proud of her or disappointed in her, because what is the use of their pride in an impostor?*

"Then I don't want to go," I admitted, for the first time, to both them and myself. "That is what will make me happy now."

My mother actually sighed with relief when I said this. I had been so wrapped up in my projections of what would please her and my father that I failed to see just how worried they had been about me. Only then did I realize that they did not want me to go to Israel, either—not at the expense of my health and happiness. They were afraid to send me so far away for so long after what had happened to me when I had been away at camp for only two months, and in the same country. Having me alive and well was more important to them than any other expectations they had for me. Although it may seem obvious that parents' instincts are to protect their children, even at the expense of their own happiness, I had not internalized that seemingly axiomatic principle until I heard my father's words and my mother's sigh.

My struggle with food was about control. That summer in camp, I had felt a taste of what it would be like to be free to make my own decisions, to explore my spirituality and religious expression on my own terms, whether that meant completely casting off Judaism or finding some way to reconcile myself with the religion of my childhood.

However, I knew that after camp I would be returning home to what I saw as a suffocating life—one more year at home, then another year at a yeshiva in Jerusalem. I felt closed in, restricted, controlled, chained, and I wanted to be free. So I grasped at the one thing that I knew only I could control: food.

In the end, however, I let the food control me. Why else would I allow my need to manage my food intake endanger my life? I was starving myself as a cry for attention. I had felt I couldn't tell my parents the truth about who I was and what I wanted, so I made them force it out of me.

A tension between the needs for autonomy and authority played itself out when I was a teenager in a struggle within myself to negotiate my relationship with my parents, especially as they represented for me the authority of the law, both religious and societal. I still feel this tension in my efforts to find individual expression within a halakhic community, as well as in my struggle to negotiate rabbinical halakhah with my own sense of what is right and just. There are times even now when halakhah feels oppressive, when I do not want to submit to the authority of the law, when I feel the need to exert control over my own life, as I did when I was a teenager. The difference is that I no longer need to resort to unhealthy, destructive means of exerting that control. I know now that I do not have to give up on God and tradition in order to express myself as an individual in Judaism, nor do I have to lose myself in order to uphold the traditions of my people and maintain my faith in God.

CHAPTER SIX

◆

Chuppah: Marriage

A woman is acquired in three ways: with money,
with a contract, or with sexual intercourse.
— Mishnah *Kiddushin* 1:1

"YOU DON'T KNOW HOW lucky you are," my friend Michelle tells me. "There aren't many men around who would be supportive of a wife with ideas like yours. Liberal religious men like Jacob are a rare commodity."

I am sitting in Michelle's apartment. She is one of the small number of women I know who pray with a tallit and tefillin every morning and are not Conservative rabbis or rabbinical students. Her husband is not supportive of her putting on tallit and tefillin. They met when she had already taken upon herself these obligations, and although they share much in common in their personalities, their priorities, and even much of their religious ideology, this has been a point of contention since they met. I respect her husband and appreciate the traits that my friend loves in him, but I can't understand how he can be in love with her and reject the part of her that pushes her in this spiritual direction. "He loves me in spite of it," she insists. "He would prefer that I stop with the tallit and tefillin and be a regular Orthodox woman," she tells me. Maybe he just doesn't yet understand that these practices are an expression of the courage, boldness, commitment, and imagination that he loves in his wife.

"It embarrasses him," she continues, "because he doesn't agree with my doing it on principle, and he feels that he's always having to answer for me nonetheless. He's in a difficult position, and I feel guilty for putting him there. But I can't be a different person, and neither can he. He puts up with it because he loves me, but he'll never approve."

Just as I would find it difficult to live with this lack of support for my wearing tallit and tefillin, if Michelle were married to Jacob, there are certainly things about him that she would find difficult to accept. Conversations like these, however, remind me not to take for granted Jacob's support for my unconventional endeavors. Although he was an activist and a fighter for social justice when I met him, women's status in Judaism was not yet one of his causes.

When I met Jacob in the hallway of my coed college dormitory during the second semester of my first year of college, he had just returned from Friday night services and Shabbat dinner, and I had just returned from an enjoyable evening at a jazz club in Greenwich Village. We noticed each other right away, and the attraction was mutual, although there were obvious differences between us. Jacob was dressed in a suit in honor of Shabbat, a black leather kippah was resting upon his short hair, and his tzitzit were wrapped neatly around the belt loops on his pants. I was dressed in jeans and a sweater and a long, threadbare, gray woolen coat that had belonged to my father before I adopted it. It seems a wonder now that we began immediately talking to each other, but somehow each of us recognized in the other something familiar. We talked for hours that night, and since then we've been together.

Like me, Jacob grew up in a Modern Orthodox home, although his was on the South Shore of Long Island, in a community that was becoming more and more "black hat" despite its original Modern Orthodox founders. Since high school, Jacob told me that night, he too had secretly not been religiously observant. He had rebelled, but now he was on his way back.

The next evening, Jacob and I had our official first date. We went to a rally for Jonathan Pollard—the convicted American spy for Israel who was sentenced to life in prison without parole—at which Pollard's sister was speaking. I was skeptical about Pollard after I had watched an unflattering interview with him on 60 Minutes. Jacob wanted me to hear Pollard's side; he was certain that I would change my view if only I heard the truth.

We decided to meet at the subway, and when I saw him skating toward me in his casual clothes—faded, torn blue jeans, ripped white sweatshirt, roller skates, and tzitzit hanging out from beneath his shirt, flying wildly in the breeze—I felt like I was seeing the real Jacob, minus the stiff suit and tie. There was something about his dress that told me he was his own person, that he too struggled with the traditional "good Jewish boy" role. Unlike most other Orthodox Jewish men I knew, he did not wear his tzitzit as a simple, unconscious habit. His fringes stood out so blatantly against the backdrop of the rest of his attire; he did not wear a dark suit and a white shirt, or even chinos and a polo shirt—the usual uniforms of a *yeshiva bachur,* a male yeshiva student. He wore his tzitzit with a radiating pride and love. He had clearly thought for a long time about these tzitzit, as he did about all the mitzvot he performed. His was not a religion of rote, nor was it one that stemmed from social pressure to fit in with the cliquish New York Orthodox scene. It was his own.

When I began college, I wanted nothing to do with religion. I did not set foot once in the campus Jewish center or synagogue my entire first semester. While Friday night services were taking place, I was either at a party, at a club downtown, or getting high in a friend's dormitory room. I was having a blast, and I was finally experiencing life without the burden of my Jewish identity.

After a few months of this, I began to miss that part of me that made me different. Actually, I realized that no matter how far I tried to run, I could never escape that essential part of myself. Judaism was too integral a part of my identity and my soul for me to be able to cast it off.

I decided to spend winter break in Israel, which, I assumed, would be the perfect place to explore these feelings. It did help, for in Israel I was able to solidify my commitment to remaining within the fold. I felt a deep emotional tie to the land that did not seem to have weakened because of my abandonment of the religious aspects of my Jewish identity.

When I returned home, however, I was still not satisfied. I knew that I wanted to find spiritual meaning in my life, for a secular connection to a land and a people, no matter how intense, was not enough to fill that spiritual void. Still, I did not feel that I had a religious or spiritual home. I knew that a duplicate of the religion of my childhood was not the answer to my quest, but I was determined to find my spiritual home in Judaism—where or how, I didn't know.

I returned to Columbia College for a second semester, wanting to find an entry point back into Judaism but without any concrete ideas of how to begin. It was then that I met Jacob. I told him that I too was on my way back, but I was not willing to return to the same practices of my parents. For him, it was enough to return to a Judaism whose trappings looked like those of the religion of his childhood, as long as the spirit of the religion was different for him, as long as he felt that he was doing the mitzvot not out of social pressure but rather out of his own convictions and love of Torah. He was in search of a Judaism that would translate into a pursuit of justice and truth, which he saw as a Judaism of social activism in the name of Torah and mitzvot. He was involved in a number of causes: promoting *aliyah* to Israel and Jewish education; fighting against Holocaust revisionism; struggling for the freedom of Soviet Jewry and Jonathan Pollard. Gender was a nonissue for Jacob; the injustice of keeping half of the Orthodox Jewish population out of public ritual life had never occurred to him, as it does not to most Orthodox men. He sat on his side of the mechitzah and never imagined that the women on the other side could be another cause on his list—until he met me.

I began to go to services again on Friday night, but I did not go to Orthodox services. Instead, I went to the egalitarian services on campus. I could not return to the Orthodoxy of my childhood. If I was going to return to Judaism, it would not be to a seat behind the mechitzah.

I knew many of the students who went to the Orthodox minyan, and, more important, Jacob went there, but I resisted going. When I tried it once, it felt oppressive, and I felt like an impostor. I did not believe that this was the way that God wanted us to pray, and I felt that even by participating I was helping to perpetuate something I felt strongly against. Jacob and I would walk, hand in hand, to the building where services were held, kiss each other "Good Shabbes" (which most young Orthodox couples on campus would never do in public, even if they were privately sexually intimate), split up for *tefillah* itself, and then meet again after it was over.

Jacob and I often argued about the topic of women in Orthodoxy, but we did not come to many agreements. Jacob understood that I felt oppressed in an Orthodox shul, but he did not, and therefore he did not join me where I prayed. He felt uncomfortable in a nontraditional setting, and I felt uncomfortable in a fully traditional one. We rarely were found in the same minyan. Even once we were married, the summer between my junior and senior years of college, we could not agree on a shul.

After I graduated from college, Jacob and I moved to Washington, D.C., where we both studied in graduate school. Our first year there, I continued to go to an egalitarian service at a havurah, and he continued to go to an Orthodox shul. However, Jacob would walk over to my havurah after services to socialize, because he felt he had more to talk about with this more politically and religiously liberal group.

During that first year in D.C., I began to wear tefillin each morning; it was Jacob who gave me my first pair and showed me how to put them on. Seeing me wearing tefillin must have been bizarre for Jacob at the beginning, especially since the elementary school he had attended was an all-male, black-hat yeshiva, but he was completely supportive and helpful.

I realize now that my decision to lay tefillin—although it is socially more radical than participating in egalitarian services, since there are so few women who do it—was easier for Jacob to support than my participation in egalitarian services. He saw it as a serious act, a statement that proved my sincerity in my pursuit of spiritual expression within the tradition. It is not so difficult to go to shul, lead services sometimes, and read from the Torah, especially when it is in a nurturing environment, a place where others support what you are doing and have decided to express Judaism in the same framework. However, when I committed to putting on tefillin every morning, even in places where people were hostile to my doing so, Jacob finally understood how deep both my pain and my love went, and how far I was willing to go to reclaim my place in the religion of my childhood.

The next summer Jacob and I took a trip to Israel. He volunteered in the Justice Minister's office, and I studied in a women's yeshiva. I also bought my first tzitzit and tallit. Jacob had been encouraging me to start wearing a *tallit katan* every day, to experience one of his favorite mitzvot. By then, he had become more than merely tolerant of my religious feminism.

When we returned from Israel, and I discovered that I was pregnant, Jacob and I decided that we had to find a synagogue on which we could agree. With a child on the way, we wanted to go to shul on Shabbat as a family. At this point, Jacob was ready to commit to praying in an egalitarian minyan, and I was ready to move on from the havurah to a more traditional community and service. We and some friends joined forces to begin a traditional egalitarian minyan in our neighborhood. It was a strictly traditional service, except for the fact that women were equal participants in the *tefillah*. When we started the service, we could barely get a minyan; six years later, the service is standing room only, with around 300 participants a week.

After a few years of hearing my arguments and seeing my struggles, Jacob had seen my point of view and made it his own. From this vantage point, it seems that it was probably only a matter of time before he would reach the conclusions that he has. Jacob is an activist and a fighter for justice. It took a woman with whom he is close to show him what it feels like to be on the other side of the mechitzah. Now Jacob says that he finds it strange and oppressive to pray in a completely male-led service. He says that it feels like a male locker room, or as if the women are in a cage, in a typical Orthodox shul, and it disrupts his *kavanah*, or concentration. He much prefers a *tefillah* in which women actively participate. Today we pray most often in various *minyanim* in our Jerusalem neighborhood in which women participate (in ways limited by halakhic considerations). This is where we both feel most comfortable now, although, Jacob actually feels less strongly than I do about complying with these halakhic limitations. Since we lived in D.C., I have become more concerned about working for change more slowly within the halakhic framework, and he has become less concerned with that issue. He would more easily switch back to a completely egalitarian prayer service than I would. He has come a long way from the elementary school yeshiva boy with a black hat who thanked God each morning that he was not created a woman.

Today, when Jacob prays each morning, he says: "Blessed are You, God, Ruler of the Universe, who has made me a man."

"We can't expect men to see the world through our eyes," I tell Michelle, "but it can happen if we patiently but adamantly nudge them in that direction. You never know how your husband will feel six years from now. Give it time."

When Jacob and I decided to get married, he did not propose. He did not get down on his knees and ask for my hand in marriage, and he did not speak to my father to ask permission to marry me. Our "deci-sion" was actually not even a decision. We had been dating for a year and a half, and a few weeks into our relationship it became clear to us both that we wanted to build a life together. When we started talking about what Jacob would do after his graduation from college (he was graduating a year before I), we assumed that his plans would include me, and vice versa. We had already become a couple for life. The wed-ding itself was something that we knew we had to go through to please our parents and make our bond religiously and civilly official, but with-out discussing it with each other, we were each already planning our lives to include the other.

About nine months before Jacob graduated, we told our parents that we intended to get married, and the months that followed until the actu-al wedding were filled with planning, arguing, and anxious anticipation. I did not want to have much to do with the details of the reception. The first time that Jacob and I sat down with our parents to discuss the event, I quite earnestly suggested that we have a brunch outside with bagels and lox and other salads and spreads. No one seemed to take me seri-ously, because my suggestion received only laughs, and after that I was not included in the "big picture" planning of the event.

Jacob and I did insist on a few things. Since we are both vegetari-ans, we refused to allow meat at the wedding. We wanted the ceremo-ny to be outdoors, weather permitting. (It rained the entire day of the wedding, so in the end it was held inside.) I was most interested in the ceremony itself. I wanted to be involved in planning what would hap-pen under the *chuppah*, the wedding canopy.

We were both twenty-one years old, and although we knew that we were on a different track than the one our parents had chosen and that we did not quite fit in with the communities in which we had grown up, we were young and still dependent on our parents in some ways. We wanted our wedding to represent us and our relationship, but we also felt that the wedding was really more for our parents than for us, and we did not want to deprive them of this pleasure. Not wanting to alien-ate our parents, Jacob and I chose an Orthodox rabbi with whom we each had an independent relationship, and we met with him at his home to plan the ceremony.

We discussed the details, and I took notes, since I planned to write a booklet explaining the ceremony to be handed out to all the guests. I had been to traditional Jewish weddings before, but the one-sidedness of the marriage act itself had not hit me as forcefully then as it did now that I was to be the bride, who would be standing there in her long white dress, a veil over her face, being "acquired."

Beneath the chuppah, in a traditional Jewish wedding ceremony, the *hatan*, the groom, speaks and gives a ring to the *kallah*, the bride, who says nothing and gives nothing. She does, however, have to visibly accept the ring, reflecting the halakhic stipulation that a woman cannot be married unless she agrees. This may have been radically progressive in the era in which this ceremony was created, but in 1990 it seemed totally archaic, offensive, and not at all representative of the mutuality and partnership that we felt in our relationship.

The ketubah, or wedding contract, would have to be signed by witnesses—who, traditionally, can only be men. In it, the groom promises to support his wife and, in the event of a divorce, legally binds himself to give her a specified sum of money. *What about my obligations to Jacob?* I wondered.

The unilateral nature of the ceremony also made me uncomfortable because of what I knew about divorce in Jewish law. According to halakhah, a divorce can be accomplished only through the giving of a *get*, or writ of divorce, which can only be given by the husband. Today, there is a large and very serious problem of *mesuravot get*, frequently called *agunot*[1]: women whose husbands refuse to give them a *get*—out of spite, blackmail, or even insanity. Such a woman cannot remarry. To offer but one example of how ugly this issue can become: one man is now trying to obtain custody of his children by saying that they will never have a two-parent home with his ex-wife because he will never give her a *get*.

The one-sidedness of divorce stems from the narrow interpretation of Deuteronomy 24:1: "When a man takes a wife, and marries her, if it comes to pass that she does not find favor in his eyes, because he finds in her some indecency, he writes for her a writ of divorce, and puts it into her hand, and sends her out of his house." The Rabbis do not extend this verse to apply equally to a woman taking a man as a husband. Marriage consists of a man "taking" a woman, and the divorce can only be initiated by him, as the verse says; *he* must place the writ of divorce in *her* hand, and not the other way around.

The unequal natures of marriage and divorce are intertwined. He "acquires" her through a *kinyan*, a legal transaction that has the effect of transferring land, money, animals, animate or inanimate objects, or even people, from one person and domain to another. In the case of marriage, it is the woman who is being transferred. The man "acquires" exclusive sexual rights to the woman. Thus he "releases" her; she cannot release him, since she never acquires him in the first place.

To our rabbi's credit, he suggested that we sign a prenuptial agreement in which Jacob would legally bind himself, in the event of a civil divorce, to pay me a large amount of money each day that he refused to give me a *get*. This is the solution that a number of rabbis have utilized to deal with the problem of *mesuravot get*: to provide a financial incentive, enforceable under civil law, for the husband to be cooperative. Although Jacob and I did sign such an agreement publicly at our wedding—and it is important that all Jewish couples getting married sign such an agreement—this is not *the* solution to the problem. The majority of Jewish marriages today are performed without such a prenuptial agreement, and it would be impossible to convince all couples to use one. Many couples do not want to begin their marriage already discussing and anticipating divorce. The only way that the prenuptial agreement could solve the problem forever would be if all rabbis refused to marry couples if the husband did not sign such a document.

Even if this could be accomplished, the agreement does not eliminate the possibility of a husband refusing to give his wife a *get*. As long as he is willing to pay or sit in jail—and some vindictive men are—she will still be harassed, blackmailed, or at least unable to remarry. The extent to which this document will prove legally binding also remains an open question. Will it always stand up in a secular court of law, or will some man's lawyer find a loophole? Is this a chance that the Jewish community is willing to take? Why should we be willing to rely on civil courts to solve Jewish legal problems?

In Israel there are two options: a civil monetary agreement, like the one Jacob and I signed; or an agreement of a more halakhic character, to be enforced by a rabbinic court. The latter option could work on a large scale in Israel, because the central rabbinate could decree that all marriages must be performed with a prenuptial agreement signed beforehand. In Israel there is no separation between secular and religious marriage, so all marriages and divorces must go through the religious courts. The rabbinate has control over all marriages, so if the rabbis wanted to solve this problem, they could.[2]

So far, the official rabbinate has not shown any interest in solving the problem—whether out of lack of courage, lack of sensitivity, or sheer misogyny. Rather than centralized marriage working to the advantage of *mesuravot get*, it works to their disadvantage. All women who want a divorce in Israel must obtain a *get* from their husbands. There is no other way out of the marriage. This applies to even the most secular men and women. The government, in essence, has handed all men the legal opportunity to emotionally abuse their wives.

Recently, three rabbis (including Emanuel Rackman, a prominent Modern Orthodox rabbi who is the rector of Bar-Ilan University) joined forces to establish a *beit din*, a rabbinical court, to retroactively declare as invalid any marriage in which a man refuses to give his wife a *get*. Their logic is that there was a lack of valid consent to the marriage in the first place, since the woman would never have agreed to marry the man if she had known that he would be emotionally abusive. This is a brave effort, one which is winning them few rabbinic friends; disappointingly, their rulings have not been accepted by the Orthodox community at large. Rabbi Moshe Feinstein, an extremely influential modern-day *posek*, allowed for this in certain cases, although he did not allow for it in the broad range of cases in which Rabbi Rackman is applying it.[3] Without widespread community support and acceptance, this bold effort is not enough to help such women.

An additional effort that is being used in Israel is to place sanctions on the man: revoking his driver's license, medical license, credit cards and passport, and making him pay high child support payments, to "convince" him to give the *get*. According to halakhah, the *get* must be given willingly. The *beit din* cannot actually force a man to give a *get*; instead, they must find ways not connected to the *get* itself to persuade him to give it. This is a brilliant strategy in many ways and one with halakhic precedent, but like the prenuptial agreement, it does not help a woman whose vindictive or cruel husband is willing to live without a driver's license, to pay large amounts of money, or even to sit in jail for the rest of his life rather than give a *get*.

All *poskim* agree that a *get* given under coercion legitimately exerted by a rabbinic court is valid. The disagreement arises over which circumstances call for this coercion at the hands of the court, since if exercised in an inappropriate situation, the coercion would result in an invalid *get*. If the woman in this situation remarried, any children from her second marriage would be *mamzerim*, children of an illicit relationship, who are not allowed to marry anyone but another *mamzer* according to Jewish law. Maimonides says that if a woman declares, "*Ma'is alai*" (this man is revolting to me), this is sufficient grounds for the court to *force* a *get*, "for she is not like a captive, that she should be forced to have intercourse with one who is hateful to her."[4] Unfortunately, his position was resoundingly rejected by other *poskim* because of the influence of Rabbeinu Tam, who ruled that a husband cannot be compelled to give a *get* except in the seven cases that are spelled out in the Talmud.[5]

The only way to unequivocally solve the problem would be to have all Orthodox rabbis of all communities come together, for the first time in Jewish history, to come up with a solution. They could agree to follow Maimonides' opinion to expand the current use of coercing a *get* at the hands of the court, or they could agree to enforce coercion only in the cases mentioned in the Talmud, which even Rabbeinu Tam advocated. Since this list includes the case of a woman who is subjected to her husband's abuse or misconduct, the problem could be easily solved, for the refusal to give a *get* when a marriage has ended is surely (religious) misconduct, if not outright abuse. The rabbis could also revive the use of *hafka'at kiddushin* (retroactive annulment), a solution for which there are talmudic precedents that were used by some medieval rabbis but which fell into disfavor. (There have been modern efforts to revive this practice, especially by some Sephardi rabbis.) Finally, the rabbis could institute a *takanah* to totally change the nature of Jewish marriage and divorce, making both bilateral in recognition of the modern social reality that women are no longer "property" to be acquired and disposed of unilaterally by fathers and husbands.

This move would not be as radical as it may seem, bearing in mind that Rabbeinu Gershom in tenth-century Germany instituted two pivotal decrees that began a progression toward a more egalitarian view of marriage: He banned polygyny, and he decreed that the woman must willingly accept the *get* for a divorce to take place. No Orthodox rabbi today is willing to organize or institute a similar effort, and few people believe that such a campaign would succeed even if there were a willing rabbi. Although it is true that the laws in this area are complicated and the consequences of a mistake being made are serious (including the possibility of *mamzerut* of future children), I believe there are other forces at work. The Orthodox rabbinical establishment does not want to give up male control of marriage. Most rabbis today also see themselves as powerless to change a law, even one with unjust consequences. Thus, it does not seem realistic to expect that the necessary *takanah* or any of the other possible solutions mentioned above will be forthcoming in the foreseeable future, unless women can exert enough pressure to force the necessary steps towards justice.

As a result of women's pressure, and in reaction to Rabbi Rackman's *beit din*, the Rabbinical Council of America, the mainstream Orthodox rabbinical association in the United States, has recently formed a task force to help *agunot* (women whose husbands have disappeared, leaving them without a husband or a *get*) and *mesuravot get*. In their mission statement, they declare that they plan to coordinate international efforts on behalf of these women. Given the track record of the Orthodox rabbinical establishment, there is little reason to hope that this task force will be brave enough to issue a *takanah*. Often when there is a push for change, a backlash results in movement in both directions: toward a reactionary approach and toward change. If this task force or another like it does not come through, we will have to wait until women have enough power in the world of halakhah to push through such a *takanah*.

Sitting in the office of the rabbi who would coordinate our marriage ceremony, I felt myself very much in a bind. I knew that we had to have an Orthodox wedding ceremony for a variety of reasons. Most important was the fact that our parents believed very strongly in its necessity, and we did not want to turn a joyous occasion into a family feud. There was also the issue of legitimacy. Neither Jacob nor I wanted anyone to be able to question the validity of our marriage, whether in the United States or when we eventually made our move to Israel, as we already intended to do. Neither of us felt confident enough in our knowledge of halakhah to break new ground in this area without the backing of a rabbi whom no one would dispute.

However, I could not completely submit to the traditional ceremony without attempting to make it more equal. I could not agree to being "acquired" without in some way demonstrating that this did not feel right. I explained to the rabbi that each of us intended to give the other a wedding ring. "Could I give mine to Jacob under the chuppah?" I asked.

"Absolutely not," the rabbi answered, explaining that the *kinyan* must be one-sided, and not even *appear* otherwise, in order for the marriage to be legally binding. According to halakhah, the act that effects the marriage can, by definition, be initiated only by the man. Even if the woman is the one who asks the man to marry her, he must be the one to give her the ring (or whatever object they are using to effect the *kinyan*).

When the man gives the woman the ring and says, *"Harei at m'kudeshet li b'taba'at zo"* ("you are hereby sanctified to me with this ring"), the woman is with that act becoming "set apart" for her husband, but he is not technically becoming set apart for her. She is off-limits to other men, but he is not equally off-limits to other women. Despite the acceptance of Rabbeinu Gershom's decree forbidding polygyny, the ceremony itself remains as it was. His edict can even be overturned in a specific case if there is a body of one hundred rabbis who agree to do so. This is sometimes done today for men whose wives refuse to accept a *get* or for men who refuse to give their wives a *get*—but who themselves want to remarry.

"You can give the ring to Jacob afterwards, in the *yichud* room," the rabbi reassured us, advising me to present Jacob with it during our traditional moment of privacy after the official ceremony ended.

We agreed to this, although I insisted that we write in the wedding booklet that I would be doing so. When I gave Jacob the ring, I said: *"Harei atah m'kudash li b'taba'at zo."* Even though halakhically my action and words had no legal significance, at least I would not feel so demeaned, and between us we knew that we saw our marriage as a two-way transaction.

"What about the ketubah?" I asked. "Can't I write up my own ketubah to Jacob? Can't I promise him whatever I want?"

"Listen, Haviva," said the rabbi, who was already used to my questions and issues, "you can do whatever you want as long as it is not under the chuppah."

Thus began my investigation into the rabbinical attitude toward marriage. I was determined to find a basis in the sources to create a more two-sided image of marriage that Jacob and I would feel truly represented our relationship. Otherwise, I would question the validity of the ceremony, because it would seem a farce, an empty show for the sake of our parents and their guests.

In the end, I came up with the following marriage statement:

> While the ketubah speaks only of the man's obligations to his wife, this does not mean that a Jewish wife has no obligations in marriage. On the contrary, a Jewish wife has always had the responsibility to perform acts that maintain a stable home and family life and express her devotion to her husband.
>
> The Mishnah in *Ketubot* 5:5 states that a wife is obligated to perform seven duties for her husband: 1) grinding grain into flour, 2) baking bread, 3) washing clothes, 4) cooking, 5) nursing their child, 6) making ready his bed, and 7) working in wool. The Gemara in the Babylonian Talmud, *Ketubot* 59b, explains that this mishnah does not follow the view of Rabbi Hiyya, who taught that a man should marry a woman for her beauty and her ability to bear children. A Jewish wife should be more to her husband than a mere ornament or "baby machine," the Gemara seems to be saying.
>
> The Mishnah then states that if a woman has four maidservants, she may lounge in an easy chair. The Gemara, however, cites the statement of Rav Isaac ben Hananya, who says that the wife must nevertheless fill her husband's cup, make ready his bed, and wash his hands, feet, and face. Rashi explains that these three actions are expressions of intimacy and love and should therefore always be performed by the wife, no matter how many maidservants she could have do so in her place. [These are the same three duties that are forbidden when a woman is in her *niddah* period, based on this same rule in the Gemara.] So, at the very least, a wife must continually perform those duties that are an expression of her devotion to him; she must never be completely idle or distant.
>
> There are many Jewish women today, such as myself, who do not wish to be idle but also do not wish to take *sole* responsibility for the maintenance of the home and family. Rather, we hope to share responsibilities in the home and also pursue our interests

outside the home. Where do we fit in terms of the traditional role the Rabbis have assigned to women in marriage? It may come as a surprise to some, but the Rabbis did take us into consideration.

The Gemara on *Ketubot* 58b quotes Rav Huna, who states in the name of Rav: "A woman is entitled to say to her husband, 'I do not wish to be maintained by you nor to work for you.'" ("Work" here includes the above mentioned duties, as well as any profits or salary that the woman could earn from those, or other, activities.) The Gemara explains that Rav Huna holds the opinion that when the Rabbis regulated the duties of husband and wife, the wife's maintenance was paramount. (Rashi comments that this is because, at the time, women could not usually support themselves.) Because this law was made for the wife's benefit, she may relieve her husband of the obligation to support her at any time. Thus, she may also relinquish her obligation to work for him, since Rav Huna holds that the Rabbis require her to do so only in order to prevent ill feeling between the members of the couple by setting up a balance of reciprocal obligations. Tosafot on *Ketubot* 63a (s.v. *Rav Huna amar mi'tashmish*) comments that Rav Huna holds that even in such a case where the woman declares economic independence, she must still perform the three previously mentioned acts of intimacy. Rav Huna's opinion is considered halakhah and is written in the *Shulchan Arukh*, the Code of Jewish Law (*Even Haezer* 69:4).

Bearing in mind the foresight of the Rabbis and the changing role of women in society (and in marriage) today, I, Haviva Rena Krasner, wish to state on this day, June 14, 1990, 21 Sivan 5750, of my marriage to Jacob Aryeh Davidson, the following:

I will love, cherish, honor, support, and maintain Jacob, as he has obligated himself in the *ketubah* to do for me. I will support his endeavors (within reason) and strive to make our marriage a true partnership of love, understanding, and friendship. As we provide both moral and economic support for each other, Jacob and I will also share the household and familial duties, so that together we can build a *bayit ne'eman b'Yisrael*, a true home in Israel.

We had my statement written up artistically and enlarged and then signed by two of our female friends, to make it a parallel document to the ketubah that Jacob was giving me and having signed by two of our male friends. I also read this statement aloud and had it signed at my *kallah's tish*, a gathering of women before the ceremony that we organized to take place simultaneously with the *hatan's tish*, the traditional gathering of men at which the ketubah is signed. We put a copy of my statement in the back of our wedding booklet so that those who were not present at the *tish* could see it and think about it.

All this was our way of expressing our dissatisfaction with the traditional Jewish wedding without alienating our parents, the community in which we grew up, and the tradition itself. We did acquiesce to participating in the traditional ceremony, despite the fact that it serves to perpetuate a system that is oppressive to women, but we also found a way to rebel at the same time that we were submitting. In essence, we created an "underground wedding" at the same time that the more official wedding was taking place. I think it was clear to the guests at the wedding that what more reflected our true feelings for each other was the one we had created ourselves.

If we were getting married today, we would do things differently. I would want an official ceremony, not an underground one, with which I could feel comfortable.

There have been many contemporary suggestions for new, halakhic ceremonies to join a couple in marriage. Rachel Adler, a feminist theologian, has created a ceremony called *b'rit ahuvim*, in which the marriage commitment is based not on the laws of acquisition but on the laws of *shutafut*, or partnership.[6] Others have proposed (based on a responsum by Rabbi Yaakov Emden in eighteenth-century Europe[7]) doing away with *kiddushin* (the traditional Jewish marital relationship) and instead using the concubine relationship as the basis for marriages today. Rabbi Meir Feldblum proposes a marriage that does not use *kiddushin*; instead, it uses a principle mentioned in the writings of some medieval *poskim*: *derech kiddushin*, a sort of pseudo-*kiddushin* that is not a rabbinic marriage, nor is it a form of concubinage or *z'nut* (an improper sexual relationship). This *derech kiddushin* would not require a valid *kinyan* or a *get*.[8]

The problem with the above solutions, especially the one based on the concubine model, is that they lower the sanctity of the institution of marriage. Although marriage was originally a *kinyan* only, in the talmudic period the Sages added the layer of *kiddushin*, or sanctification, making the woman not merely acquired but also set apart. These models remove that layer of sanctity, making the marriage a partnership or some other kind of relationship (whether it be sexual or something else). In addition, some people may feel so sentimentally attached to the words "*harei at m'kudeshet li*" and other aspects of the traditional marriage ceremony that they will not want to depart from the traditional model.

The problem of *mesuravot get* may be reason enough to compromise the sanctity aspect of the Jewish marriage and our sentiments. Time will tell. It is mainly in the hands of women whether new models will be put to the test. An ideal solution would address all of these issues, making the marriage a bilateral act while maintaining its sanctity.

For those who feel the *kinyan* aspect of the ceremony is essential to its validity, I propose another model based on a discussion in *Kiddushin* 7a. It seems there that for the purposes of marriage, a *kinyan* is valid even if what the man is giving the woman is of nonmaterial benefit, *hana'ah*. The case in the Gemara is of a woman giving a gift to an important man. The Gemara states that in such a case the *kinyan* would be effected based merely on the *hana'ah* (pleasure) that the woman would get from such an important man having accepted her gift.

If it is possible to make a *kinyan* based on *hana'ah*, the woman could first give the man a ring. Then the man could take a *neder*, or vow, that from that moment, all other women besides his intended wife are off-limits to him. The woman then would declare in her own words that she has derived great pleasure from the fact that her beloved (who is, of course, the most important man in her eyes) has accepted her gift and taken this *neder*. At that point, the man would give the woman a ring and say, "*Harei at m'kudeshet li b'taba'at zo u-v'hana'ah zo*" ("you are set apart for me by this ring and this nonmaterial benefit"). This way, both the man and woman would be giving a ring, both would speak under the chuppah, both would be bound on some level in a monogamous relationship, and the ceremony could actually have the added element of being a romantic expression of love rather than only the highly legalistic and businesslike ritual that forms the basis for the current mode of *kinyan*.

This ceremony, however, would not solve the problem of the unilateral nature of the marriage, since a *kinyan* is still the basis of the ceremony, and a *kinyan* is by definition unilateral. Nevertheless, it does give a different feel to the ceremony, basing the *kinyan* on a love commitment in addition to the ring. If the man did in fact take a lover or another wife, he would be in breach of his vow of faithfulness to his wife. A divorce would also include a ceremony to annul the man's vow.

This is not an ideal solution, but it is a more palatable one for couples seeking a halakhic ceremony, for it would better reflect their mutual love commitment. It is a beginning, a way to think critically about the traditional Jewish wedding while preserving its important features. The Orthodox community is not ready to accept the models of *derech kiddushin*, *pilagshut* (concubinage), or *shutafut*. There are some rabbis who may be willing to add to the traditional ceremony in some of the ways suggested here. One step at a time, we can work toward a more ideal solution.

I am a volunteer for an organization called Mevo Satum (Dead End), which helps women whose husbands refuse to give them a *get*. I met today with a woman who has six children and can't pay her rent. Her husband, who was physically and mentally abusive to both her and her children, informed her after fifteen years of marriage that he was leaving. He moved out, and since then he has not been meeting his alimony or child support payments. He was the one who left, yet he is refusing to give his wife a divorce. He has no interest in reuniting with his wife, but as long as she has no *get*, he is in control. He can try to blackmail her for custody of their children, little or no child support payments, or whatever his cruel heart desires.

This woman says she will not give in to his manipulations. Her children are afraid of their father, so she will never let her husband have custody. She will fight in the courts for a fair agreement in which her husband will at least have to pay for the roof over their children's heads. With no work experience or marketable skills and with six young children, she cannot make ends meet on her own.

Even if the court rules in her favor, it would be difficult to force him to pay. He apparently lives off money he raises for a school for girls that he claims to run. He claims that he has no money, yet he travels to France, his place of birth, for vacations. This woman's steadfastness may cause her the loss of her *get*. The angrier her husband gets, the more stubborn he will become. He may never give her a *get,* but she has no choice. She will not agree to give her abusive husband custody of their children, even if it means that she will never be able to remarry.

"So how can your organization help me?" she asks me.

I tell her that we can try to raise charity money for her, and we can help her to obtain psychological counseling for herself and her children. We can send her to a self-defense course free of charge. We can help her to find a new and better lawyer. We can even stage rallies outside her husband's apartment and school to shame him into submission. What she needs most, however, we cannot do. We cannot make him give her a *get*.

CHAPTER SEVEN

◆

Taharah and *Tumah*:
Purity and Impurity

*For three transgressions a woman dies in childbirth: for being
careless regarding the laws of niddah,* challah, *and lighting
Shabbat candles.*
— Mishnah *Shabbat* 2:6

As I PREPARED FOR my marriage to Jacob, I began to study the laws of
taharat hamishpachah, or family purity, which determine a couple's
sexual intimacy based on the woman's menstrual cycle, when she is in
a state of niddah.

In the Torah, there is a section dealing with the things that can render people *tameh*, or ritually impure, which means that they cannot
enter the Temple until their status has changed to *tahor,* or ritually pure:
menstrual blood, afterbirth, semen, unusual penile or vaginal discharges,
leprosy, and contact with a corpse. There are a number of verses that discuss the menstruating woman. Leviticus 15:19–24 declares a menstruant
t'meah (the feminine form of *tameh*) for seven days and outlines the consequences of her ritually impure state: anything she sits on or touches
(including a person) will become *tameh*, and anyone she has sexual relations with will become *tameh*. Another verse, Leviticus 18:19, forbids a
man to "approach a woman who is in niddah in order to have sexual
relations with her." Since the destruction of the Temple, the general laws
of *tumah* and *taharah* have fallen out of usage, including those relating
to menstrual blood. However, the verse forbidding approaching a menstruant to have sexual relations with her is still relevant today, and it is
upon this verse that the laws of *taharat hamishpachah* have been based.

As with all areas of Jewish law, this biblical verse gives rise to
lengthy elaboration and broadening of the plain understanding of the

restriction, and even more volumes of legal discussion. From this one Torah law, the Rabbis in the Talmud and those who came after instituted a complex system of rules: prohibitions of a man having intercourse with his wife if he suspects that she is going to bleed soon, of touching his wife when she is a niddah, and of sleeping in the same bed with his wife when she is a niddah, even if he does not touch her. There are rules about "stains," addressing, for example, the case when a woman finds blood on her garments but not an actual flow of blood. Is she, too, considered in a state of niddah? There are rules about a woman checking herself internally for blood, since any blood, once it has left the uterus, is problematic.

Some of the traditional practices connected with these laws—such as bringing blood stains to a rabbi and sticking a white cloth (called a *bedikah*, or checking, cloth) inside your vagina to check for blood—seemed to me, as my impending marriage approached, insensitive and outdated. What rabbi could know better than I what was my period and what was some other kind of blood? I am enough in tune with my body to know when my period is starting, so I didn't think that I needed to stick a cloth inside myself. Especially because the legal system in which niddah is embedded is so thoroughly a male product, I resented the way that these laws and practices seemed to question a woman's ability to know her own cycle, rhythms, and bodily messages.

The extremely detailed and meticulous nature of the directions I read in various books about *taharat hamishpachah* only supported my initial intuition. It became clear to me that the Rabbis were uncomfortable, to say the least, with the idea of menstruation and the internal nature of a woman's genitalia and organs. Why else would they require so many fastidious examinations? I began to research the rabbinic expansion of the Torah's more limited prohibitions and requirements.

When I looked into the origin of waiting seven "clean" days (that is, days free of blood flow) after a woman's period is over before resuming sexual relations, I learned that the Torah says that a woman who bleeds *dam niddah* (normal menstrual blood) must wait seven days (which, for most women, would be mostly days of bleeding) before immersing herself, whereas a woman who sees *dam zivah* (blood other than normal menstrual blood) must wait seven additional, clean days after the bleeding has stopped.

When I asked a friend of mine who is a rabbi why we today wait these extra seven days after niddah blood as well, he told me that we are not sure today which blood is *dam niddah* and which is *dam zivah*. I decided that I would treat the blood I saw each month as niddah blood, menstrual blood, and not worry that it might be *zivah* blood, since I never bleed between periods. I felt I could be certain that the blood I saw every month was a normal period and not the abnormal bleeding referred to in the Torah. I resented what I saw as men projecting their alienation from female biology onto women. It didn't surprise me that they weren't sure how to define the blood that flows from women, but that doesn't mean that women themselves aren't sure.

The Talmud[1] explains that the Rabbis instituted the practice of waiting *six* clean days after even one or two days of *zivah* bleeding (which would render a woman a *zavah k'tanah* and should only require waiting one clean day), because they were concerned that this woman might be a niddah rather than a *zavah k'tanah*. Jewish women, the Gemara continues, decided to wait one additional clean day after seeing even only one drop of blood (making it seven clean days), because they were also concerned that they might be in either a niddah state or a *zavah gedolah* state (which is defined by three days of nonmenstrual bleeding), when a woman must wait seven clean days after the bleeding has stopped. It was the "daughters of Israel" who extended the stricture to cover all of the bases, so that for any sighting of blood a woman would have to wait the maximum number of days required in the Torah. I wondered why women would not only have accepted but actually added on to this rabbinical stricture. It made sense to me that the Rabbis might have been worried that the women could not distinguish between niddah blood and *zivah* blood, or keep track of what was their normal menstrual cycle and what was abnormal bleeding, but I could not fathom why the women did not feel sufficiently confident about their own ability to distinguish between a drop of blood and three days of bleeding.

Considering that the letter of the law was difficult enough without the additional seven days of separation, I decided not to observe them, since I understood them to be an unnecessary restriction added on by the Rabbis and women of ages past. Trying to keep them, I told myself, would only make me so resentful that I would probably end up aban-

doning the entire enterprise. So I began keeping the laws of family purity by waiting only seven days in total before going to the mikveh, following the Torah's rules for niddah blood.

As time went by, though, I began to feel a need to stay more within
the bounds of mainstream halakhah. In addition, I came to look forward
to my monthly mikveh visits. I loved the feeling of being surrounded by
the water and then emerging fresh and renewed, like a rebirth each
month. I also loved the mini-honeymoons that followed, when I would
return home to Jacob after a week of sexual abstention (which for new-
lyweds can seem like an eternity!), and we would excitedly make our
way to the bedroom. These were special, loving reunions for us each
month, when we would have a chance to rediscover each other sexually, and when we learned to appreciate our sexual relationship more
because of the separation. Rabbi Meir alludes to this idea when he says
the following:

> Why does the Torah ordain that a woman be a niddah for seven
> days? Because being in constant contact with his wife, [a husband]
> might develop loathing toward her. Thus, the Torah declared that
> she should be ritually impure for seven days, so that she would be
> beloved to him like she was beneath the marriage canopy.[2]

I, of course, would expand Rabbi Meir's statement to include the
wife's attitude toward her husband as well, although I would not go so
far as to say that either spouse might develop "loathing" toward the
other as a result of constant sexual availability. However, I admit that
there is something to what he is suggesting, that abstinence does
increase the sexual drive, that absence does indeed make the heart grow
fonder.

Since my experience of keeping the laws of family purity was for the
most part positive, I began to consider keeping the laws in a more traditional way. I tried to look at the collective decision of the "daughters
of Israel" differently. I had regarded the fact that these women took
extra days upon themselves as a desire to be "more kosher than kosher,"
as the saying goes. I was not interested in taking upon myself unnecessary strictures. The Torah's prohibition seemed difficult enough to keep.

However, once I became accustomed to keeping these laws, saw that
it was not as impossible a task as I imagined, and even began to appre-

ciate the rhythm of this type of sexual relationship, I became open to see-ing more positively the decision of the women in the Talmud. As I began to see them differently, I began to regard following in their footsteps not as a burden but rather as a liberation, and to see their act as self-empow-ering, since it was a halakhic change instituted by women in an area of law about women's bodies. Although it is true that, according to this passage in the Gemara, it was the Rabbis who began the idea of adding strictures in this area of halakhah, it was the women who made the deci-sion to be so careful as to leave no room for doubt whatsoever. It is so infrequent that we hear about women in talmudic times, especially about women's initiative in halakhic matters, that I felt I had been pre-sumptuous to dismiss their decision.

Furthermore, we do not know the women's motivation for adding this stricture. It may have stemmed from a desire to limit the time peri-od in which they were halakhically sexually permitted to their hus-bands, which would, in effect, translate into women taking control over their own bodies—even though women today sometimes experience these laws as restrictive and as part of a male system. The motivation may also have been to formalize, or make part of mainstream halakhah, a women's tradition that already existed in practice. This is rarely recorded in the history of halakhah; women's traditions were too often discredited as foolish traditions or superstitions with no halakhic basis. By perpetuating this tradition of the "clean days" today, we are uphold-ing a women's tradition that would otherwise be lost to us. It is worth noting that the idea that this was a women's initiative is mentioned only in the Babylonian Talmud; the Jerusalem Talmud[3] does not mention women at all in relation to this legal development.

In solidarity with Jewish women of old, as well as out of a desire to uphold an ancient tradition, I decided to keep the extra seven clean days, or at least give it a try. I still did not do the required examinations or bring my underwear to a rabbi. Nor did I separate from Jacob in any way other than refraining from sexual intimacy during my (minimum of) twelve days of niddah before I immersed myself in the mikveh and we could sexually reunite.

About a year after I started keeping the seven clean days, I began a program of study at the Drisha Institute, a yeshiva for women in New

York City. We studied Talmud in the mornings and halakhah in the afternoons. My second year in the program, our afternoons were devoted entirely to the study of the laws of *taharat hamishpachah*.

I spent an entire year of afternoons, from 1:30 to 5:00 P.M., studying Jewish legal texts relating to the laws of niddah. My *hevruta,* or study partner, and I sat each afternoon studying what the Rabbis had to say about the prohibition in the Torah of a man having intercourse with a woman who is in niddah. It was one of my most difficult religious undertakings, reading these texts day after day, knowing that the rabbinic discussions form the basis of traditional Jewish practice in this area. In order to be able to face these texts each afternoon, I had to reconcile myself to the fact that despite the misogyny and the lack of an accurate understanding of female anatomy on the part of the Rabbis in the Talmud (as well as medieval and later Jewish legal scholars), we still use these texts today to determine the laws of *taharat hamishpachah*.

There are a number of problematic texts from a feminist—or even a medical—point of view. This is what Rabbi Meir had to say about a woman without a regular menstrual cycle: "A woman who does not have a regular menstrual cycle—her husband cannot have intercourse with her, and he must divorce her without giving her the divorce payment promised to her in the ketubah upon divorce."[4]

In order to explain the statement of Rabbi Meir in the Mishnah[5] that when a woman is urinating and sees blood, if she is standing she is *t'meah*, and if she is sitting she is *t'horah* (feminine of *tahor*), Rashi, the most influential commentator on the Talmud, states that a woman's bladder is connected to her uterus by a tube and that there is only one hole from which either blood or urine can leave a woman's body. Therefore, if a woman is standing while urinating, urine can back up into her uterus and blood may come out with her urine. So if she finds blood in the toilet bowl when she is urinating while standing, she can assume that it has come from her uterus. On the other hand, if she is sitting while urinating, she can assume that it has come from a wound in her urinary tract, since the urine will not back up into the uterus while she is in this position, and the urine will flow quickly, not allowing for any blood from the uterus to mix in with it.[6] The reality, of course, is that a woman's bladder is not connected to her uterus, and that women have two orifices: the urinary meatus and the vagina.

Fortunately, the halakhah in this case follows not Rabbi Meir, but Rabbi Yossi, who says that whether the woman is standing or sitting, she is *t'horah*.[7]

Maimonides believed that a woman's menstrual cycle works in the following manner: seven days of menstruation followed by eleven days of nonmenstruation. Therefore, any blood that flows during the seven-day period is niddah blood, and any blood that flows during the eleven-day period is *zivah* blood. According to him, this seven-eleven cycle begins the first time a girl menstruates and continues in this fashion forever.[8]

Nachmanides, a major twelfth- and thirteenth-century rabbi, disagrees. He asserts that we should calculate a woman's cycle in the following manner: When she bleeds the first time, she is in her niddah period for seven days, so any blood that flows during that seven-day period is niddah blood. Anything that flows afterwards is *zivah* blood, even if it is a continuous flow from her niddah period, until the flow stops or until she has eleven days of bleeding, whichever comes first. Then, the next time she sees blood, or on the twelfth day of her bleeding, she is in a niddah period again for seven days.[9] Maimonides and Nachmanides agree that a woman's basic menstrual cycle is an eighteen-day one, but they disagree exactly how the cycle works. According to Maimonides, the woman is always on a seven-eleven cycle of days. According to Nachmanides, the cycle starts again only when the woman sees blood after eighteen days have passed.

The halakhah was decided according to Nachmanides, whose opinion is closer to the reality of the average woman's cycle than Maimonides opinion, but it is still based on a mistaken notion. Despite the fact that we know that a normal woman's cycle is longer than eighteen days, Nachmanides' perspective is accepted for the purpose of determining practical halakhah. Since all blood is today considered *zivah* blood, we no longer pay attention to the seven-eleven cycle, but it is still the basis of the laws in this area of halakhah, and it has never been refuted in the halakhic literature. The law in this case, as in others like it, has its own reality with its own set of rules, even if they contradict what we know to be the scientific truth. (This tension between the biological and halakhic realities may have been the impetus for the "daughters of Israel" to treat all blood as *zivah* blood, since they may have understood from their own bodily cycles that with the seven-eleven approach, there would certainly be mistakes in distinguishing between *zivah* and *niddah*.)

My *hevruta* and I tried to keep a sense of humor about our endeavor, because if we did not, there were times that we might have ended up crying. Early in the year, we began keeping a list in the backs of our notebooks of derogatory terms that the Rabbis use for a woman's anatomy. These are some of the terms the Rabbis have for a woman's genitals: *kever* ("grave"), *shinayim* ("teeth"), *alma* ("[her] world"), *panehah shelimatah* ("her lower face"), *oto hamakom* ("that place").

There were times that a sense of humor was not enough, and I had to accept that I often felt so much at odds with Judaism's most respected and revered scholars, upon whose opinions religiously observant Jews base the way we live our lives today. Yet we cannot merely cast their writings aside. They are too enmeshed in our tradition. They *are* our tradition to a great extent. In order to free Jewish law from sexism entirely, we would have to start anew, create another religion, and that is not an option for me. I want to live as part of the religious traditions of my ancestors. I realized that I would have to find a middle road, a way to remain rooted in the tradition while doing so with a critical view of the Rabbis' limited scientific knowledge and social enlightenment.

There is no blanket solution to this dilemma with which I still find myself grappling constantly; no one cohesive philosophy of Judaism and the *halakhot* of niddah emerged for me upon completion of this yearlong course of study. Each month that I am not pregnant or nursing, when I see my own menstrual blood, I need to work through these issues all over again. These laws fascinate me so much—probably because they involve so many of the theological issues that I am constantly grappling with and trying to sort out—that I have chosen to write my doctoral dissertation on the topic of niddah. I also study with women before their weddings to teach them the practical applications of the laws. When we study together, I attempt to convey to them the deeper meaning and textual basis of the laws of *taharat hamishpachah*, as well as their historical development, so that they can grapple with their own levels of practice. There are no easy answers, but I offer my own insights and approaches and listen to each woman's own thoughts and ambivalences. Together, we explore.

Today I continue to keep many laws and customs that I find problematic because I see the value in holding on to traditions that have been kept for generations, through the rich and sometimes very difficult history of the Jewish people. I do so if I can find a way to make them meaningful in my life, despite the problems that I have with aspects of these practices. It is always important to understand and acknowledge the origins of the *halakhot* and the rabbinic understanding of them, no matter how problematic or even offensive they may be. I am never in favor of apologetics or revising history to make our laws and scholars into something they were not. Putting anachronistic words or interpretations into the mouths of the Rabbis seems to me more disrespectful than disagreeing with them. We can imbue a ritual with new meaning in a way that is both conscious and intellectually honest without insisting that the new meaning is what the earlier commentators had in mind. Part of Torah's timelessness is its ability to adapt across cultures and eras. We need not be apologetic about that.

There are, however, *halakhot* to which I simply cannot reconcile myself, and I advocate changing them both in practice and on the books. These laws clash with fundamental ideals of what is moral and good and sully our religious tradition.

The first mishnah in Tractate *Horayot* says that if the court rules that it is permissible to violate one of the mitzvot of the Torah, and an individual acts upon this ruling, the individual is vindicated. However, if a student sitting in the court knows by his or her own reasoning that the ruling of the court has erred, if this student then goes ahead and acts upon the faulty reasoning of the court, the student is liable. Rabbeinu Asher, a thirteenth-century German and Spanish scholar, states that anyone whose opinion differs from that of the court is dependent upon his own mind—that is, must decide for himself.[10]

Obviously, this situation is different from our modern reality. In the time of this mishnah, there was a Sanhedrin, a clear halakhic authority, as well as an assumption that there was an objective, correct way to rule on a halakhic matter. If the student *knows* that the court has ruled incorrectly, only then is he or she expected to act upon his or her conscience. Today, we have no single halakhic authority, and no one can claim to know for certain the objectively correct halakhic ruling; there is no notion of halakhah as a monolithic legal system with one correct interpretation.

However, despite the differences between our modern reality and the assumptions of this mishnah, we can still learn from the viewpoint of Rabbeinu Asher. We too must use our own reasoning and moral judgment and not blindly follow what mainstream halakhic authorities tell us is the only way to interpret and apply our legal tradition. If we feel in our hearts and know in our minds that their rulings do not coincide with what we perceive as the ethical ideal, we have a moral obligation to follow our consciences in an intellectually honest fashion. Unlike the student in the mishnah, we cannot be certain that we are correct, but we can feel confident in our own vision of what is moral and good, and we have an obligation to ourselves and to the integrity of the Jewish tradition to follow that path.

Yet although this philosophy of personal autonomy within the halakhic system is fine for personal, private mitzvot, and even for many communal mitzvot (such as the issue of women's participation in communal prayer), it cannot work for public, legal issues such as the problem of women whose husbands won't give them a divorce. With a collective (even if not majority) moral consciousness, those who want change will have to put pressure on the system, so that it will progress—as it has throughout the history of our people. These changes will have to be made by working within the halakhic system, following its traditional modes of discourse, to arrive at teachings that we can honestly respect. Blu Greenberg, one of the founders of the Orthodox feminist movement, has often said, "Where there's a rabbinic will, there's a halakhic way." How is a "rabbinic will" created if it doesn't exist on its own? It is forced by the people, through action and protest and breaking the halakhah as it now stands, in order to preserve the Torah and not eradicate it.

As I began to learn more about the intricacies and origins of the laws of the private mitzvot associated with *taharat hamishpachah* and became aware of how problematic much of the rabbinical material on the subject is, ironically, I also became more strict in my personal observance of these laws.

Once I understood that according to the Rabbis' understanding of a woman's cycle, the blood's status as either niddah blood or *zivah* blood depends not on any difference in the blood itself but rather upon whether it flows on a *zivah* day or a niddah day within the seven-eleven cycle, I also began to understand why there was a need to simplify matters. At a time when there were no calendars or clocks, it must have been extremely difficult for women to keep track of their cycles.

The notion of the seven-eleven cycle originates much earlier than the medieval period, when Maimonides and Nachmanides lived. We find evidence of it in the *Sifra*,[11] a halakhic *midrash* on Leviticus that was probably compiled in the fourth century. This may have been one of the reasons that niddah and *zavah* were conflated: it made life simpler for women and also appeased the Rabbis, who were worried about women not being able to keep track of their cycles. However, it is troubling that the Rabbis based their system on the mistaken notion that a woman's cycle lasts eighteen days. It is also problematic that the conflation of niddah (which is still observed because of the prohibition, not related to *tumah*, of sleeping with a niddah) and *zavah* (which has no biblical sexual prohibition and is mentioned only in the context of ritual purity laws[12]) has kept alive the notion of *zavah*, while the categories of *zav* (a man with a nonseminal emission) and *shikhvat zera* (seminal emissions) have both fallen away in practice. Misogynist nations about women's bodies and blood most likely played a role in this.

Nevertheless, it would be problematic, impractical, and difficult to totally uproot and rework the laws of *taharat hamishpachah* after so many years of their observance in this fashion. A mass movement to change these laws might provide a basis for making changes, but this is not a reality. If anything, more couples in all religious movements are taking on this practice than did so in my parents' generation. If the case were successfully made that many Jews who are not keeping *taharat hamishpachah* would do so if the number of days were decreased, that would provide a good reason to consider implementing changes on a large-scale, formal level. (I believe that if a couple will not keep these laws at all if they have to keep the twelve-day minimum, they should be advised to at least keep the Torah's seven-day prohibition.) When there is a morally compelling reason to revise these laws for a particular application, that is another story entirely, of even greater urgency.

For a woman who ovulates before the twelfth day[13] of her cycle and is trying to conceive, for example, it is terribly cruel to expect her to wait until after she has ovulated before resuming sexual relations with her husband. There should be two options for this woman. One, if she bleeds fewer than five days and does not have sex right before the onset of her period, we could let her start counting her clean days earlier. Two, if this is her regular menstrual period, she could keep *niddah d'oraita*, the biblical version of the niddah laws, and wait only seven days before immersing in the mikveh and resuming sexual relations with her husband. Since we know that the conflation of niddah and *zavah* were a later rabbinic development, we can and should be more flexible in this extreme individual case.

However, on a communal level, once we have accepted the seven-eleven understanding of the cycle for halakhic purposes, it is easy to see (based on this premise) how one could miscalculate days. If I had been trying to keep track of my cycle based on the seven-eleven idea, I too might have thrown in the towel and decided to just consider all blood *zivah* blood, requiring seven clean days. Once it was decided that all uterine blood found outside the uterus is problematic, and with the looming punishment of *karet*, it is easy to understand why the "daughters of Israel" would have wanted to be cautious.

The more impulsive part of me would like to just say, "Let's throw it all away and start from scratch!"; the more rooted part of me cautions, "What about tradition? What about community? What about the legal system?" That is why, even with what I know today, I keep those extra seven clean days. Yet I ask myself: *What is the point of all my studying if I am only going to perpetuate the status quo?*

Here is my attempt at an answer: first, just because I choose to keep this particular halakhah does not mean that I think all rabbinical laws must be followed without innovation. Second, knowing what I know, if a woman with needs other than my own—a woman having trouble conceiving, for instance, or a woman who simply cannot, for whatever reason (ideological, emotional, or physical), keep those extra seven days—comes to ask me for advice, I can tell her what I know, counsel her knowledgeably, and let her decide for herself.

After nine years of marriage, keeping these extra seven days is still difficult, even though I have been pregnant or nursing for the majority of those years and therefore have not been in niddah very often. However, it is not nearly as difficult as when we were first married and could barely keep our hands off each other. These extra days give me some time to myself, alone with my body, at a time when I am not menstruating, and thus without the undertones—mistaken or otherwise—of my period somehow making me dirty or taboo.

I do find the whole idea of keeping a cycle of separation and reunion healthy, revitalizing, and renewing. I appreciate the importance of structure in our sexual relationship. Although spontaneity has its value, when there is no structure and no preplanned cycle, two individuals in a relationship can often end up out of sync sexually. When one is too tired, the other is in the mood. With the niddah schedule already in place, we tend to be in the mood at the same time more often. A set of laws that at first seemed to hamper our sex life has had the opposite effect.

Now that I have been married for nine years and have a six-year-old daughter, a four-year-old son, and a one-year-old daughter, I realize that five to seven days without sex is not such an anomaly, so that without the extra days, that short a time wouldn't be enough to make a real spiritual difference.

More difficult for me than refraining from sex during niddah is refraining from the other forms of physical contact that the Rabbis prohibit: the *harchakot*—literally, "distancings"—which are laws limiting physical interaction between husband and wife during niddah.

When we were first married, Jacob and I did not observe these strictures. We understood them as created to prevent the act of intercourse itself, and we decided that we didn't need the Rabbis' assistance in this area; we could control ourselves. Moreover, not touching at all for two weeks each month seemed excessive for us, because it meant, according to the most strict interpretations, not even passing keys to one another, and according to the more lenient interpretations, not even hugging. It meant not being physically intimate at all, not even as friends. That did not seem in the spirit of the original prohibition, which we saw as trying to prevent sex, not all intimacy.

Two of my closest friends who observe this aspect of *taharat hamishpachah* insisted that I was missing something special by not doing the same. Both told me that their reunions with their husbands each month are so much more intense and their nonphysical communication so much more developed. I thought seriously about trying some *harchakot*. I had found with most practices that you can't responsibly dismiss them until you try them.

For at least two years I toyed with the idea of trying the *harchakot*. I knew that Jacob and I did not need them to prevent us from having intercourse; we had proven that we could control ourselves. But I was willing to try the *harchakot* for the more spiritual reasons that my friends had shared. Then I became pregnant, and after my daughter Michal was born, I nursed her for a year. Since I did not menstruate when I was nursing, I was able to put off the decision for some time.

When I stopped nursing and my period came back, I decided to experiment with the *harchakot*. I wanted to try those that deal with not touching; the others—such as laws against passing objects between husband and wife, setting up barriers between each other when eating, and not sitting on each other's bed—seemed too extreme for us and would only make the entire trial backfire. Jacob still felt negative about keeping these laws at all; he believed that they were unnecessary and even worried that they could be harmful to our relationship, because of the way that they would distance us from one another. But he agreed to try them at least once.

It was an extremely difficult two weeks, made more so by the fact that Jacob went away on a one-week business trip to Israel five days before my period came. That meant that when he came home, I was in niddah, and we couldn't even kiss each other hello. We did make some mistakes, of course, when we forgot that we weren't supposed to be touching, but as soon as we touched, we remembered, and with an almost embarrassed laugh pulled away.

All through those days of separation, I often found that I had to stop myself from giving him a hug, a kiss, or a playful tap on the behind. I missed cuddling while we watched a video on Saturday night, or sat by a fire in the Berkshires on Thanksgiving weekend. Of course I missed sex, but that I would have missed even without the *harchakot*. This was an entirely new experience.

Our reunion after this first period of distancing was even more sexually and emotionally charged than after our previous niddah periods. I was as excited to embrace Jacob and to hold his hand when I came out of the mikveh as I am when we have been separated by oceans and time zones. In addition, since this particular month my day for ritual immersion, or *tevilah*, fell on a Friday, our reunion was even more spiritually imbued. We invited no company for Shabbat dinner Friday night and accepted no invitations. It was a quiet night, just for us, after Michal went to sleep. Our physical and sexual reunion felt doubly holy to us because it occurred on a Shabbat night, which was made even more precious by the manner in which we connected.

I have achieved an additional appreciation of our relationship through keeping these laws. Like most laws of separation and distinction in Jewish practice, which highlight the permitted against the backdrop of the forbidden, they help me to appreciate the times that Jacob and I *can* be together both physically and emotionally. I had not realized just how often I reach out for Jacob's physical comfort and presence. Perhaps I even took his physical availability for granted. Although I once thought that I did not need these laws, I am now grateful to be reminded of just how lucky I am to enjoy a hug or a squeeze of the hand.

Jacob and I continue to adhere to the *harchakot*, but not in the strictest manner. We cannot bring ourselves to refrain from all of the rabbinically prohibited interactions during our separation period (such as eating off the same plate, making our beds in each other's presence, or passing objects), because we do not experience all of these as sexual. We stop only touching that is *derech hibah*, or sexually related. This rationale dictates that each couple must determine for themselves what constitutes sexually charged contact, and each couple must determine how much physical distance their relationship can handle without causing a harmful rift; the calculation may change over the course of a marriage. This is the approach that we are most comfortable with, because it seems the most reasonable and practical. It is the best way for us to balance our desire to uphold tradition with our need to find a logic in our practices that will make them meaningful for us.

After our first encounter with the *harchakot*, I immediately became pregnant with Adin, and for nine months we did not have to deal with this issue again. Then came labor and childbirth, and although neither of us entertained for very long the idea of not touching during the birth, I did feel that I was being inconsistent in some respects—at least during the pushing stage, when there is definitely blood from the uterus. According to mainstream halakhah, when a woman begins hard labor, her husband is not supposed to touch her. In fact, during the birth itself, he may not even look at her vagina to see the baby coming out. If you plan natural childbirth, your labor partner may not be your husband.

I could not reconcile myself to this halakhah for a few reasons. We both believed that Jacob should be involved in the birth of our children; he felt alienated enough from their gestation process that I did not think it would be healthy for his identity as a father if he were alienated further by being shut out from their births. We see ourselves as partners in parenting. Second, I knew that I would need Jacob during my labor. It seemed cruel for him to abandon me while I suffered through the process of bringing *our* child into the world. The least he could do was to be there for me emotionally and physically. Third, since I understood the primary reason for the *harchakot* as being a preventative measure against intercourse itself, I thought it extreme that the Rabbis should go so far as to extend these laws to the labor room, where intercourse would be physically impossible!

All the other positive reasons for keeping the *harchakot*, connected to the creation of an even more heightened cycle of separation and reunion, did not seem to apply to the birth experience. I was not sure that I would want to be reunited with Jacob at all after having to go through labor alone! I could see no way that separating during the birth of our child would strengthen our relationship. Moreover, not having sex for six to eight weeks (the average time it takes a woman to stop bleeding after giving birth) seemed like enough to give a charge to our reunion without also forbidding touching.

Jacob very much wanted to be involved in the entire birth process; if we were to keep this restriction, the initiative would have to come from me. I would have to tell him to leave the labor and delivery room. He would comply, he informed me, but against his will. I was not prepared to banish him.

In the end, Adin was born by cesarean section, so we never did make it to the pushing stage. I did labor first for six hours, however, and I needed Jacob's support in every way.

When I was in the hospital in Israel for Meira's birth three years later, I saw many ultra-Orthodox women laboring without their husbands. They were screaming in pain while their husbands waited outside. It seemed like such a lonely, frightening experience. I spoke to an ultra-Orthodox friend of mine, who told me that she finds the birth experience (without her husband) to be a very personal, introspective time for her, a spiritually powerful time. I hadn't considered this before, but I am certain that not all women experience birth alone positively. Many of the women I saw looked very scared, and they appeared as if they would have appreciated the assistance if their rabbis would have allowed their husbands to participate.

Even for women who don't mind laboring alone, is it really fair to their husbands? Is that the best way to start off the parenting journey? For couples who view the mother as the primary caretaker, perhaps that is appropriate, but for couples like Jacob and myself, who understand our parenting to be a joint venture, having me labor alone would contradict what it means to have and raise children.

There are those who would pick up on precisely this point, arguing that the Rabbis did not want us to view parenting as a joint venture, that we are wrongly trying to impose our modern (and therefore foreign) ideas on the ancient Jewish tradition. We should, they would argue, readjust our contemporary mindset to fit that of the Rabbis rather than change the halakhah to fit our modern views. If halakhah goes against our modern ideas, then our ideas are wrong.

I do not accept that approach. Judaism is a constantly evolving religion that must change with the times so as to keep its relevance and not die out, and so that it can effectively continue its mission of repairing the world. As society evolves, Judaism needs to incorporate those advances into its own laws while being careful not to discard tradition altogether. We need to keep this delicate balance. Otherwise, we are left back in a time of slavery and polygyny, where parents could have their rebellious son put to death and a girl could be betrothed through intercourse at age three years and one day. A couple that wishes to keep the *harchakot* to the extent of not having the father be in the labor room should be free to make that choice, but couples who have accepted birth and parenting as something to be shared should know that there are ways to understand the halakhic sources that allow for a man to assist his wife in labor.

According to the *harchakot* laws, the husband is not allowed to touch his wife after the delivery either. Because he cannot sleep with her then, he also cannot touch her, as is the case with a niddah. According to the traditional application of the law, after all three of my cesarean sections, Jacob should not have been touching me. In fact, we should not even have been passing the baby between us. Even after the births of Adin and Meira, when we were already keeping some of the *harchakot*, Jacob did touch me. We had decided before I went into labor with Adin that we would touch during the delivery, leaving open what we would do after the delivery. As with the delivery itself, Jacob made it clear that he wanted us to have physical contact after the delivery as well. Again, it was up to me to decide. I told him that I would decide when the time came and I knew better what my needs and feelings were.

It turned out that after six hours of labor, my doctor performed a cesarean section because Adin was in distress, and after he was born there was really no question as to whether Jacob would touch me. I had just been through labor and major surgery, and I needed physical help. I couldn't get out of bed for almost two days, and when I did, I needed assistance in walking, getting up, lifting things, and sitting down. Every move was incredibly painful, and it took a few weeks before I could be completely on my own with my children.

There were ways that I could have received help without Jacob touching me: I could have had nurses help me in the hospital, and I could have hired a nurse to help me at home until I recovered, but I wanted Jacob's help and sympathetic attention. I believed that any good reasons the Rabbis might have had for making these laws could not be more important than my need for Jacob's assistance and support, or more important than Jacob's need to be part of the experience of his child's birth. The narrow view of fatherhood at the time that most rabbinic laws were codified influenced the Rabbis' thinking and their vision of the birthing process, as did the fact that births were considered women's domain in all traditional societies. Birthing women were attended by midwives and other women, not by the fathers of their children. The fact that the father was left out of the picture then does not mean that we should perpetuate that ideology today against the wills of couples who take a different approach.

I could not understand the reason for the *harchakot* immediately after birth. If the baby is born vaginally, the mother is too sore to have sex so soon after; and if the baby is born by cesarean section, she is simply in too much pain. Bearing these physical realities in mind, I thought that any positives of the laws regarding not touching during and after childbirth could not possibly outweigh the negatives.

After having studied the laws of *taharat hamishpachah* in more depth, I realize that the issue is more complicated. The *harchakot* can be seen as a preventative measure for the biblical prohibition of sex during niddah, or as a rabbinical prohibition in and of itself. The Rabbis may have felt that sexual intimacy in and of itself (even without the possibility of leading to intercourse) should be forbidden during niddah, based on the verse in the Torah in which it is written that a man should not "draw near" to a woman who is in niddah. Either of these interpretations is plausible. If one understands the *harchakot* to be more than a preventative measure designed to guard against sexual intercourse itself, a halakhic argument that would allow for a husband's physical assistance during labor would have to deal with the question of whether or not his assistance is vital enough under the circumstances to override the *harchakah*.

Such an argument could be based on the opinion in the Gemara[14] that if a laboring woman cries out that she needs a candle lit on Shabbat, the candle should be lit for her, overriding the normal restrictions against lighting a fire.[15] In fact, Maimonides says that even if she is blind, the candle should still be lit for her, because what matters is her need for it. Every birth is potentially a life-threatening experience, and Maimonides' opinion reflects the belief that the mother's emotional state is of utmost importance in preventing the birth from becoming such an experience. Whatever she requests should be done. This is the mitzvah of *pikuach nefesh*, or saving a life, and *pikuach nefesh* overrides even a Torah commandment like Shabbat observance.

We might argue that a woman can get through childbirth without her husband's assistance. In fact, having the father in the labor room at all is a phenomenon that began only in the past few decades. Although the laboring woman may think that she needs her partner, we know that she doesn't, the argument would go. Maimonides, on the other hand, asserts that even a woman's *emotional* needs—which only she can determine—override Shabbat. Whatever will help this woman get through this enormously draining, painful, potentially life-threatening experience should be done, even if it means violating a Torah commandment. He was, it seems, aware of the highly subjective needs of a laboring woman, which to some observers may seem ridiculous but to the woman herself could provide just the boost she needs for that last push.

In Tractate *Yoma* 83a, Rav Yannai says that if a medical patient says that he needs food, and the doctor says that he doesn't need food, we listen to the patient. He cites Proverbs 14:10, "A heart knows its own bitterness." This should apply even more to the case of a laboring woman, where so much depends upon her willpower and stamina. In a natural labor with no complications, everything depends upon the laboring woman's psychological and emotional state. If she says that she needs her husband to be there, no one else will do. If we add to this the fact that a husband is required by Jewish law to provide the best medical care for his wife, if she says that she needs his support and assistance during labor, isn't granting her this wish the "best care"? Could his refusal to assist her be considered akin to torturing her, which is against Jewish law even in relation to animals?

The ideal halakhic approach to birth would be to think of the father as an available resource to get the mother through the birth. If she needs him, she should call out for him, and when she does so, he would be halakhically mandated to help her. Dr. Noam Zohar argues in his article, "A Labor and Delivery Preparation Course," that assisting his wife in childbirth is actually a mitzvah for the husband.[16] I would add that a woman should use her husband's assistance before using an anesthetic, since no anesthetic—even an epidural—is risk free, but her husband's support is.

I am, in the end, genuinely ambivalent about the issue of *harchakot*. Although I appreciate that our relationship is enhanced by our self-imposed separation, I can also argue against this same separation. I wonder if the payoff is worth the deprivation. I have read many theories about the benefits of the *harchakot* for a couple's sex life and marriage in general, and I have experienced them, but I still wonder if this is ultimately a healthy practice. Could this kind of repression be harmful to our relationship? I wonder to what extent the origin of these laws is based on the notion of a woman's blood as taboo, and if a distancing imposed from the outside is a healthy thing for a marriage. Is a heightened sexual relationship two weeks out of the month worth the sacrifice of all physical contact for the other two weeks?

I am not sure if it is, but halakhah's answer to the question is that whether it's worth it or not, it's required. The Rabbis who designed the *harchakot* may have strongly believed that human beings involved in a long-term romantic relationship need to have their attraction reinforced through physical distance or separation. They may have been concerned that constant sexual availability could lead to the sexual and emotional rut that many married couples fear, and some experience, after years of marriage. The Rabbis do not tell us explicitly why they instituted the laws and practices of not touching. It is implied that they are a preventative measure against the act of intercourse. However, there seem to be additional factors at work, layers that were added over time: enhancing a husband's attraction for his wife, a manifestation of negative feelings about women's blood, and a carryover from the laws of transferring *tumah* through touching. We are left without a clearly stated rationale—only hints and the laws themselves.

When Jacob and I finally began preparing for our big move to Israel, beds became an immediate point of contention. We had been arguing for a while about whether we should turn in our old full-size bed for a set of twin beds. Since one of the distancing laws requires that while a woman is in niddah she and her husband sleep in separate beds, the common practice among people who keep the *harchakot* is to have twin beds that they push together during non-niddah days and push apart during niddah days. However, Jacob has always felt that the restrictions during niddah on physical intimacy that is not clearly sexual are excessive, and although he has been willing to go along with my desire to follow some of the *harchakot*, he has never felt comfortable doing so.

Why is there a practice of having separate beds? The Torah states that when a woman is *t'meah* from menstruation, everything on which she sits or lies becomes *tameh*, and anyone who sits or lies on her chair or bed, or who even touches her chair or bed, becomes *tameh*.[17] There is perhaps an associative connection between this law and the rabbinical ruling that a woman in niddah and her husband must sleep in separate beds. Since there is no longer any practical application of the laws of *tumah* for anyone today, including a woman in niddah, a man need not fear becoming *tameh* from a woman. The Rabbis ultimately consider the laws of separation during niddah as a category of law unto itself. Thus, even if particular laws reflect *tumah* prohibitions, they are for the ostensible purpose of separating to avoid sexual intimacy during the niddah period.

The Rabbis considered sharing a bed a sexually charged act. A story in the Talmud describes an otherwise righteous and pious man who died because he slept in the same bed as his wife during the seven clean days, even though he was careful not to touch her.[18] Although I am not afraid that we will be struck down by God, the importance in the eyes of the Talmud of sleeping in separate beds during the two weeks of separation became clear to me after I read this horrifying story, adding—despite my reservations—to my growing appreciation of a general distancing between husband and wife beyond the mere act of intercourse.

When I explained the results of my learning to Jacob, he was not convinced. He argued that the Rabbis' idea of what constitutes sexual intimacy does not necessarily match our own feelings of what is sexual in our relationship. I agreed with him, and as I spoke found myself suggesting my own theory.

I believe that the Rabbis understood all acts of intimacy between husband and wife as sexually driven, but they did not want to create a situation where the only option would be for husband and wife to completely separate—that is, live in separate houses—during niddah. (In the Jewish community in Ethiopia, the women did live in separate "women's houses" during niddah, a practice that has disappeared in the community that has relocated to Israel. There is also a reference in the Mishnah[19] to "chambers [for ritually impure women]," so it is possible that at one point in the history of rabbinic Judaism there were separate houses for women in niddah.) The Rabbis created a system of laws restricting all relations that they considered especially sexual while maintaining a semblance of normalcy in the household. In fact, there is a disagreement in the Talmud[20] as to whether a woman can wear makeup and jewelry when she is in niddah. The Sages at first say that a woman is forbidden to wear makeup or jewelry during niddah, but then

Rabbi Akiva argues that if this is the practice, men will divorce their wives. Despite its troubling message about men's willingness to divorce their wives over superficialities, this is an important text, because it reflects a development in the laws of *harchakot* toward normalizing the relationship between husband and wife, to some extent, when she is in niddah—so much so that the wife may even make herself sexually attractive to her husband.

This normalizing has many possible explanations: a desire to do away with the most extreme layer of the blood taboo, the need to keep the family unit cohesive, or reasons of modesty (so that no one would know when a woman was menstruating). Perhaps the Rabbis simply didn't know how to deal with the practical aspects of separating women from their families. Who would take care of women's household and economic responsibilities? In fact, there is a discussion in the Talmud[21] about which of the seven duties that a woman is obligated to perform for her husband may no longer be performed when she is in niddah. The decision is that she cannot perform the sexually charged acts—making his bed, pouring his drinks, and washing his hands and feet—but she must continue to perform the others.

That is why, I suggested to Jacob, separate beds in the same room are allowed, but passing a baby to each other is not allowed. A couple would separate in a way that allowed them to live and function together, even in the close quarters that most families had in the time that these laws originated. The beds could be pushed apart, and the baby could be put down by one parent and picked up by the other.

Based on this understanding, I draw the line at kissing and hugging and touching for a nonutilitarian purpose. Anything beyond that—such as the rabbinical injunction against a husband eating his wife's leftovers or passing her something, even a baby!—seems unnecessary to me, irrelevant in the society in which I live. Marriage has changed from a mere socioeconomic arrangement to include a partnership of love and emotional support. Marital partners are more familiar with each other and less formal, and everyday interaction between men and women (even those not married to each other) is commonplace and normal except in extremely conservative communities. Not every exchange between a man and a woman, or a husband and a wife, is experienced as sexual. Some of these laws are unnecessary restrictions and would

only cause tension in our marriage, but I am willing to expand somewhat my definition of what is considered sexual, in order to align
myself with the halakhic tradition. I will meet the Rabbis part way.

I began studying the laws of *taharat hamishpachah* in depth right
after Adin was born, and because I did not menstruate while I was nursing Adin, the issue was moot. We kept our double bed and put off making a decision about it until I began menstruating again.

Then we decided that the time was ripe to follow our dream and
move to Israel. We began packing, which meant discarding anything that
was not worth paying to have shipped overseas. That included our bed,
but what would we purchase in its stead? I argued for a set of twin beds,
but Jacob reacted strongly because it would change our relationship not
only during niddah but also during our non-niddah period. He feels
strongly about sharing a bed, so we decided that we would sleep together in our full-size bed except when I am in niddah, when one of us would
sleep in a guest bed. (Our plan for when Meira stops nursing and my
menstrual cycle resumes is to replace Meira's crib with a daybed in the
small room off our bedroom, where Meira now sleeps.) We would rather
sleep truly *together* when it is permitted, and bear the cost of this by having to be farther apart when it is not.

Jacob still doesn't think any of this is necessary; he would prefer to
sleep in the same bed all the time, and do everything but engage in actual sexual activity (foreplay and intercourse) when I am in niddah. He goes
along with me grudgingly, because of my strong desire to comply with the
rabbinical restrictions in this area. Despite the fact that I know a reading
of the Gemara in *Shabbat* 13a could allow for a woman in niddah to
sleep with her husband as long as both husband and wife are wearing
pajamas, I have come to appreciate the time of distancing, and I like the
experience of returning to the marital bed after a period of separation.

Adopting stringencies merely for the sake of being stricter is dangerous; it opens doors for people to adopt stringencies that are harmful
as well. Some very traditional Jewish communities even have separate
shopping hours for men and women in supermarkets. That is clearly
not required by Jewish law, but if one takes the idea of *tzniut*, or modesty, to an extreme, any conclusion can be justified. This dangerous
extreme eliminates all normal relations between men and women and
makes everything sexual—even grocery shopping!

It is difficult to find a comfortable balance between throwing myself totally into the mitzvot and being wary of extremes. It is a walk on a tightrope. I try to move forward with grace and balance, hoping I don't fall.

About a year after our move to Israel, Jacob and I had the most serious argument we'd had since the move, and perhaps even since we've been married. We accused each other and aired some deep-rooted complaints about our relationship. In the end, we came to a place of mutual understanding and agreement.

This was an extremely emotional experience for us both, made much more difficult by the fact that I was in niddah. When we were finally at the point of kissing and hugging as part of making up, we could not. It was awkward and painful. We had said some difficult and hurtful things to each other that had to be said, and after that there was nothing I wanted to do more than to put my arms around him. We said the words, "I love you"—according to the strictest opinions, this is also forbidden during niddah, but we do not go that far—yet that did not seem enough. I wanted to show Jacob how much I love him, despite all that I had said. I felt an actual physical need to reach out and touch him, and to feel him touching me, not in a sexual way but in a loving, caring way.

I asked him, "Can I just give you a hug? Just one hug?"

To my surprise, Jacob answered, "No."

"Please," I tried again.

"Nope," he said, smiling. The argument was over, and we were clearly making up, but I still felt I needed some physical contact.

"Why not?" I asked. After all, I was the one who wanted to keep the *harchakot*, I thought.

"Because you're in niddah, and you don't want us to touch when you're in niddah."

"I know," I pleaded, "but I think it would be okay now. I want to make an exception."

"Nope," he insisted. "No exceptions. You'll have to wait."

We did not hug to make up that night. We did not hug again until ten days later—a very long ten days—but we made it through that time by using verbal ways of expressing our love and commitment, and I am glad that Jacob made me stick by my decision. Although I felt at the time that I *needed* that hug, I guess I did not. Our relationship is strong enough that we can make up without kissing, even after the most serious of arguments. That's comforting to know.

I was in niddah when one of our closest friends committed suicide. Jacob and I had met each other through this friend, and he was one of the two witnesses who signed our marriage ketubah. He moved to Israel one year before we did, and he lived a block away from us here in Jerusalem.

At the funeral, Jacob broke down in tears, and I reached out and held him close.

A friend, a woman with whom I studied the laws of *taharat hamishpachah* before her wedding when she was still living in Israel, sent me a desperate e-mail from New York, where she now lives. She is in her forties and recently married, and she and her husband want to have children before it is too late. They had been trying to conceive since they were married more than a year ago, without success, so her doctor performed a series of minor surgical procedures to correct the situation.

As a result of these operations, she has been spotting, which has prevented her from being able to go to the mikveh so that she and her husband can resume sexual relations. Finally, she had been "clean" for the required seven days and had been planning to go to the mikveh, but that night before she logged onto her computer and sent me her desperate message, she had found another stain on her underwear. She was upset and wanted to know if she had to wait another seven days before she could go to the mikveh. She didn't know if I would receive her message in time, and she would eventually have tried calling, but luckily I was on-line at the time.

I checked some of my old notebooks and sources, and I was able to give her the green light on going to the mikveh, because she was wearing pink underwear at the time that she found the stain. A stain found on colored cloth is not considered problematic, since it is impossible to know if the stain is actually blood because one can never be certain of its true color. Since concern about stains of blood without a prior sensation (as opposed to a flow of blood coupled with a sensation) involves a rabbinical prohibition rather than a biblical law, and since sexual satisfaction of one's spouse and procreation are mitzvot, the halakhic approach is to be lenient. I was not sure at first if pink is a dark enough color for the principle to apply, but after I consulted my notes and my books, I was able to reassure her that she was free and clear.

That e-mail communication gave me a boost that lasted for a week. I felt empowered by my ability to give her a ruling, albeit a simple one, in an area of Jewish law. I felt infused with purpose. I had been able to help her through a stressful time and reassure her that by having sex with her husband she would not be violating this serious commandment.

I knew that my friend would not have felt comfortable speaking to a male rabbi about her predicament—especially if she had to bring him the stained underwear so that he could evaluate its status by examining its color. She had told me this when we studied together. She knew that I was familiar with her fertility situation, and she knew that I understand how difficult it is to keep *taharat hamishpachah*, especially during one's first years of marriage. She knew that I would be sympathetic but honest. She knew that I would look for a way to prevent her from having to wait another seven days, but she also knew that if I couldn't find a way, I would tell it to her gently but straight. It is a delicate situation that requires the intimacy that a friend—and for some women, only a close female friend—can best provide.

When I received my friend's e-mail the next day thanking me for my help, I thought, *This is the way it should be: women asking other women about their bodies. Who can know better about a woman's body than another woman? We should not have to submit this thoroughly female area to men nor be subjected to the embarrassment of showing our stained underwear to male rabbinic authorities.* I was so glad to have been able to help.

My friend has since adopted a precious girl from China and is still undergoing fertility treatments. I keep her, and other friends who are having difficulty conceiving, in my prayers.

CHAPTER EIGHT

◆

Mikveh: The Ritual Bath

*I took a gift I was given and wrapped it—in many layers of
various patterns, shades, and hues—to give to you, my soul sister.
Because all Jewish women should know of their right to
experience total immersion.*
— Rivkah Slonim
Total Immersion

BEING A "MIKVEH LADY" was never a role I imagined for myself. A
mikveh lady, to me, was an older woman, stocky and wearing a *sheitl*
to cover her hair. Yet when I accepted the key to the only mikveh in
Washington, D.C., that is what I became. My daughter Michal had just
been born, and I had the summer off from graduate school and teaching to spend with my new baby. I thought, *Why not try it? Why not
assist other women in discovering and experiencing the joys of mikveh?*

This is not your average mikveh. It is located in a Conservative synagogue, which is rare. Most *mikva'ot* are under the auspices of
Orthodox institutions. As mikveh coordinator (the title I gave myself),
I had the key to unlock the mikveh for anyone who wanted to use it,
for purposes of *taharat hamishpachah*, conversion, or any other reason.
I would meet the person at the mikveh, explain to him or her the laws
of mikveh and *tevilah*, ritual immersion, and for my female clients, witness their immersion.

It was also my job to make sure that the water level was high
enough, in both the mikveh itself and in the *bor*, the pit that contains
the pure rainwater. In addition, it was my responsibility to make sure,
when the mikveh was in use, that the plug was out of the hole that connects the *bor* to the mikveh, so that the pure rainwater and the mixture
of rainwater, tap water, and chemicals (to keep the mikveh sanitary)
could "kiss." At the same time, I had to be careful to put the plug back

in before turning out the light switch that also turned on the filtering system, so that water from the mikveh wouldn't back up into the *bor*. In other words, I had to be sure to keep a kosher mikveh.

The rabbi of the synagogue in which the mikveh was located also trusted me to make decisions about who could use the mikveh and when. At "my" mikveh—I felt a proprietary interest in it—women could enter at any time of day or night. As long as I was available, whether it was light or dark outside, the mikveh was open. I decided that since this mikveh was not in a conspicuous or busy place, and no one would know if a woman was entering the synagogue specifically to use the mikveh, modesty was not an issue. I had been told that the reason that women can go only at night to the mikveh is for *tzniut*, or modesty, reasons, because people will see a woman emerge from the mikveh building and know that she will be having sex with her husband that night. The rather convoluted reason given in the *Shulchan Arukh*[1] is that a woman's daughter might miscalculate the number of clean days since her mother's period ended, assume that her mother is going to the mikveh during daylight of her seventh day (the last day of her seven clean days) instead of daylight of the eighth day (the day *after* her seven clean days), and conclude (mistakenly) that this shortening of her time in niddah is permitted.

This reason is no longer applicable in our time. It presupposes an intimacy and familiarity in the lives of mothers and daughters that is rare in modern society. Unlike the daughters of women who lived in premodern times and stayed at home with their mothers during the day, the daughters of the women who used my mikveh either were in school during the day, lived away from home, or were too young to even know what a mikveh is. Although traditional sources do not make an exception even for a woman who has no daughters at all, this was not a law that I felt comfortable enforcing and defending.

Another reason to go at night rather than the next day is that one should not delay the sexual reunion of husband and wife. This reason does still apply today, and so I told the women that they should come at night, but if they said they couldn't or wouldn't, I let them come the next day. I saw no reason to delay the reunion any more. And I did not consider it my business to tell these women when to have sex with their husbands.

It was my policy as the mikveh coordinator to keep it kosher and available. My goal was to encourage women to use the mikveh; I did not want to scare them away with unnecessary rules and restrictions, nor did I want to make the use of the mikveh so much of a burden that they might not use it at all. More than one woman told me that, if it weren't for my mikveh and the fact that it was available during the day, she wouldn't have made this ritual part of her religious practice.

If a woman is afraid to go to the mikveh at night because of danger or cold weather, she can go during the day, according to halakhah. If she goes during the daytime—on the eighth clean day after her menstrual flow has stopped, not the seventh—for reasons other than these, her immersion is still kosher after the fact.[2] There are even circumstances in which some rabbis permit women to go on the seventh day as long as she will not see her husband until that night. My policy of daytime availability was not one that would invalidate a woman's *tevilah* or make the mikveh itself not kosher for others. Some women did come during daylight hours—before work, on their lunch break, in the morning while the kids were in school, or even in the evening after work but before dark. In many cases it was much more convenient to come during the day—when their children were at school or in child care, or when it felt safer to ride the Metro—especially during the summer, when daylight lasts so long. When a woman said that she was sure she was not going to see her husband until that night, I let her come even during daylight hours on the seventh day. I explained the halakhah and the reasons for the laws, and then I entrusted them with deciding when to come. I did not want to be like some mikveh coordinators with whom I was familiar, whom I considered patronizing and even dictatorial. My clients were adult women who could take responsibility for their own religious practices. I provided them with the information to make a responsible decision, but I did not see my role as policewoman.

Women used the mikveh I tended for purposes other than *taharat hamishpachah*—an option traditionally available to men only. There were women who came on Rosh Hodesh (the celebration of the new month), birthdays, and graduations. One woman even came to mark the time when she and her husband began trying to have a baby. She came after work on her way home for her first night of "unprotected" sex with her husband, and the glow on her face was like that of a new bride.

The Rabbis discouraged women from using the mikveh for reasons other than *taharat hamishpachah* because they did not want unmarried women to use the mikveh after niddah and then feel that they had a license to engage in premarital sex. One of the obstacles to men and women having intercourse before they are married is that unmarried women are in a perpetual state of niddah because they have been menstruating but have never gone to the mikveh; traditional brides-to-be go to the mikveh before their weddings.

I encouraged men to also use the mikveh before their weddings; men, too, can use the experience as an opportunity to prepare themselves spiritually for this momentous event. One man came with his future father-in-law, and when they emerged from the room, I noticed that both of them had wet hair. I asked why. "Well," the older man answered, "it looked so great in there, I decided to give it a try."

If a woman said that she wanted to use the mikveh but did not want to have me present to witness her immersion, I did not force her. Some women find the ritual uncomfortable because they do not want another woman, usually a stranger, gaping at their nude body. I have mixed feelings about this issue for my own mikveh use; I want to be certain my *tevilah* is kosher, and I even experience a kind of female bonding with another woman present, but when the woman is not a friend, I do feel inhibited and rushed.

The only reason that I needed to be present was to be sure that there was a "kosher" immersion—meaning that the water touched every part of the woman's body, and that all of her hair went under the water. For the few women who felt strongly that they did not want me present, I explained to them that they should go as far down as possible into the water and dunk again if there was any doubt in their minds as to whether they were completely submerged. The only exception was with candidates for conversion, whose immersion I always watched.

Many women said that they felt safe and comforted by my presence and that they enjoyed the connection they experienced between women at the mikveh. A few women brought friends or family with them to be their witnesses instead of using me. I felt most sure that my policy was a beneficial one when a woman who had recently undergone chemotherapy decided to go in alone because she did not feel comfortable having me see her without her wig. From the anteroom, I heard her splashing and singing the blessings in the most beautiful, sweet, and melodic voice, and I hoped that her prayers for complete healing would be answered.

Although I did have several regular monthly mikveh users, the mikveh was used mostly for conversions. It was my job to open the mikveh, explain the mitzvah to the convert, and (if the convert was a woman) to watch her immersion to make sure that she completely submerged. To my surprise, I was often assisting in up to twenty conversions a month. Many of these conversions were not in the context of an upcoming marriage. I felt privileged to be part of bringing these souls into the Jewish people.

Since most rabbis, even non-Orthodox rabbis, in the Washington area are men, I often was the only woman present besides the female convert herself, and it was my job to introduce the mikveh to these women on the threshold of their conversions and to be present with them as they became Jewish.

A great feeling of power filled me as I watched these women dunk and then recite the blessings, while the male rabbis listened from the anteroom through a crack in the door. What a reversal from when I used to stand behind the mechitzah in the shul of my childhood, straining to see the action in the men's section up on the *bimah*.

One unanticipated benefit of the job of mikveh coordinator was social. Whether the immersion was for conversion, a marriage, or a monthly visit, I met many interesting people and made many close friends through the job.

The doctor of the woman who had recently finished chemotherapy had predicted that she would experience premature menopause. It was a minor miracle that she needed to use the mikveh at all. Each time we said goodbye, I said, "I hope to see you next month, *im yirtzeh Hashem* [God willing]."

Then there was the woman who had been trying desperately—with fertility drugs, ovulation tests, the works—to conceive after a number of miscarriages. Her mikveh immersions each month had a dual meaning: first, in their traditional function as a ritual of transformation from the status of sexually off-limits to sexually available, and second, as a way of preparing for and hoping to create a new life. She would call me from the doctor's office to say that she was at her most fertile, could she come today? I would do my best to rearrange my schedule, or else I would find a way to get the key to her so that she wouldn't miss the opportunity. To her I'd say, "I hope I *don't* see you next month." A couple of months before I had to give up my job as mikveh lady because I was moving back to New York, she stopped calling. I found out later that she was pregnant. Tragically, the baby, a boy, died of SIDS (Sudden Infant Death Syndrome) before his *brit milah*. I was happy to learn that they have since had two healthy, beautiful children.

I'll also never forget the blind woman who came for conversion accompanied by her seeing-eye dog. I had never been alone with a blind person before, and I had certainly never helped one to navigate a pool of deep water. As she instructed, I oriented her to the room, told her where she could find the shower, the sink, the closet, and the toilet, and then I left her to her privacy. As I waited for her in the anteroom with her dog, I heard the toilet flush and then the shower running in the next room. I was relieved that she had found her way around this unfamiliar place, and I was impressed with her ability to do so. The task of finding one's way in a world of complete darkness seemed daunting to me. When she called out that she was ready, I went in, checked to see that she was prepared, and then directed her down the steps and into the mikveh. I wondered what it would feel like to descend into water in complete blackness—a true act of faith.

When my next appointment came, also a convert, I found that I had to reorient myself to giving instructions to a sighted person, because the last experience had been so intense. After she left, and I had the mikveh to myself, I took my daughter to a woman in the synagogue office upstairs and immersed myself. However, this time was different: I kept my eyes closed.

A most fortuitous meeting occurred about a month before the end of my stint as mikveh coordinator. A woman about my age was converting under the sponsorship of a female rabbi who is a friend of mine. I was a bit concerned, because the woman was in a wheelchair, and I wasn't sure how she was going to get down the steps and into the water. I knew that because of my FSH I would not be able to carry her in myself, but the woman assured me that she could do it herself.

Sure enough, when the time came for her to descend, all she needed was help getting out of her chair, and she was able to make her way down the steps herself on her backside. I was inspired watching this woman, with a condition that was obviously much more debilitating than mine, doing her best to overcome or live with her disability.

She did have trouble getting out of the mikveh. Try as we might, we could not get her back from the floor into her chair. She never lost her calm or her sense of humor, even as she pulled herself, dripping wet and nude, on her backside along the tile floor and into the anteroom so that we could pull her up onto the couch—a lower surface than the chair—so that she could slide herself into her wheelchair.

After she was dressed and on her way out, it occurred to me that this woman's disease might be the same as mine, only in a more exaggerated form. I can't pucker or whistle or hold my breath, but she couldn't move her lips at all, and whereas I can't lift my arms higher than my chest, she could barely lift hers at all. My legs, thank God, are not affected, but she is in a wheelchair. I asked her, "Do you have muscular dystrophy?"

She answered, "Yes."

"What kind?" I asked.

"FSH," she said.

"So do I," I said.

"I know," she said, "I noticed right away."

I was so thrilled to finally meet someone with my rare disease, and I was thankful for her honesty. So many times people had told me that they didn't notice my crooked smile, my winged scapulas, or my drooping shoulders, and I was actually relieved to have someone tell me straight out that she noticed it as soon as she saw me. Sometimes I almost questioned the reality of my disease. Did it even exist, or was I imagining it? Here was a woman with the same disease, acknowledging my different appearance and, implicitly, my years of difficulty.

Even more, I was faced with what I myself could become if my disease continued to progress. It was frightening in a way, but I also felt so thankful to have the strength that I had at the time, to be able to carry Michal as much as I could. Most of all, I was inspired by this woman, who seemed so comfortable and at ease with her condition. I hope that if I should need to test my emotional strength in those areas myself, I will remember her and be able to follow her example.

Another woman, who preferred to go into the mikveh alone, was a special inspiration to me. It was not for reasons of modesty or shyness that she chose to have me wait outside, but so that she could have a private spiritual experience, she told me. She said that she was not worried about her *tevilah* being kosher, because she dunks very deep down into the water seven times. I would let her into the room and then wait in the anteroom as she did her seven immersions, one for each of the seven lower *sefirot* on the kabbalistic Tree of Life, the seven emanations of God in the human world. I've never seen anyone who enjoyed the mikveh so much. When she emerged, a lovely calm would always be surrounding her. Sometimes she could spend an entire hour on the preparation—cutting her nails; scrubbing her skin; removing her make-up, jewelry, and contact lenses—her fifteen-minute immersion, and getting dressed. She would apologize when she finally poked her head through the door, her freckled skin aglow and her auburn hair still damp. "It's just so hard for me to get out," she'd say.

On her last visit to the mikveh with me as her mikveh lady, I asked her the usual question of whether she wanted me to watch her dunk. Surprising us both, she said that she wanted to try it with me present. I followed her into the mikveh room, took her towel, and watched her descend into the clear aqua water. Seeing her in that water was a truly religious experience. *This is what this mitzvah is all about*, I thought. She was experiencing everything that immersion in a mikveh is supposed to symbolize or create: a return to the womb; a celebration of life; a connection to the cycle of life, to God, or to one's own spiritual center.

When I finished watching her seven dunks, I left her alone in the mikveh to "just hang out," as she put it. When she was finally dressed and ready to have me lock up behind her, she surprised me once again by saying, "That was wonderful, to have you in there with me." She said she felt like this also when she was a bride being watched by a *shomeret* (a spiritual guardian of sorts) the day of her wedding. She felt protected and nurtured. I was glad to have been able to provide that feeling. I had never thought consciously of my role as mikveh coordinator as a *shomeret*, but I welcomed that idea. It felt natural and appropriate, something I had already experienced but hadn't yet clearly formulated.

We then talked about mikveh and what it means to us. I was aware of the connection between *tumah*, or ritual impurity, and death (which I had explained countless times to my first-time mikveh users) and of the idea of the mikveh ritual as a celebration of the lifecycle and a returning to the womb, but I had only recently connected the two concepts to understand immersion in the mikveh as a miniature death and rebirth each month. It was a feeling that I had experienced in the mikveh myself—complete weightlessness, senselessness, and nothingness, a simulation of death and birth in some spiritual way—but hadn't ever seen it described that way in any of the sources I had studied.

When I told all of this to her, my new friend, she became excited and told me that this is exactly how she experiences mikveh. Discovering that someone else experiences such a private and vital ritual in the same way that I do was a special and transforming moment for me.

It was clear that she and I had connected on a deep level that day. The mikveh had become the locus for our mutual spiritual growth and meeting. Two busy women with separate lives and different backgrounds, we had come together through this quintessentially women's mitzvah.

My first immersion in an Israeli mikveh after our *aliyah* was a letdown. When I arrived at the mikveh, it was 8:30 P.M., and when I walked in the attendant looked annoyed and told me that I had fifteen minutes to shower, immerse, and dress. I had assumed that the mikveh would be open at least until 11:00 P.M., since *mikva'ot* usually open only after dark, and with a whole neighborhood of Jews I figured the mikveh would have to be open for hours to accommodate so many women. I was lucky that I had decided at the last minute to put off my study session with a friend until after the mikveh. If I hadn't, I would have had to put off my reunion with Jacob for yet another day.

What followed was perhaps the least spiritual mikveh immersion I have ever experienced. I was so busy rushing that I had no time to focus on the deeper meaning of my preparation and immersion. Usually, as I prepare to immerse, I reflect upon the past month, my accomplishments and failures, and how I can work toward improving myself in the month to come. I also think about my relationship with my husband, since my ritual immersions are in preparation for our sexual reunion. I like to set this time aside each month to meditate on that extremely important aspect of my life. As I clean myself physically, I think about how I can cleanse myself spiritually and emotionally as well. However, this month I had no time for any of this inward reflection. I was not relaxed enough to focus on anything but the physical cleaning of my body.

When I walked back out into the cool Jerusalem night air, I missed the mikveh that I had used in Washington, D.C. I would never have guessed that in Jerusalem, the center of Jewish spiritual life, I would long for a mikveh in the *galut,* in the Diaspora.

When we moved into our new house in Jerusalem, I switched to another mikveh. It is run by Sephardi women and has a different feel than the one I went to when we first moved here. The atmosphere is open and celebratory, nonjudgmental, and flexible. The building is old and rundown, unlike that of the other mikveh, which is newly renovated, but there is a warmth at this mikveh that is lacking in the other. This space feels safer and more nurturing to me, more like a women's space should be.

One Friday night two months after I had given birth to Meira, it was my time to go to the mikveh. Conveniently, we were at the home of friends who live across the street from the neighborhood mikveh. They have services on Friday night once a month in their home. Meira and Adin were with Jacob on the other side of the mechitzah, and I was sitting with Michal. When we began to pray *Ma'ariv*, the evening service, I told Michal that I needed to go out for a while and that she should tell Jacob that I was leaving and would be back soon. She asked where I was going.

"To the mikveh," I answered. I had already explained to her what the mikveh was when we had our heart-to-heart "Where do babies come from?" talk when I was pregnant with Meira, but I had never told her exactly when I was going to the mikveh because I usually went after the kids were asleep. On Friday night, however, one must use the mikveh as soon as it gets dark, since the woman who runs the *mivkah* has to get back to her family for the Shabbat meal.

When I was a child, mothers in my parents' community did not tell their children where they were going when they went to the mikveh. The entire subject was a secret because it was associated with sex. When the time came for my parents to discuss sex with me, they bought me a book; this was as close as they got to actually talking directly with me about sex. In high school, when I learned about mikveh and the laws of family purity, suddenly I understood why once a month my mother would go out, her destination unknown to us children, and return with wet hair.

There was no reason to keep this mitzvah a secret from my own children. When Michal asked about it, I did not hesitate to explain.

"No. Don't go!" Michal pleaded.

"I have to."

"But I want you to stay here with me," she said. I was beginning to grow anxious, since I did not want to miss the short period of time that the mikveh would be open.

"Do you want to come with me?" I suggested. I did not know how the mikveh attendant would react to this, but I assumed that if she did not want Michal to come in with me, Michal could sit outside in the waiting room.

"Yes! Yes!" Michal said, clapping her hands in excitement.

"So tell *Abba* quickly that I am taking you with me, and let's go."

As we crossed the street and entered the mikveh building, I told Michal how I had taken her to the mikveh when she was a baby and dunked her in the water to mark her entering into the brit between God and the Jewish people. She smiled broadly to learn this piece of her personal history.

When we entered the room outside the mikveh, where the mikveh attendant sat at a small table, reading from her *siddur*, I asked if Michal could watch me dunk.

"Why not?" the attendant answered in Hebrew, shrugging her shoulders.

We went into the changing room, and Michal watched me undress, her face glowing. When the mikveh lady called me, telling me to come out, Michal's grin grew even wider. She followed me out to the mikveh and watched with wide eyes as I removed my towel, descended into the water, dunked, said the *brachah*, and dunked another six times (a custom I had adopted from my friend in Washington). Then, as I dressed, Michal helped me by passing me items of clothing. She was so attentive to me, so focused on my needs—a rare treasure to experience from a small child.

When we left the mikveh building, my hair wet and my cheeks red from the heat of the mikveh, the January Jerusalem night air felt cold against my skin, still damp from the warm mikveh waters. I love the feeling of freshness and renewal each time I leave the mikveh. My pores feel so clean and open, and I am overcome with a burst of energy. The world seems brighter, filled with possibilities.

"Can I go with you again next time?" Michal asked.

I thought for a minute, reflecting on this mother-daughter outing. I knew that I would not want to bring Michal every time that I go to the mikveh. It is an important private experience. It gives me a spiritual space to reflect each month, away from Jacob and the children. Yet it *had* been very special to have Michal with me this time. We don't get much time alone together since the arrival of Adin and Meira. Having Michal with me at a mikveh was especially meaningful; we were returning to the place where she was brought into the covenant, when she was still small enough for me to hold in my arms. *Next year Michal will be entering first grade. She is growing up so fast*, I thought. Time was passing so quickly, and I realized that moments like these would be the ones to stick out in my mind among the years of Michal's childhood. *I should take her again*, I decided.

"Sure. Next time I go on a Friday night," I said, taking Michal's hand in mine. Together we skipped back to shul.

CHAPTER NINE

◆

Torah: Learning

Teaching your daughter Torah is [like] teaching her tiflut *[folly].*
— Rabbi Eliezer in Mishnah *Sotah* 3:4

Better to burn the words of the Torah than to teach them to women.
— Tosafot on *Sotah* 21b (quoting Rabbi Eliezer)

From what do women merit? From calling their children to the synagogue, from delivering their husbands to the study hall, and from waiting for their husbands to return from the study hall.
— Rav in *B'rachot* 17a

I AM SITTING WITH my father on Friday night studying Talmud. We do this together almost every Friday night. My older brother is not, as they say, among the big students of Talmud. He has never derived the pleasure that I always have from studying these texts, which are the basis of the Jewish legal system to this day. My father, who is a lawyer, also enjoys the logic games and legal arguments that make up the Talmud, so—after our family dinner is over and the table is cleared—we spend an hour or two studying Talmud together.

This Friday night, as my father and I pore over a page of this ancient Aramaic text, my father turns to me. "You'll be the lawyer in the family," he says.

It wouldn't have crossed his mind to say that I would be the rabbi in the family, since women in the Orthodox world don't become rabbis. Only men can aspire to that most respected and powerful role in the Jewish community. But he clearly wanted me to "think big," to push myself to reach my potential.

Did he realize that by sitting there with me week after week, perusing these texts that only a generation before had been barred to girls like myself, he was teasing me in an almost sadistic way? I am sure that he didn't, and I certainly don't fault him for giving me as much as he could. He knew that as a woman I would not be able to take my love of Talmud study as far as a man might, but that was no reason to deny me access to the text.

Had my father known the frustrations I would eventually encounter in wanting to use my knowledge to guide and teach others, would he have thought twice about exposing me to these texts? I would like to think not.

According to the Talmud,[1] women are exempt from *talmud torah*, the study of Torah. The Sages cite a teaching from the *Sifre*[2] (a halakhic commentary on Numbers and Deuteronomy, compiled in the third century C.E.), on Deuteronomy 11:19, "*V'limadtem otam et b'neichem.*" This quote can be interpreted in two ways—"You shall teach your *children*" or "You shall teach your *sons*"—because in Hebrew one uses the male plural form when speaking about groups that include both sexes. The *Sifre* (as well as the Talmud, which quotes the *Sifre* without bringing an alternative reading) chooses the latter interpretation: "'And you shall teach *b'neichem*'—your sons and not your daughters."

Maimonides takes this thinking one step further and offers the minority opinion of Rabbi Eliezer, that teaching your daughter Torah is teaching her *tiflut*, or folly, to support the idea that not only are women *exempt* from studying Torah, they are *prohibited* from it. He explains that women shouldn't study Torah because "their minds are not suited for Torah; rather, they will turn the words of Torah into words of folly with their flightiness of mind."[3] However, Maimonides is using Rabbi Eliezer out of the context of his original statement. Rabbi Eliezer's comment is cited in the Mishnah[4] during a discussion about a *sotah*, a wife accused of adultery who must drink a special concoction. If this (physically harmless) concoction harms her, she is proven guilty, but if she is not affected, she is proven innocent. Because it is believed that a woman's merits will delay the effects of the *sotah* waters, Rabbi Eliezer says that if one teaches his daughter Torah, it is akin to teaching her folly. His comment is generally understood to mean that if she knows that her merits can delay the effects of the *sotah* waters, she could use this knowledge to get away with adultery. Thus, her father would be teaching her lasciviousness.

The Hafetz Hayyim, Rabbi Israel Meir HaKohen, who lived in nineteenth- and twentieth-century Lithuania and was a highly influential ultra-Orthodox leader and *posek*, advocated teaching girls *Tanakh* (the entire Hebrew Bible) and its commentaries. His argument was that because women were now being educated in secular knowledge, they would leave Judaism if they were not also taught Torah.[5] Today it is the accepted practice in most Orthodox communities (except for some ultra-Orthodox groups) for women to study *Tanakh*, but women who study the Oral Torah (especially the Talmud and other legal texts) are still in the minority, albeit a rapidly growing minority. In many Orthodox communities, women who choose to study these texts intensively are considered revolutionary and are usually careful to insist that they are studying purely for the sake of heaven, and not to obtain power or access to leadership positions.

Rabbi Eliezer feared that knowledge in a woman would lead to sexual promiscuity. Today, it seems, the fear is that it will lead to powerful women. Times may have changed, but the desire of many men to keep women under their control has not. Some day soon women will reach positions of equal power, even in the mainstream Orthodox world— even if it means first claiming that power for ourselves without the consent of the male rabbinical establishment.

As I was finishing high school, it was becoming popular for Orthodox families in the United States to send their children to spend a year in Israel studying Torah intensively before college. Today, at least half of Orthodox Jewish high school graduates spend a year in Israel studying in a yeshiva. They study only Jewish texts, to provide a balance to the mainly secular subjects they will be learning in college, and to infuse them with Judaism before they go out as young adults into the secular world. Many of the high school graduates who do this return transformed into intensely religious first-year college students. Some are simply more zealous in their observance and their desire to learn more Jewish texts. Others return as ultra-Orthodox Jews—the boys wearing black hats and suits and growing *peyot* (sidecurls), and the girls wearing long sleeves and long skirts with stockings.

My parents gave me the choice to go to a women's yeshiva in Jerusalem or go straight to college. The only yeshiva we considered was

Brovender's (now named Michlelet Lindenbaum), the only one at the time with a post-high school program for American girls that taught Talmud.

I felt Israel beckoning me, and the learning appealed to me. Throughout all my rebelliousness, I still loved to study Jewish texts. My thirst for knowledge did not abate even though I had lost all faith in the divinity of the Torah and the relevance of rabbinical law. I still wanted to know what the Torah and the Rabbis said, even if I did not feel bound by their opinions. Although I considered myself outside the authority of halakhah, I had abandoned Jewish law in practice only. I was still very much engaged with the system in which I was raised. I still had a desire to read everything that my tradition had to say, even those things that upset me most. Even later, in my most antireligious stage in my first semester of college, I would take a graduate-level Talmud course. In my love-hate relationship with Torah, I couldn't get enough of Talmud.

I applied to Brovender's, and during the interview I offered no information about my personal religious beliefs and observances. They assumed that I was a devout and religiously observant young Jewish woman, and I did nothing to suggest otherwise. I focused on how excited I was to learn Jewish texts all day and how much I longed to live in Israel. With all this talk, I managed to convince myself as well. I decided that I would continue to live my dual life for one more year. I would live at the school and abide by their rules, but on weekends I would visit my nonreligious cousins and in that way break free.

Even in the yeshiva, I told myself, they couldn't control my thoughts or my words; they couldn't control what I would say, the questions I would ask. I could use the year to explore my feelings about Judaism. Asking questions could not be a crime, for which they would kick me out. They didn't have to know that I acted on my doubts; I would do that only outside of Jerusalem.

I never made it to Israel to study after high school. My eating disorder helped me to realize that I needed to explore my religious beliefs and commitments in a religiously neutral environment.

More than a decade later, I am here in Jerusalem, studying for s'micha, rabbinic ordination. I am not studying at an institution with an organized training program for rabbis. I am not studying to become an "Orthodox rabbi," a "Reform rabbi," a "Conservative rabbi," a "Reconstructionist rabbi," or a rabbi with any other label.

I did dream of receiving s'micha from an Orthodox rabbinical seminary when I was living in Washington, D.C. Michal had been born that summer, and I was on a spiritual high. In addition to my graduate studies and teaching Creative Writing, I had made a life for myself as a religious and spiritual leader in our Jewish community. Besides being the mikveh coordinator, I had founded (along with Jacob and other friends) and helped run a still thriving traditional, egalitarian minyan in the heart of D.C. I taught in a volunteer adult Jewish educational center, and as a religiously observant woman with a knowledge of Jewish texts who also wore tzitzit, tallit, and tefillin, I had become a role model for feminist Jewish women seeking religious expression within the tradition. I was tasting what it felt like to be an influence in people's religious lives, so when I found myself asking what I wanted to do once I completed my graduate degree, the most obvious answer was: become a rabbi.

Where could I study and be ordained? My choices were limited to the Conservative, Reform, and Reconstructionist movements, since within Orthodoxy women may not yet become rabbis.

The first question I needed to ask myself was: am I still Modern Orthodox? I had departed from many of the practices and philosophies of the community in which I had grown up. The Modern Orthodox movement, if it was still alive at all, had *regressed* to a more narrow outlook rather than *progressing* toward the kinds of changes and pluralistic attitudes that were by then central to my practice of Judaism. I saw the movement's leadership as being too afraid of what those to the right of them thought, and I feared the situation would only become worse. Today there are two new organizations which suggest that, simultaneous with the shift to the right within Modern Orthodoxy, there is also a shift to the left: Eida, which is run by Rabbis Avi Weiss, Yitz Greenberg, and Saul Berman and is trying to revive the liberal Modern Orthodox movement; and the Jewish Orthodox Feminist Alliance, the brainchild of Blu Greenberg, which organizes the Feminism and Orthodoxy conferences and advocates for feminist advances in Orthodoxy.

At the time, however, I did not identify with the existing Orthodox movement as I weighed my options. Nor did I identify with any of the other movements. Reform and Reconstructionist Judaism had completely abandoned a belief in the binding nature of halakhah. The Conservative movement was philosophically, perhaps, the closest to my own *hashkafah,* or religious ideology, but so few Conservative Jews lived out a commitment to halakhah that I knew I would not feel comfortable calling myself a Conservative rabbi.

I had also found both institutional Orthodoxy and Conservative Judaism to be spiritually lacking. The emphasis was on what one should and should not do, but not on the reasons why. My religious role models—my teachers, my congregational rabbi, the adults around me—placed little emphasis on the purpose of the mitzvot, and they rarely mentioned their personal relationships with God. Talking about these issues was considered too "touchy-feely," something for kabbalists and Hasidim, not rationalist Jews. The havurah that I had attended in Washington was different, but with the opposite problem. There was a lot of meaning, but little if any attention was paid to halakhah. I had felt the most spiritually satisfied there, but the lack of a halakhically committed community was, in the end, the catalyst for my leaving.

I felt in some deep way that if I explicitly left Orthodoxy, I would be selling myself short. By naming myself something other than Orthodox, I would be admitting that my Jewish vision and practice of a progressive yet traditional halakhic Judaism was beyond the Judaism of my childhood. I believed then, and I believe now, that a Judaism committed to tradition as well as to the idea that change is positive and necessary is continuous with the Judaism of the sages in the Talmud. I was not willing to give up maintaining this position within the Orthodox community.

Nor did I want to limit my audience by labeling myself as something other than Orthodox, because, unfortunately, most Jews who identify as Orthodox see anyone who does not claim that label as distorting the Torah. I wanted to push the limits of the Orthodox community, and I knew that if I received ordination from another movement, Orthodox Jews would have an easy way of dismissing me. I had visions of joining with others to create a new Liberal Orthodoxy the way my parents' generation had done with Modern Orthodoxy (albeit learning from their mistakes).

Yeshiva University in New York was originally founded with the mandate of the Modern Orthodox movement. The institution, like the movement itself, was in the process of moving to the right, but I still had reason to hope that they would consider my application. Despite the trend of rightward religious movement, great strides had been made in terms of women's learning. I was not asking to be counted in a minyan, to be a witness, or to lead *tefillot*—all things that would require some halakhic innovation to be implemented. I was asking only to study what the men were studying and to receive the same degree and title that they do.

S'micha originated with Moses, when he conferred his God-given authority to Joshua. God commanded Moses, "Take Joshua, son of Nun, a man of spirit, and lay your hand upon him."[6] Thus began a chain of authority passed on from master to disciple throughout the generations. At some point during the end of the Geonic period (the sixth-eleventh centuries), the chain was broken, so what we have today is not the authentic and original s'micha that once existed. Nevertheless, the concept itself still exists, and rabbis confer s'micha on their students, with the title "rabbi" attached. This title has accompanied s'micha since before the time of the Mishnah. Despite the fact that rabbis today have not received their s'micha from a direct line back to Moses, it is still taken quite seriously, denoting knowledge, authority, and leadership. S'micha carries no ramifications for performing ritual. A rabbi is not required to act as a witness or to lead *tefillot*. Women's inability to fill these roles according to the interpretation of halakhah should not be used to prevent women from receiving s'micha.

A more overarching problem comes from a citation by Maimonides, who says that there cannot be a queen of Israel because the Torah says *melech*—that is, a king, not queen.[7] He expands this to include all positions of leadership in the Jewish community, which would include for us today, among other things, presidents of synagogues and Jewish organizations, the prime minister of Israel, and members of the Israeli Knesset. Many rabbis do not apply this opinion today because positions of leadership are now based on the consent of the governed rather than on monarchical authority, and because the status of women today in society at large has changed so that it is not considered unseemly if a woman acts in a position of power.

The biggest obstacle to women becoming rabbis in the Orthodox world is sociological, not biblical or legal. It simply is "not done." However, it was "not done" in the other denominations, either, until women pushed for it. I believed that the time was ripe for someone to press the question in the Orthodox movement in a very practical, direct way: by applying to YU's rabbinical school. Unfortunately, because the movements that do ordain women have become so far removed from Orthodoxy, it is easy for many Orthodox Jews to create an aura of heresy around the idea of women rabbis and to demonize even those female rabbis who *are* committed to halakhah. I wanted to send a clear, tangible message to YU that there are women who are committed to Torah, Judaism, and halakhah who also want to become rabbis. I hoped that my application might motivate them to do something to accommodate me and women like me.

My upbringing had conveyed the message that although I could not be equal to my male peers in ritual, I could be in my studies. My application to rabbinical school was an extension of this mindset, a logical conclusion for me of the educational philosophy of Modern Orthodoxy. Women like me who love to study Torah were left high and dry after high school.

This is slowly and gradually changing, now that there are serious institutions for women's Torah study, and some liberal Orthodox institutions are experimenting with new leadership roles. In 1998, there was an encouraging development. Two women, Julie Stern Joseph and Sharona Margolin Halickman, were hired by Orthodox shuls to be "congregational interns." This title is purposely vague. They are not rabbis and have not completed a full rabbinic education. These women, as well as the rabbis of these synagogues, are careful to say that they are not in training to become rabbis. Their responsibilities are teaching, delivering *divrei torah* (learned talks during services), visiting sick female congregants in the hospital, and counseling women in the congregation about the laws of *taharat hamishpachah*.

Although this is a step forward, I also fear that it will distract people from the issue of the ordination of women as Orthodox rabbis. Aside from giving *divrei torah*, the role these women are filling is no different than that which a *rebbetzin*, a rabbi's wife, may fill. The main and not inconsequential difference is that these women will be paid. Despite this development, there has yet to be any formalized role or title for learned women in the Orthodox world.

Jacob called the Rabbi Isaac Elchanan Theological Seminary of Yeshiva University to ask them to send an application in the mail, intentionally leaving out the crucial piece of information that it was for his wife. After I had sent in the application, a friend, who at the time was an editor at a popular English-language Jewish magazine, told me that the next issue would include an article by Blu Greenberg defending the idea of Orthodox women rabbis and predicting that women's ordination would eventually happen. When I told him about my application, he asked me to write a piece explaining why I applied to YU.

I had not considered publicizing my application, but once he mentioned the idea, I thought some publicity might help to bring the issue out into the open. I also hoped that if YU did not accept me, the article could serve as a call that might be answered by someone who *could* help me to actualize my goal.

When the article came out, *The New York Times*, *The Washington Post* and a number of Jewish newspapers around the world wrote stories about my application, and for a while I was the topic of much discussion, debate, and criticism in the Orthodox world. It was an exciting but emotionally draining time for me. Suspicious, antifeminist Jews said unkind things about me, mostly with the intention of delegitimizing me and, by extension, my goal. However, I also received many supportive letters, phone calls, and comments that reassured me that I had taken a positive step. "I wouldn't have had the courage to do what you've done," was a common response from liberal Orthodox women, "but I'm glad someone did!"

Needless to say, I was not accepted to YU. In fact, the school did not even acknowledge my application. When I would call to find out what was happening with my application, the receptionist always said that there was no one in the office who could speak to me, and when I sent letters, I received no response. Months later, a friend of mine who began his studies in the rabbinical school that year told me that during student orientation, the president of YU had told the first-year rabbinical students that he had sent me a rejection and that I had responded with a nasty letter. When I wrote to demand an explanation, I received a letter from his secretary denying saying such a thing.

Perhaps there was a misunderstanding; perhaps he did not say what my friend heard. I will never know for certain, but neither I nor my application were taken seriously by the school, despite the seriousness with which I filled out the application and challenged the school's silence in the media. In the Purim issue of the school's newspaper (a comic issue in the spirit of the classic Purim *shpiel*), a cartoon appeared with a picture of a tall, blonde woman in a miniskirt, her head not covered, sitting in a waiting room, waiting to be interviewed to fill the position of dean of the rabbinical school (YU was actually seeking a new dean of the rabbinical school at the time, a position that would presumably be filled by a rabbi.) The caption read something like: "Ms. Krasner-Davidson [the name I used in the United States], you're next!" It wasn't so much the fact that they were making light of my application that bothered me, but rather the cynical portrayal of me as the opposite of a serious religious woman (and, incidentally, physically very different from my petite stature and brown hair). When I applied, they had asked for a picture, which I gladly sent, and many of the newspaper articles about my application were accompanied by photographs, so this was apparently an intentional statement conveying at least what some of the students thought of me.

At the time, I felt very much that to the extent to which I was taken at all seriously, it was out of fear of what I represented: change. Yeshiva University is no longer the Modern Orthodox institution it was founded to be. At one point in time, it may have been at the forefront of the movement to combine enlightened thinking with a religious life, but today the administration is too much afraid of change to wave the banner of the Modern Orthodox movement. I am glad in many ways that they did not accept me. Before my experience with my application, I had not realized the extent to which the school had abandoned the Modern Orthodox outlook. After my experience, I not only realized that YU was not the right school for me ideologically, I also was so disappointed in the way that they avoided dealing with me and this important issue that I realized I would not want to associate my name with YU even if they would accept me.

Although I have given up on the Orthodox establishment, per se, I

will not let others label me or define me out of Orthodoxy. I am studying with Rabbi Aryeh Strikovsky, a brilliant and modest rabbi who has
Orthodox s'micha from an Israeli Orthodox yeshiva. His s'micha will
guarantee me nothing in terms of acceptance as a rabbi in the Orthodox
community. Some people will call me "that crazy feminist," "that
Reformit," and other labels to discount me so that they don't have to
listen to what I say. If I do, God willing, receive his s'micha (the program of study is long and an arduous undertaking), I will probably
close as many professional doors as I open, but I am committed to con-
tinuing on this path. There should be a woman studying for Orthodox
s'micha. The time is ripe. I have the motivation, the desire, and a rabbi
who is willing to take this step—there is no reason not to move forward.

During my last two years in the United States, I lived in New York
and studied at the Drisha Institute, a yeshiva for women in Manhattan
on the Upper West Side. The first day that I entered this institution to
begin my course of study, I was nervous. After the previous year, in
which my unsuccessful application to YU had become controversial in
the Orthodox Jewish community, I had decided to enter the Scholars'
Circle program, an intensive three-year program parallel to that of a
man studying for s'micha, even though I could receive no formal degree
or title at the end of my studies. I did not know how the other students
would feel about my attending, or if the other women studying there
had been basically supportive of my application to YU. Every woman
in the Scholars' Circle program that year except one had a husband or
husband-to-be who was currently studying for s'micha at YU or had
already been ordained there. I hoped that even if my fellow students did
not agree with what I had done, at least they would be open to studying and entering into dialogue with me.

No one was overtly hostile to me when I first arrived. In fact, with
the exception of my second-year *hevruta* (who was not in the program
during my first year), none of the women mentioned my application for
the entire two years that I studied there. In some ways, this was worse
than being challenged directly.

When I arrived the first day, it was not clear to me which program
I would be in that year. The rabbi who is the founder and head of the

school, David Silber, had told me on the phone that he thought I should study for a year in a lower-level program before beginning the highest-level Scholars' Circle, since I had never studied rabbinical texts this intensively before. When I arrived, however, there was no other program besides the Scholars' Circle, so Rabbi Silber told me to join the other women.

I went into the *beit midrash*, where it is customary for people to study in *hevruta* pairs in preparation for *shiur,* the group lesson. Most of the learning time, in fact, is spent studying in pairs. Class time is not the focus of the studies; rather, the personal mastery of the texts is most important.

As soon as I entered the *beit midrash,* the study hall, I saw that I was the odd woman out. There were three pairs of women studying already, and I had no study partner. I went back to Rabbi Silber and asked him what I should do. "Ask to join another *hevruta,*" he answered.

The first pair I asked said no. I was taken aback, but they said that they had been studying together for years and thought it would be an uncomfortable situation to suddenly have a third. Fair enough. I went over to another pair, who also said no. Their reason was similar; they had also been studying together for a while. In addition, they explained, with my lesser skills, I would hold them back. I went to the third pair. They too had studied together in the past, they said, but I could sit down and we would see how it went. I guessed that they, too, wanted to say no but felt they couldn't because there was no one left for me to ask.

I studied with this pair of women for a few weeks, and from my point of view it was going reasonably well. I did not participate in the give-and-take as much as the other two women because I did not feel as confident or comfortable as they did with the texts. Socially, I was also an outsider, because they were friends from before the program. I wanted to learn, however, and I knew that with time my confidence would grow and I would get to know the other women. Even if I never became close with them, my purpose was to learn, not to make friends.

One day, when I sat down at the table with my book in hand, my study partners told me that they had decided it wasn't working. They did not want me to study with them any longer. They felt that a threesome—especially when one of the three was on a lower level than the other two—ruined the dynamic.

I spent the rest of that year studying by myself.

It was not until the end of the following year that I would discover that my imminent arrival at this yeshiva had caused a stir among the students in the Scholars' Circle program. Some objected to my acceptance into the school because of my politics and my activism. They were concerned that I would make the institution, and therefore them, look too radical. Rabbi Silber, however, had stood by his decision to accept me. Now I understood the cool reception I had faced when I arrived. I had experienced how easy it is to hurt others in the name of Torah. I kept asking myself: *What is the point of learning Torah if we don't integrate common decency into our lives?* It's easy to treat well those whom you perceive to be like you; the test is to do the same for those who are different.

In traditional Jewish learning, each student wants the *hevruta* relationship to be just right. The learning levels of the partners should be compatible, and the personal relationship should also be in sync. Like any relationship, it requires work and some amount of compromise from both sides. I wanted a shot at making it work. I will never know precisely what combination of legitimate self-interest and unkind inflexibility left me studying alone for almost a year.

I have a tremendous amount of respect for these women and their mastery of texts, and for their religious commitment in spite of the barriers to their ability to reach their complete potential within their communities. I feel warmly toward several of them on a personal level. They may have been frightened about the political consequences of befriending me. Their decision to study in this pseudo-s'micha program was already a radical enough step for most of them, many of whom come from the Yeshiva University community. They may have been worried about the consequences of our being in the same program. Would my presence radicalize the program to such an extent that it would ruin their chances of being accepted as teachers in their communities?

Yet while I have some sympathy for what may have caused their negative reaction to me, I also cannot help but hold them accountable for the way that they treated me, alienating me both emotionally and physically. Even with the insight of the past years, I still believe that they should have made an effort to reach out to me, to try to understand me (one classical interpretation of "loving your neighbor as your-self"), to welcome me as a stranger, even an unwanted one. Because these are good women with a moral conscience and a desire to do what is right, I expected more.

Tragedy struck in Israel during the spring of my second year at Drisha. Two Number 18 Jerusalem city buses were bombed during rush hour, and many of their passengers were killed. This was followed by another bombing in Tel Aviv in the busy Dizengoff Square, killing mostly children dressed in their Purim costumes. It was a mournful Purim—the holiday of Jewish merrymaking at its most extreme—for Jews all over the world.

Two young Jewish students from the United States, in love with each other and with life, were on the first bus that was bombed. They were on their way to Eilat for a vacation. One of the students was Sara Duker, who was studying science at the Hebrew University in Jerusalem for the year. She was an outspoken religious feminist, and just the night before her death, she had spoken to a women's *tefillah* group (in which I now participate) about her decision to wear a tallit when she prayed.

The other American student, Matthew Eisenfeld, was her boyfriend and a rabbinical student at the Jewish Theological Seminary; he was spending a year at its Jerusalem branch. Matt was intellectually sharp and an idealist. He believed in the goodness of all people and the search for Torah in all places. Like me, he was seeking a religious home among the various higher institutions of Jewish learning. He was at JTS, but I had heard that he was seriously considering switching over to the Institute of Traditional Judaism (ITJ), a rabbinical school for men founded by Rabbi David Weiss-Halivni, who left the Conservative movement because he believed that it was going too far too quickly with its halakhic changes, especially its decision to ordain women. Matt was an outspoken pluralist when it came to embracing all Jews, and he would have been an incredible asset to the Jewish community. Instead, his life was cut short by terrorism.

I had met both Sara and Matt briefly, but I did not have the opportunity to get to know either of them personally. I felt certain that if they had lived longer, we would have become friends and colleagues. I felt a real personal loss when I read of their murder, and I mourned the loss of all that they would have continued to offer to the Jewish people. Their murder occurred on the heels of the Rabin assassination, and when I heard the news of Matt's and Sara's deaths, I noted the tragic loss of two Jewish pluralists who loved all of the People of Israel at a time of extreme divisiveness.

The night that we heard the tragic news, a couple of friends of mine—one a rabbinical student at the Hebrew Union College (the rabbinical school of the Reform movement), and one a rabbinical student at ITJ—drafted a letter expressing their grief at Matt's death. They were planning to have the letter signed by students at the various rabbinical seminaries, as well as at our women's yeshiva, and then send it to the Jewish newspapers in the New York area. The purpose of the letter was for students of Torah from all branches of Judaism to unite to honor the memory of a fellow student of Torah, as Matt would have wanted. The letter was specifically about Matt because it was drafted by rabbinical students who wished to acknowledge the death of a colleague.

I brought the letter to school the day after the bombing, thinking that it was a simple and very fitting gesture. We should do something, after all, to express our grief, I thought. The atmosphere was solemn, as everyone was mourning the loss of so many innocent Jewish souls and contemplating what this event would mean for life in Israel, both in terms of the prospects for peace and the everyday reality of riding the buses and walking the streets.

Assuming that every woman there would want to sign, I showed the letter to the other scholars. One woman asked for time to think about whether she wanted to sign; another said right away that she wouldn't. A third said that she would have to speak to her husband. I could not believe what I was hearing! The next woman I asked wanted to discuss the letter. "What is the purpose of it?" she asked. "Why not write something about everyone on the bus?"

I answered that that was not the purpose of the letter. Of course all the deaths were tragic. In fact, there were ways in which I identified more with Sara than with Matt, but the purpose of this letter was to show our special feelings of loss when a student of Torah like ourselves, aspiring to leadership in the Jewish community, was so cruelly murdered. "I felt a tie to him. He was one of us. Don't you feel it?" I asked.

"Not really," this woman admitted. At a dialogue group (between the students who signed and those who refused to sign this letter), which met in my apartment later that week, I discovered what the barrier was for my colleagues: they did not feel a kinship to students of Torah in other Jewish denominations. They did not feel or know that there were non-Orthodox Jews who were studying the same texts, loving the same Torah, and devoting their lives to the dissemination of that same Torah. For many of us, the saying *"shivim panim laTorah"* (seventy faces to the Torah) includes all interpretations of the Torah, no matter with which community the interpreter identifies. For others, I have learned, this notion applies only within a limited framework of discourse, within Orthodoxy alone.

By the end of the day, there were two names on the letter: mine and that of my *hevruta*, Mia, with whom I was blessed in my second year at the yeshiva. It seems that there was the same problem at YU. There, even the s'micha student who brought in the letter to be signed—the friend who had told me what was being said about me at YU—was persuaded by one of the rabbis to erase his name.

When the letter appeared in various Jewish newspapers that Friday, my name and Mia's were printed among all those names from the other rabbinical seminaries: HUC, JTS, the Reconstructionist Rabbinical College (RRC), and ITJ.

What am I doing here? I asked myself. This time my doubt came from more than just a feeling of not belonging. Now I was *embarrassed* to be associated with this community that called itself Orthodox. After many years of frustration and anger, my disappointment with the movement was so profound that I began to seriously reconsider my decision to try to remain within it.

I never did finish the Scholars' Circle program. I completed two years of the three-year program, but during my second year it became clear to Jacob and me that if all went as planned, we would soon be able to finally actualize our dream of moving to Israel. We wanted to move as soon as possible, before Michal, who was three years old at the time, grew old enough that the language and social adjustment would be difficult for her. Our plan was to move that summer, so I would fall short of completing the program by one year. It would not have made sense, we decided, for us to remain in the United States merely for me to graduate, since I would receive no s'micha and no degree. I could just as well continue my studies in Israel. We would live in Jerusalem, where there is no shortage of places to study Jewish texts.

The last few months that I spent at Drisha reinforced my decision to leave. The first class of three women would be graduating that summer, and all the scholars (myself included) were involved in a seemingly endless number of meetings about the wording of the certificate they would receive. At the first meeting, we drafted a certificate that said that we had studied Talmud intensively for three years as well as mastered three areas of Jewish law: Shabbat, kashrut, and niddah. This seemed like the obvious information to put on the certificate, since that is indeed what is required of each woman in order to be able to graduate. This first draft of the certificate also included a one-sentence explanation of the Scholars' Circle program and its purpose: to prepare women to become educators and leaders in the Jewish community.

At the second meeting, however, one woman raised an objection. She said that she had spoken to some students (read: men) at YU who thought that people there would find the inclusion of the specific areas of study in the program objectionable, on the grounds that it would highlight the fact that we were learning the same things that they were. In essence, it would look too much like a s'micha certificate.

This issue was put to a vote, and out of eight women, only Mia and I voted to keep the language, so it was changed. Instead, it would say merely that we had studied Talmud and Jewish law.

I was enraged at the lack of courage I was witnessing in my colleagues, who were unwilling to publicly stand behind what they were doing, to acknowledge that they were studying the same texts as their male counterparts at YU. Yet even another objection was raised at the next meeting. When a different woman spoke to some of *her* friends at YU, they found another word in the proposed certificate problematic: the word *leaders*. Women, in the opinion of these unnamed sources studying at the training ground for Modern Orthodox rabbis, cannot be "leaders" in the Jewish community.

To my shock and chagrin, we were voted down on this issue as well. Not one of our colleagues, who had chosen to devote their lives to the intensive study of traditional Jewish texts, was willing to defend her right to be a leader in the Jewish community.

It became clear that this was not the place for me, and I began to look forward to my departure, even though I had only one more year of study in order to complete the program. Drisha is a wonderful place that provides an incredible service to women who want serious and high level study of religious Jewish texts, and perhaps today I would feel more comfortable there. I hear that the student body now is very different from what it was when I studied there, that the women there now are more pluralistic, open-minded, and activist feminists than the majority of women who studied there during my tenure. For instance, there is now a daily women's prayer service each morning at the institution, with the traditional reading from a Torah scroll on Monday, Thursday, and Rosh Hodesh. When I studied there, I was the only woman who prayed regularly with a women's prayer group, and most women said that they would not do so because they were ideologically against it. The climate that existed among the student body was neither bold enough nor pluralistic enough for me to feel comfortable, and my leaving felt timely.

By the time I arrived in Jerusalem, I was disillusioned with Orthodox programs for women that awarded no clear respectable degree at the end. I realized that I could no longer remain in an environment that asked me to set aside my feminist commitment and my self-respect. Many institutions and individuals were afraid of a backlash against women's Torah learning in general, but I was willing to take that risk. I was not willing to make the sacrifice that was being asked of me: to delegitimize my own learning.

It is still not clear to me whether my colleagues at Drisha had essentially similar goals to my own but chose a slower, more moderate, method of working toward change, or if they sincerely believed that they were simply women studying Torah in a social vacuum, with no political ramifications or motivations for their actions. In any event, these knowledgeable women will most likely accomplish a quiet, modest revolution; they will study, teach, and be leaders—whether or not they use that or any title. I respect their approach for the communities in which they want to live, and I wish them the best. I have chosen a different path, with more radical goals and a more egalitarian vision.

In Jerusalem, I decided to study at a non-denominational institution while I decided about my future. It is one of a small, growing number of places of learning where all are welcome: secular, religious, non-Jew, man, woman, Reform, Orthodox, Conservative, and Reconstructionist. When you walk into the beit midrash for the first time, it is a jarring sight to behold. There are men with *kippot* sitting and learning with bare-headed men, women with head-coverings learning alongside women in sleeveless shirts, men with *kippot* learning with women with *kippot*. Such people would rarely even be talking to each other about the weather here in this highly segregated city, let alone sitting together and poring over a page of Talmud!

I am at a session at a conference in Jerusalem. The topic is the status of women in Orthodoxy. The speaker is a well-known liberal Orthodox rabbi who received his s'micha from Yeshiva University before he moved to Israel. He is a renegade; he supports openness, pluralism, and progressive ideas. As he himself has said, he is pushing the limits on some issues, and on others he refuses to get involved. He chooses his battles.

An eccentric man with a commanding presence, this rabbi states his position. First, he goes through a historical analysis, positing unequivocally that sexism is at the heart of rabbinical literature: that the Rabbis certainly thought of women as inferior, light-headed, frivolous, and a distraction to men, who should be busying themselves with holier pursuits than talking to or even looking at a woman.

He argues that because this is now troubling to us in the modern Orthodox community, rabbis go through mental gymnastics to reinterpret the tradition. He paces across the front of the room, gesticulating wildly. "It's apologetics at its most distasteful to say 'that's not what the Rabbis had in mind at all.' " The claim that the Rabbis thought women were on a higher spiritual level than men and therefore don't need so many mitzvot is, he argues, ridiculous.

I am nodding my head in agreement. It is so refreshing to hear a man—an Orthodox rabbi, no less—saying this. I am heartened as he says that it is an insult to make women sit behind a mechitzah, to tell us we can't touch the Torah. How can we deny women *aliyot*, he challenges the audience? How can we in good faith not include them in all ritual and not open the doors of all positions of power to them? There is certainly a halakhic way to rectify this. It's misogyny, not the law, he argues, that's preventing these changes.

Right on, I am thinking.

"However, I am not in a position to do anything about this," he says, his voice less forceful now. I was afraid this was coming. He explains that he is neither comfortable making women sit behind a mechitzah, denying them access to the Torah, nor with changing these practices. The latter would, he claims, delegitimize him in the eyes of most of Orthodoxy. Change has to come slowly and organically. That is something, he explains, that he has learned over the years. "Too much too soon, and you're written out."

I agree with him on the overall issue that change should be organic, but I differ with him in his assessment of what the "Orthodox community" is ready to accept. It's true that mainstream Orthodoxy is not ready to have women be called up to the Torah, but there is a growing liberal community that is committed to both halakhah and the idea of egalitarianism. It is a community that is willing to work slowly within halakhic bounds for change in the area of women's involvement in *tefillah*.

I think back to the time, only a few months before, when some friends and I went to meet with this rabbi to ask if our minyan could meet in the building of his institution. Our minyan is a traditional *tefillah* with women participating in the Torah service and the parts of the *tefillah* that do not require a minyan but not acting as *sh'lichot tzibbur* (leaders of the *tefillah*). The former is easier to justify halakhically than the latter, and we wanted to begin slowly with instituting change. I had heard him speak out in other contexts for more women's involvement in *tefillot*, so I had thought that since our minyan was in line with the ideas I had heard him espouse, he would be delighted.

However, I was wrong. He had said no, for the same reason he is giving now in this lecture, that he does not want to lose his legitimacy in the Orthodox community. But I think: *A community that feels as he does already exists. The question is: is he willing to be our rabbi? If this is the position he takes, why not turn his beliefs into actions, as he has throughout his life? He will never be accepted by the mainstream Orthodox community in any event, not only because of his stands on women's issues, but also because of his positions on pluralism, interreligious dialogue, and left-wing religious politics, for instance. Why not serve the community that believes in his vision and is asking for his leadership?*

"Women learning—it's so important." Yet you won't give a woman *s'micha*, I am thinking. As if to respond to my unspoken challenges, he continues on, saying that s'micha for women is a "non-issue," that there's absolutely no halakhic problem. A rabbi is a teacher and a leader, and there is no reason that a woman can't fill both of these roles—but, he tells us, in the end *s'micha* means nothing without a community that will accept the rabbi's authority.

It is certainly true that no one can be a leader without a community to lead, and no one can claim to have authority without people who accept it —but that is not a good enough reason to deny women the opportunity to receive s'micha itself. Those who won't accept a woman's authority won't accept it with or without s'micha, and those who will certainly won't be put off by her s'micha per se. The seal of approval of an established rabbi can only help a woman to be accepted. The community that this particular rabbi serves is open to change. Most of those who see him as their teacher and a leader have a relatively progressive view of religious transformation, and his actions and those of rabbis like him have significance for their lives and visions. If he believes that granting women s'micha is the right thing to do, he should follow his conscience; more than a few people will come along for the ride.

When it comes to women's issues, only the most activist Orthodox rabbis will put themselves on the line to do what is just, and there are not many. Rabbis Saul Berman, Yitz Greenberg, David Hartman, Emanuel Rackman, Shlomo Riskin, Avi Weiss, and the late Eliezer Berkovits[8] have been outspoken on these issues, but not even they have ever agreed to give women s'micha, or even significant ritual roles, when they served as congregational rabbis. If we want to see major changes for women's status in the Orthodox world, it will be up to women to agitate for and make change.

It is 1997, soon after the First International Conference on Orthodoxy and Feminism, held in New York under the chairwomanship of Blu Greenberg. With more than 1,000 attendees, it was an incredibly empowering and heartening experience. I am back in Israel, speaking on a panel about Orthodoxy and feminism. I was asked to speak on this panel to carry over some of that excitement to the Holy Land.

The room is packed, and there are three of us on the panel: Rabbi Seth Farber, a young male Orthodox rabbi and self-identified Orthodox feminist; Dr. Beverly Gribetz, a woman a generation older than I, who has been involved since the first phases of the Orthodox feminist movement (she received a Ph.D. in Education, writing her dissertation on teaching Talmud, at the Jewish Theological Seminary of New York and was the first woman to teach Talmud in a Jerusalem high school, in the face of voices and placards of protest around the city); and me.

We speak about Orthodoxy and feminism, our visions for the future, and our practical game plans for the present. Then it is time for questions and answers. One woman asks the entire panel: "Are there any limitations to the incorporation of feminism into Orthodoxy? If so, what are they?"

I answer first. I explain that I don't see any ultimate limitations, but I do see change occurring over a period of time—a gradual, cautious, and organic change, introduced step by step so that we will not sacrifice essential traditional values or ignore the reality that a community must first be sensitized before it can be open to altering the status quo. I also speak about feminism as a value that must be incorporated into Orthodox Judaism, quoting a speaker at the conference, Dr. Tamar Ross, a professor of Jewish thought at Bar Ilan University. She is a religiously observant woman; every inch of her hair was covered by a scarf as she spoke about successive revelations throughout Jewish history, and feminism as one of them, and how history unravels the meaning of the initial Revelation at Sinai over time. Although this idea is merely a different way of phrasing the traditional idea of the Oral Torah, and she qualified her remarks by saying that later revelations are not equal to the initial Revelation, hearing her incorporate feminism into her vision of the divine plan was a huge relief to both my feminist and my religious ears, after having heard so many times from those claiming to speak for the religious camp that feminism will only work against the divine plan. I quoted her, and then added my own development of her idea: that if we see feminism as a divine revelation, there are no limits in the vision, as long as we work with our traditional texts and within the halakhic system. The question is at what pace should the change occur; only time will tell which changes will take hold and which will not.

I then explain where I see the next steps taking place—not in all communities, I add, since some communities are ready to move onto new issues while others are still battling out issues of women's *tefillah* groups or even women studying Talmud. Some communities are ready to begin incorporating women's participation into the prayer service. The halakhic barrier to women reading from and being called up to the Torah in a communal service is *k'vod ha-tzibbur*, the "honor of the congregation," which could mean either that men will feel ashamed because it will appear that none of them could perform this honor or that it will be embarrassing to have women (who were on a lower social level than men during the time of the Talmud, when this issue was raised) read Torah with at least ten men present. If the members of the community decide that it will not shame them to have a woman perform certain ritual roles in the shul, this would negate the problem of *k'vod ha-tzibbur*, and a woman could read from the Torah even with a minyan of ten men in the room.

There are many parts of the service that do not involve men's and women's different levels of obligation for prayer: leading the *Kabbalat Shabbat* service (added to the Friday night service by medieval kabbalists to usher in Shabbat); leading *Pesukei D'Zimra* (the prayers before *Shacharit*); opening the *aron kodesh*, the Holy Ark where the Torahs are kept; and lifting and dressing the Torah after it has been read. Mixed readings of the *megillot* on Tisha B'Av, Purim, Shavuot, Passover, and Sukkot are entirely appropriate. On Purim, a woman's *hiyuv*, or obligation, to read the Book of Esther is equal to that of a man's, and on the other holidays, there is no *hiyuv* at all to hear these readings from the *megillot*. It is custom, not law.

Then there are the issues related to women learning Torah. Although women are allowed to study Talmud, in most mainstream Orthodox communities they are generally not given access to institutions with the highest level of religious text study. These places prepare men to be leaders in Torah as teachers, legal experts, and spiritual guides. I raise the issue of female rabbis. "Why," I ask Rabbi Farber, "if there is no halakhic barrier to women becoming rabbis, are Orthodox rabbis today denying women the right to become rabbis? Why are you against giving s'micha to women who study the same texts as male rabbinical candidates?"

I sit down and wait for his answer.

"Authority makes someone a leader," he begins, not a piece of paper. Women have to first gain that authority and respect. He tells me pointedly that I am doing a disservice to the Orthodox feminist movement by seeking s'micha now, that I am deflecting attention away from the really important issues and giving the opposition easy ammunition to discount the cause.

I often think about this point. I am not so sure of myself that I can afford to dismiss this criticism out of hand, but it seems to me that there is more than methodology and strategy at the heart of his position. Although I know that there are many women who agree with his stance, I also know that it is difficult for men to hand over their power to women and to dissolve all gender inequities when it comes to leadership. Why has there never been a female president of the United States? It's not a legal issue or even an issue of principle for most people; it's a cultural issue. It just doesn't seem "right," because people still think of men when they think of power and supreme leadership.

This rabbi, and all the rabbis who addressed the issue of female Orthodox rabbis at the conference, hide behind the guise of methodology, I can't help but conclude. They probably don't even realize their own gender biases. With the best of intentions, they are holding back from women what is rightfully ours and preventing our communities from benefiting from our leadership. We have, with our learning, already earned the right to study for s'micha, but until we are granted that right and are given the title, we will remain second-class; we will never become policy makers but will forever be put in a position of having to lobby those in power for our cause.

I seek, at the end of my official period of studies, a title to match my learning. If my authority is not recognized, I am prepared to deal with that. If nothing else, the knowledge that a woman has received s'micha from an Orthodox rabbi will make the idea seem less radical for women who come after me.

As I walk home from this panel, I realize that it *is* important that we have many different voices in the Orthodox feminist movement. As with any movement advocating social change, there will be some people at the more radical end of the movement and other people who are more conservative in their vision. The Orthodox movement has almost as broad a range of individual opinions as the Jewish community as a whole; just as feminist values have found their way to Orthodoxy from the other, more liberal, movements, they will find their way to the more conservative wing of the Orthodox movement from people like me who are part of its liberal wing. We need those people who are always pushing for the next step, as well as those people who say, "Hold on a minute!" I wish we could more often work together and recognize each other's contributions toward our common goal, rather than arguing so much about whose approach is better.

As I met people here in Israel and mentioned to them my desire to study for s'micha, but not in the Conservative or Reform movements, one name only was on people's lips: Aryeh Strikovsky. I went to meet him. *What will he look like,* I wondered, *the only Orthodox rabbi living today who is willing to give women s'micha publicly?* I had no idea.

However, I am quite surprised. My first glimpse of Rabbi Strikovsky (although he prefers to be called Aryeh) is of him sitting over a large volume of the Talmud, holding the page up about an inch away from his eyes as he struggles to decipher the small print. He is an unimposing man: short, thin, with a gray beard and glasses so thick they magnify his squinty hazel eyes to double their size. Even with glasses, when he reads (which he does all day), he often needs to hold the book up close to his face as though he is examining each letter with a magnifying glass. He is very nearsighted, which may contribute to his somewhat otherworldly, mystical demeanor. Yet he is enough of this world to take an implicit stand against the other Orthodox rabbis of his time. One would not guess from his unimposing and seemingly inwardly focused appearance that he is such a brave man, willing to stand by his ideology no matter how controversial it is in the world in which he lives.

I speak to Aryeh for a few minutes, tell him of my desire to study with him for s'micha, and he wastes no time. Already he is giving me assignments, telling me where and when he teaches. He has three jobs teaching in various institutions, and he does not have the resources or the students to open his own yeshiva to grant s'micha to women. We will start with my participation in one *shiur* a week and learning with him privately one more day a week, and we will see after that how the relationship develops.

He does not want to discuss details of tests and curriculum. "Don't worry about that now," he tells me. "That's a long way into the future. First we'll learn together. When you're ready, I'll give you a test, but that's at the end of years and years."

He tells me of another female student of his to whom he would like to give s'micha, but she is not interested. I meet her the first day of *shiur*. She is a grandmother, has been studying with him for ten years, and is very sharp, remembering quotations and page numbers and names seemingly effortlessly. If it has taken her ten years, with her kids grown and out of the house and with her quick apprehension, I wonder how long it will take me.

Slowly, I am getting to know my teacher. Born in Israel, he began studying Torah seriously at an early age. As a child, he came in second place in the worldwide Bible contest. His s'micha is from Yeshivat Hevron in Israel. He has an encyclopedic and creative mind, and at some point, I imagine, he became bored with the narrow yeshiva style of learning—which utilizes only traditional rabbinical Jewish text interpretation and no sociology, history, anthropology, or manuscript study—because he went to Yeshiva University in New York to get a doctorate in Bible and then began to study Talmud in the critical method. In New York, he studied at YU with the late Rabbi Joseph Dov Soloveitchik, (known simply as "the Rav"), whom he reveres and often quotes in *shiur*. He says that Rabbi Soloveitchik influenced his thinking enormously.

I wonder what Rabbi Soloveitchik would have thought of his student's decision to teach a woman for s'micha. It is interesting that so many of Rabbi Soloveitchik's students went on to have such varied outlooks within the Orthodox movement. On one end of the spectrum is Rabbi Aryeh Strikovsky and Rabbi David Silber of Drisha, and on the other end there are those at YU who have issued a *p'sak* against women's prayer groups, as well as those who have been quoted as saying that "any rabbi who will grant a woman s'micha is by definition not Orthodox."[9]

When Rabbi Strikovsky teaches now, he incorporates his eclectic and broad education into his *shiurim*, and he is open to all students, to anyone who wants to come and learn. Despite his modest demeanor and conservative lifestyle, his approach to the study of Jewish texts is not like that of the traditional yeshiva. He believes that there are many ways to illuminate the Torah and that all methods of study that have the intention of gaining a better understanding are fair game. To him, Torah is for everyone: religious, secular, women, men, Reform, Orthodox. I have not yet discovered if he realizes how radical he is in the context of his *dati* world. He must realize it to some extent, because he teaches only in liberal institutions, but I also think that he is baffled by how others who are learned in Torah could come to conclusions other than his own. It seems axiomatic to him that women should receive s'micha, and he derives his beliefs on this and all religious issues from delving deeper and deeper into the texts of the great Rabbis of the past and present.

As he explains his position, he quotes Rabbeinu Tam who says that women can be judges, as Devorah was during the period of the Judges in Israel. "What does *judge* mean?" he asks. "What was Devorah's position? First, she was a leader of the people. Second, she adjudicated matters of law: Torah law, Jewish law, halakhah. If a woman can reach this level of learning and leadership ability, of course she can receive s'micha," he offers matter-of-factly.

Aryeh does not seem to be a political man. His agenda is driven purely by the pursuit and dissemination of Torah knowledge and values as he understands them, and he will not be limited by other people's sociological baggage. From his own experience of teaching women and being taught by them (for example, the late Professor Nechama Leibowitz, the renowned Bible scholar, who was buried the day before I first wrote these words), he believes that the time for women's ordination has come, and that is all the evidence he seems to require.

I realize that an amazing opportunity is being placed in my lap. Here is a brilliant and pious Orthodox rabbi who is open to giving me, a woman, his personal s'micha! It is almost too good to be true. There were women in history who acted as rabbis in their communities before the Conservative and Reform movements even existed. The Maiden of Ludomir did so in the Ukraine in the nineteenth century, as did Osnat Barazani in Kurdistan in the seventeenth century, but they never received s'micha. Two women did receive personal s'micha from Rabbi Shlomo Carlebach, but this was in secret, and, unfortunately, Rabbi Carlebach was a controversial figure in the Orthodox movement for other reasons. Rabbi Zalman Schacter-Shalomi has ordained many women, but he only started doing so once he had left Orthodoxy to start what became the Jewish Renewal movement.

Thus, as far as I know, Rabbi Strikovsky is the first Orthodox rabbi who has publicly declared that he is willing to grant a woman his personal s'micha. Although he does not have a school to call his own, he is willing to devote his time and expertise to teaching women for s'micha. What he is offering is in many ways the opposite of what I would get at an Orthodox women's yeshiva: rabbinic ordination, but no official program. Receiving s'micha will depend on my commitment and perseverance, because, it seems, he is not going to push me. I will have to be self-motivated.

Once I do receive s'micha, what will it be worth? Who will accept it? Yet how can I refuse his offer? It seems to be a long-term and nebulous commitment I am making, but it has no drawbacks. At very least I will be learning from a great man. Here I am, walking somewhat blindly down this road.

When I began on this journey, I had no *hevruta*, no study partner to share the journey. Then, two years ago, my friend and *hevruta* joined me: Devorah Schoenfeld, a brilliant young Torah scholar whose commitment to and immersion in the Torah she teaches is inspiring. We discovered one another a year into my studies with Rabbi Strikovsky. Devorah had studied with him before, but she stopped, feeling uneasy about the lack of clear direction in her studies with him. After we first met and spoke for a while, she decided to give it another try. Having another woman to study with who shares my aspirations makes a huge difference to me; I don't feel quite as alone as I did at the beginning of my journey. My path is still a lonely one in many ways, but Devorah and I help one another get through the more discouraging times. Just the knowledge that another woman exists who is willing to go out on a limb and study for Orthodox s'micha is a great comfort. I'd rather be one of a pair of the first publicly known female Orthodox rabbis than the one and only. Maybe another woman, or other women, will receive Orthodox s'micha before me. That might be the greatest comfort of all.

Two years after we moved to Israel, I heard about a program at a women's yeshiva in Jerusalem, training women to become experts in the laws of *taharat hamishpachah*. The year before, I had started working toward my doctorate at Bar-Ilan University, and the planned topic of my dissertation was the laws of *taharat hamishpachah*. Since studying *taharat hamishpachah* intensively at Drisha, I had been interested in specializing in this area of law.

I knew that this particular women's yeshiva was perhaps the least liberal of all the Jerusalem women's *yeshivot* where women study Talmud. I also knew that the founder and director of the school was not supportive of my bid for Orthodox s'micha, and that neither she nor the other women there label themselves as feminist, a phenomenon in the women's Torah learning movement that I find particularly frustrating. How can women in this movement claim to be making their advances in a vacuum? How can they benefit from the advances already made in the feminist movement without acknowledging those who paved the way for them? Nevertheless, I was excited about the idea of studying in this program. I felt I could set aside my politics and focus on the learning. If I went into the program knowing that the other students and the teachers would be more conservative than I am, I could handle being different. As long as I knew what to expect, I thought, I wouldn't be disappointed, and I would also probably be less judgmental.

I applied to the program but did not hear from the school. Soon it was summer, and I still had not received a response. I called. The founder and director of the yeshiva was not there, so I left her a message. She did not call back. I left another message, and still another, but to no avail. Finally, I call her at home.

"Haviva," she says. "I have been meaning to call you, but I just didn't know what to say. I will be frank with you, and I hope you will appreciate my honesty."

"Sure," I say.

She tells me that my application presents her with a big problem, that she can't accept me to the program for political reasons. She says she thinks that what I am doing is wrong and will be detrimental to the women's Torah learning movement. She doesn't want people to associate me and what I am doing with her institution. "It would undermine all of what I am trying to achieve here. I hope you understand."

"No, I don't understand," I say. Even after my experiences at Drisha, and even after hearing a similar comment at the panel on fem-

inism and Orthodoxy, I am still shocked. I had not thought of us as
adversaries. I knew her approach was different than mine, and I was
not blind to the fact that I was considered radical by many in the
Orthodox world. Nevertheless, I had hoped that an institution devoted
to advancing the level of Torah study for women, an institution that
would have a program training women at such a high level in halakhah,
would see me as a sister in a similar struggle. "I am shocked and upset
by your response," I say. "Why do you think that I want to come to
study at your school?"

"I assume you want to be a *poseket*," she answers, explaining that
she intentionally doesn't advertise the program as a training program
for *poskot*. She does not want to be perceived as radical. "You know
we don't give s'micha here."

Had she misunderstood my intentions as merely a desire for a title?
I try to explain my motivation for wanting to join her program: I want
to be an expert in the laws of niddah for my community—a community that the other women in her school would probably never reach. I
tell her that my friends already ask me questions about *taharat hamishpachah* and that I want to be able to answer them more knowledgeably;
I talk about how much this topic fascinates me and that I am planning
to write my doctoral dissertation on the subject. I am completely honest with her, and apparently I make an impression, because she asks me
to come in for an interview with her the next day.

As soon as I hung up the phone, I called Devorah, my *hevruta* partner, and told her about my telephone conversation. I asked her to drill
me, a mock interview of sorts. I was nervous about the interview. I was
beginning to get my heart set on participating in this program. I had
managed to convince the yeshiva director to at least let me apply. Now
that I was so close, I didn't want to ruin it. Moreover, I knew that this
interview, which would be with her and three rabbis who teach there,
would be a chance for me to communicate to them the feelings, aspirations, and concerns of the Orthodox feminist movement. I did not want
to seem too radical, but I also did not want to cower in their presence.
*Should I put all of my hair up into my hat? Should I hide from them
the fact that I pray with tefillin? Should I mention my tzitzit and tallit?
Should I tell them about the* tefillot *I participate in where women read*

Torah? I mulled over these questions the night before my interview.

The next morning, when I got dressed, I wore a black cotton beret, with lots of curly, long, dark hair hanging out from underneath it. I decided to be myself, even at the risk of not being accepted. When they asked me about my studies for s'micha, I told them everything, and they sat and listened, apparently quite fascinated. It seemed this was all new to them: Orthodox women reading from the Torah, wearing tallit and tefillin, wanting to be rabbis. They had associated all of these activities with "angry feminists." They were surprised to meet a religious woman with a love of Torah and mitzvot who wanted to perform mitzvot usually associated with men, not to overthrow Judaism but to draw closer to God.

I was a bit taken aback by their seeming ignorance of my world. In fact, one of the rabbis in the interview had for a few years been the rabbinic advisor for my Jerusalem women's *tefillah* group, now called Shirat Sarah (named for Sara Duker). However, when I spoke about the women's *tefillah* movement, he seemed to be totally in the dark. It was a strange experience, explaining myself to this group of people. I was sure that they should have been aware of these issues, perhaps even sympathizing with some of my views. After all, this was an institution advocating higher learning for women in the area of Jewish law—a radical stance in the more right-wing Orthodox world.

I did not see my struggle as so far removed from theirs. I thought we were fighting for the same things, only I was perhaps a few steps ahead. Yet unless they were feigning ignorance in order to separate themselves from such "feminist" activities for political reasons, they were not fighting for the same things as I and many of my friends. They saw themselves as a one-issue movement—working toward the goal of educating women in Torah on a high level—and nothing more. They were not interested in women's participation in ritual, nor were they interested in achieving any status or title for women who accomplish this study. Their entire enterprise, they said, was *rak l'shem shamayim*, "only for holy purposes" (literally, "for the sake of heaven")—implying, of course, that women who openly seek titles or leadership positions and want to participate in more Jewish ritual have ulterior motives that are not "for the sake of heaven."

The interview lasted more than two hours, and despite the distance between us, I had a positive feeling when I walked out. I felt that they appreciated my honesty and even came to understand me on some level, that they no longer saw me as the enemy.

In a few days, I phone the school and speak to the director. She informs me that I was not accepted into the program. "We were very impressed with you at the interview. We know it was not easy for you to come and talk to us so honestly, and we appreciate it." However, she tells me, they decided not to accept me, for the same reasons she had originally given me. They do not want to risk having me associated with the school. I represent something politically from which she needs to separate her institution. "I am sorry. But we do thank you for coming to talk with us."

I was upset that they let politics interfere with justice and the dissemination of Torah, and to have my feelings confirmed that they saw women like me not as allies but as adversaries. However, the interview was not a waste of my time. The director may never see me as an ally, but the lines of communication are now open between us. If I succeeded at all in bringing her and the rabbis present at my interview closer to understanding women like me, who love Judaism and Torah but feel alienated from the traditional role that Judaism has allotted to us, it was worth the time and effort.

Unfortunately, when I called again recently to ask her to reconsider her decision, now that more than a year has passed and the first class of women has graduated, she said she feels even more strongly about not accepting me. When I asked if I could at least attend some of the more unique lectures—such as those dealing with halakhah and gynecology, or distinguishing colors of blood that would render a woman a niddah from those that would not—she answered quite emphatically in the negative.

"I hope you will understand me, Haviva," she said, letting me know that she does not want me at her institution in any capacity. She can't afford to have my name at all associated with it. While she wishes me well, she told me, she believes I made a grave mistake by publicly declaring my desire for Orthodox s'micha. Unless I'm willing to publicly announce that I'm wrong and have done teshuvah, I cannot study at her institution.

"I can't help it," a friend tells me. "I'm just obsessed with the details of her suicide. Did she leave a note? Did she clean up her room before she did it? What was she thinking? I sympathize so much with her, it's eerie. At the same time, it's like if I can figure out why she did it, I'll be able to reassure myself that her decision to end her life has no relevance for me."

We are sitting in the beit midrash of the Shalom Hartman Institute in Jerusalem, an institution of higher Jewish learning for religious and secular men and women. We are talking about the funeral of a thirty-four-year-old woman that we had both attended the previous week. This woman's death is still a shocking and tragic enigma to us.

Miriam was a brilliant lawyer and Jewish scholar who was planning to move to Israel in a few months to clerk for the Chief Justice of the Supreme Court. She committed suicide last week. Her parents flew her body to Israel for burial.

She had been my teacher in high school, although she was only seven years older than I. It was her first teaching job directly out of college, and she later went on to teach at Michlelet Lindenbaum as well as at a number of other schools in Jerusalem. She left the world of Jewish learning, went back to the United States to study at Yale Law School, and then worked for a prestigious and WASPy law firm on Wall Street. Just recently she had decided to return to Israel and re-enter the world of Jewish law, not through the yeshivas but through the courts. Miriam's name was well known in the small circle of women who study Torah seriously. I was disappointed when she, with such a brilliant mind and so much to contribute, left the learning world, and I had wondered if she would ever return. I was jealous of her brilliance and felt at times that if she, to whom learning came so easily, didn't stick with the struggle of women's learning, how could I manage to persevere? I had seen her a few times while I was living in New York and studying at Drisha during the two years before I moved to Israel, and she did not seem content in her new career. She alluded to the fact that she might give it up and return to a career in Torah, which she apparently was in the process of doing.

So why did she do it? my friend and I ask ourselves now. I too have felt an overwhelming need to make sense of her decision to end her own life, and I have been feeling guilty about it, as though I am somehow intruding on her private space by trying to tie up her life in a neat package. Nevertheless, I probe, trying to make sense of the tragic news.

At the funeral, her father made it clear in his eulogy that his daughter had had a painful neurological disease that no doctor had been able to treat, and that seems like the most obvious and likely reason for her suicide. Yet perhaps because I identify so much with this woman who struggled with many of the same issues that I do, I feel a need to find out if that was the only reason. Does someone with a painful yet non-terminal illness end her life for that reason only? I can't stop wondering if the other struggles in her life added to her feelings of hopelessness, so much so that she saw no reason to continue to fight for her life.

There are times when I feel terribly alone on my path. I can imagine that her circumstances—her extreme brilliance, being a single woman with no children in a community that is so family-oriented—may have magnified to an utterly hopeless degree the loneliness and despair that I sometimes feel.

At a Talmud *shiur* given in Miriam's memory, Dr. Beverly Gribetz said, "We, women who are involved in Torah learning, should all ask ourselves if we have made a place for the truly brilliant among us."

There is a tradition recorded in the Talmud that Beruriah, the daughter of Rabbi Chanina ben Teradyon and the wife of Rabbi Meir, was a scholar in her own right. According to a passage in *Pesachim* 62b, she "studied 300 teachings from 300 teachers in one day."

The Rabbis did not leave it at that. On the side of the Talmud page, Rashi, whose daughters reportedly wore tefillin, tells this story of her end: One day Beruriah told her husband, Rabbi Meir, that she could not understand the principle in Jewish law of *nashim datan kalot,* "Women are light-headed." Rabbi Meir told her: "You will soon understand." Rabbi Meir—the same sage who said that a woman without a regular menstrual cycle should be divorced without her ketubah money—went out and found his most handsome student and told him to seduce his wife. Beruriah succumbed and killed herself as a result.

What was Rashi's motivation in choosing to record this particular story for generations to come? His daughters were known to be extremely learned; there are those who say that they even completed his commentary after his death. Did he feel the need to prove that even the most knowledgeable women will still be limited by their "light-headedness"? Or did he mean for us to understand this story critically and ironically? We will never know. There the story stands in the border of the Talmud page, for all to read. No matter what Rashi's intentions were, he transmits to us a tale of the tragic end of a brilliant learned woman.

I am sitting in class, a Talmud *shiur*, surrounded by women, except for the one man in the room: the teacher. It is my second year at Drisha.

We are studying Tractate *Bava Metzia*, which deals with the topic of lost objects. Rabbi Silber is discussing the case at hand as he nibbles on his bar of milk chocolate with raspberry cream filling—the usual breakfast of this revolutionary Orthodox rabbi, who can find any passage for you in the entire biblical text of Torah, Prophets, and Writings but can never seem to find his own keys.

"Karen, that ingrate," he says in a singsong voice, looking at the woman sitting to his right, "steals my pen. She lost her pen and is too lazy and cheap to buy a new one, so she comes to my desk before I arrive in the morning and steals my favorite pen, the one my uncle gave me for my bar mitzvah." There are chuckles and giggles from the women around the table. It is an intimate group of, at most, ten students—on a good day, when there are no sick children, wedding preparations, or women home with morning sickness—and we have all spent the past two hours studying this case in pairs before *shiur*.

"I bring a case against Karen in court," he continues. "The pen is solid gold, and it's worth enough to bring a case. Witnesses come to back up my claim. Shira and Mia, you're the witnesses." He looks around the table. "In my school women too can be witnesses. We're an equal-opportunity yeshiva."

According to halakhah, a woman cannot be a witness in a court of Jewish law, except in certain circumstances and cases. When particular information has to be given, such as whether or not a woman's husband is dead or alive (so that the woman can be free to remarry), a woman's testimony is accepted. When it comes to convicting someone of a crime, however, a woman cannot be a witness. This clarification is further modified: The Rema[10] says that when there is no man available to give testimony, even in a monetary or personal injury case, a woman's testimony should be accepted.

Certainly in areas of personal status, such as a woman's own niddah status, a woman's testimony about herself is accepted. In fact, even in ritual matters, such as determining if a piece of meat is kosher, a woman's testimony is considered credible. Today, in Israeli religious courts, women's testimony is accepted under the category of *mesiach l'fi tumo* (relating according to his innocence), which is applied in a case where someone whose testimony is not officially accepted by the court innocently says something that gives the court relevant information for its case. Following this principle, the information is allowed to be submitted to the case. In the case of women in Israel today, a legal fiction is created, since the women do not innocently relay their information but are aware that the information they are relaying will be used by the court. However, despite this loophole, the fact remains that according to Jewish law, women are not considered valid *eidim*, or witnesses; they can never be compelled to give testimony in a court of law. They are not *obligated* to be witnesses, so therefore, although their unofficial testimony is accepted at times, they are never witnesses in the complete sense of the word. This can be used to invalidate their testimony at any time.

If only it were so easy, I think to myself as I hear my teacher so easily dispense with this loaded issue. *Sure, in his utopia, women can be witnesses in the full sense of the word, but how does that help us in the real world? How does that help women like me—who are committed to Jewish law, who continue to perpetuate Jewish tradition, but who continually come up against barriers that shut us out of full participation?*

It is not until this moment on this day that the contradictions in my situation fully hit me: here I am, a woman devoting my only free time, when my kids are at school and in day care, to studying Jewish texts. Here I am, a woman immersing myself in Judaism, committing myself to Jewish law, bringing up my children according to these traditions and values, and the system doesn't consider my testimony equal to that of a similarly alert, observant, and astute man. My gender makes my testimony at best secondary, even to the more liberal legal commentators on this issue. The Rema is relatively progressive on this issue. Many traditional halakhists don't accept women's testimony even in the areas where he permits it.

What am I doing here? I wonder. For the moment, it all seems a waste. The texts are only words, the words of sexist rabbis living in a time when women came close to being mere chattel. *Why am I studying these texts? Why do I feel bound by them? Why am I perpetuating this unjust system? Why am I reinforcing its use?*

The walls of this tiny classroom begin to close in on me. I must get out. I walk out of class and give no excuses. I have not heard anything that Rabbi Silber has said in the past few minutes. I have no idea how the case ends, and I do not care. I head downstairs in the elevator to go into the crisp autumn air, take a walk down Central Park West, and make sense of my situation.

I press the elevator button for street level. I note that the button for our school is still scratched out. This is a game that we play with an unidentified vandal. He (or she) scratches out the name of our yeshiva on the elevator button, and we replace it. This particular vandalized button has not been replaced yet; it has been sitting there, illegible, for at least a month, for everyone who uses this building to see how we are regarded by our own. If it were an anti semitic statement, why would the vandal choose our button? There are a whole range of buttons with Hebrew words like ours. The building is a synagogue! No, this vandal is targeting us because he or she is against what we stand for: women learning Jewish texts.

The elevator stops at the bottom floor and the doors open, but I do not get out. Instead, I press the button with the words scratched out. I will go back up and sit down in the classroom. I have no other choice. At times it almost feels like a game, but it is also a struggle for the future. Who will determine what Judaism will look like for my children, and their children, and their children's children? This vandal? The rabbis who won't allow women into their rabbinical schools? The communities who support these rabbis and perpetuate their beliefs? If I walk out now, I let them win. I will stay.

CHAPTER TEN

◆

Israel: Building

On that day, I lifted up my hand to them to take them out of Egypt,
to a land I had sought out for them, flowing with milk and honey,
which is the beauty of all lands.
— Ezekiel 20:6

We came to the land to which you sent us, and it flows with milk
and honey . . . The land through which we have passed
to spy it out is a land that eats up its inhabitants.
— Numbers 13:27, 13:32

I AM STANDING AT the *Kotel HaMa'aravi*, the Western Wall, which was a retaining wall of the *Beit Hamikdash*, the Holy Temple, and remained standing after the Temple's destruction in 70 C.E. The Kotel was under Jordanian rule from 1948–1967, when it was recaptured by Israel during the Six Day War. Since then, it has again been accessible as a holy spot to which Jews from all over the world can come to pray. Many also leave personal notes tucked into the crevices of the ancient stones.

I am on the women's side of the seven-foot mechitzah, which separates the women from the men in the plaza in front of the Wall. I am with a group of women, huddling together against the cold. Winter has just arrived here in Jerusalem, and with it a chill that these ancient stones surrounding the Kotel plaza soak up. To warm both our souls and our physical bodies, we sway and rock and hug ourselves closely. We are a mass of women, and we are praying.

It has been three months since my husband, our two children, and I made *aliyah*. It is the first day of Kislev, the month in which we celebrate the holiday of Hanukkah, when the small group of Jewish Maccabees defeated the large and strong Greek army. It is a month to contemplate modes of empowerment aside from physical strength, and to remind ourselves that a struggle for what one believes in, no matter how seemingly hopeless, is worthwhile.

I come here each month with these women on Rosh Hodesh, the holiday celebrating the New Moon, which according to rabbinic literature was given specifically to women as a reward for not having donated our jewelry to the building of the Golden Calf. Each month, we come to the Wall—the place that modern Jews around the world have implicitly chosen as our holiest spot—to pray as a group of women. Coming from various religious communities and backgrounds, we join into one cohesive unit for this prayer service to be uplifted and empowered by our collective presence. This monthly gathering is one of the things I enjoy most about living here in Jerusalem. I feel privileged to be part of this sincere and intensely spiritual group that is committed in a very deep sense to *tikkun olam.*

We are singing, albeit in hushed voices. It is against current Israeli law for us to pray here together with our voices raised. This was not always the case. Almost ten years ago, when a group of women came with a Torah scroll to the Kotel to pray, they were attacked by a group of *haredim.* Since then, there has been an ongoing case in the Supreme Court, which will ultimately determine whether or not a group of women can pray aloud together with a Torah scroll and *tallitot* at the Kotel. In the meantime, the Court has forbidden all of these activities. The *haredim* have monopolized this space that belongs to the entire Jewish people, and the Israeli government has allowed them to capture it as their domain. In *haredi* society, women do not pray collectively, nor do they raise their voices in prayer. Women, according to their interpretation of Judaism, should be quiet, private beings. Modesty, as they define it, means being internal and quiet; modesty, as they see it, is a women's trait and virtue. If you are a woman, and you are outspoken, you are going against the purpose for which you were put on this earth by God. You are rebellious, provocative, even dangerous.

Within two minutes of beginning our service, I hear shouting from the other side of the mechitzah: "*Goyim* [Gentiles]! *T'meot* [Impure]! *Naziyim* [Nazis]! *Asur* [Forbidden]!" The hatred in these voices makes me shudder, and at first I pretend to myself that they are not yelling at us. Then I realize that these men in black—black hats, black coats, black suits, black shoes—are throwing objects at us over the mechitzah: metal chairs, tables, and whatever else they can find. These men might well kill us in the name of the God to whom we have all come here to pray.

Immediately, a security guard orders *us* to leave the premises—not those who are attacking us, who are causing the violence, but us, the victims of this violence. They are breaking the law, but we, who have hushed our voices in order not to break the law, are being banished.

"*HaKotel shelanu* [The Kotel is ours]!" one *haredi* woman yells out to me in triumph as we leave, and I feel a heaviness bear down on my heart. Even ultra-Orthodox *women* feel threatened by our presence. It is not enough for them to restrict themselves so extensively; it is not enough that they have accepted for themselves a Judaism that represses their voices. They need to force their own stringencies and narrow interpretation of what constitutes a Jewish lifestyle upon us. They join the men of their community in claiming public Jewish space as theirs alone.

"Welcome to Israel!" a friend standing next to me snickers in Hebrew as we make our way to another spot to continue our prayer service. "I was born here," she adds. "What's your excuse?"

When I was ten years old, my whole family (my parents and two brothers; my sister Rebecca was not born yet) went to spend four weeks in Israel in honor of my brother Jonathan's bar mitzvah. My parents decided that he should have a bar mitzvah at the Kotel. I had been in Israel about six years before that, but I didn't remember much. On my second trip, we spent the entire time living in an apartment in Jerusalem, in a neighborhood bordering on the one in which I live now. My best friend from preschool until second grade had moved to Jerusalem with her family and was living nearby, and I spent most of my time with her and her friends, like a native Israeli kid. We took the buses by ourselves, wandered the city's parks, went to Scouts, had a bonfire in the woods, and ate charred potatoes that we had wrapped in foil and thrown into the fire.

I fell in love with the country, especially Jerusalem, that summer. It was a Jewish country, where I was part of a majority for the first time in my life. Even more, I felt that Judaism was alive in Israel. Now that I saw the contrast between life in Israel and Jewish life in *hutz la'aretz*, outside Israel, I came to feel that there was something empty and lifeless about the way that Jews in the Diaspora practiced our religion. It was almost as if in New York they were pretending, going through the motions, but here in Israel it was the real thing. I had this strange feeling that back where I came from, in exile, we were only practicing for the real show, the redemption, when we would all return home, but we were missing the point: the beginning of the redemption had already arrived. We now had a home, the show was already on, and there we were, still going through the rehearsals. I felt like screaming out, "Wake up! Don't you see that we can go home? God is waiting for us to take the plunge!" I couldn't understand why everyone wasn't running to catch the next flight for Ben-Gurion Airport.

When the time came for us to go home to the United States, I couldn't resist. I had no choice but to return with my parents. Before we left, I tucked a note between two stones of the Kotel, promising that I would someday return to Israel to live.

The next time I went to Israel was the summer after my sophomore year of high school. Although I no longer believed in God or rabbinic law, I nevertheless felt drawn to the Jewish State. I had dreams of one day living on a kibbutz, so I decided to spend that summer working on one. I had no choice but to go to a religious kibbutz, since I was in no position to do anything to which my parents did not agree. I chose a kibbutz on the West Bank right outside Jerusalem, where there was a special program for high school volunteers from *hutz la'aretz*.

I spent my free weekends with my nonreligious cousins in Tel Aviv and Netanya, riding in the car, going to the beach, and doing other things that are violations of traditional Shabbat observance. Sometimes I'd go with friends to the beach in Tel Aviv, where we'd rent one room in a hotel and all pile in for the weekend. We'd go drinking or dancing in clubs, and since there is no minimum drinking age in Israel, it was all legal. I knew that my parents would not have approved, but I didn't let that worry me. They were an ocean away, in a different time zone—while I was out partying at 2:00 A.M., they were just sitting down to dinner—and I was having a blast.

This trip as a teenager gave me a different view of the country than I'd had when I came as a preadolescent. I still wanted to return to Israel to live, but I wanted to be in Tel Aviv, near the beach, and live the life of a culturally Jewish Israeli. It was enough to live in Israel and speak Hebrew, I decided. Who needs all that religion, all those outdated and oppressive laws and restrictions, all that empty talk of God and holiness that religious Jews buy into because it makes them feel special, "chosen," and better than everyone else?

Living as a secular Israeli seemed to me the best way to keep my Jewish identity without having to accept the whole system of Jewish law, ritual, and belief that I had rejected from my childhood. Living in New York, the only way I saw to be a Jew was to affiliate religiously; in Israel, I discovered, by merely living in the country, you are automatically steeped in things that are Jewish, including the Hebrew language and Jewish holidays. Even if you don't keep Shabbat as defined by the Rabbis, it is a day of rest for the entire country. Even if you don't keep the holidays according to the letter of the law, even non-religious Israelis eat *matzah* on Passover and don't drive their cars on Yom Kippur. The whole country lives according to the rhythm of Jewish life, whether or not each individual chooses to observe the details in his or her private sphere.

On that trip to Israel, I made another promise to myself to return someday to live there. This time, I left no note in the stones of the Kotel. Instead, I wrote my name and the year, 1985, with my toe in the sand on the beach in Tel Aviv.

In Israel, we are used to labels. For a variety of reasons—historical, sociological, and political—individuals are often seen through the lens of categories, including this pervasive pair: *dati*, "religious," and *hiloni*, "secular." I don't fit easily into a category. I am clearly a religious person: I keep Shabbat, eat kosher, cover my head, dress modestly, keep the laws of family purity, pray every day, spend a large portion of my time studying Torah. Yet I am also a woman who wears tzitzit, puts on tefillin each morning, reads from the Torah scroll, delivers *divrei Torah*, studies Talmud on a high level, can answer (at least at a basic level) questions of Jewish law—all things that traditionally only men do. Along with the handful of other women like me, I am an oddity. I don't fit into the categories that already exist. I push the limits of what it means to be *dati* and what it means to be feminist, and I implicitly force people to question their assumptions.

The flip side, I know, is that by my mere existence I incite wrath and fear. There are always those who react against change and blurred distinctions, as though the very foundations of their lives were under fatal attack. Here in Israel, where one's very life and the future of the country often seem to be threatened, people are even more afraid to shake the conceptual foundations that give them a sense of stability.

I am not alone in breaking new ground. The divide here between religious and secular people is very wide, but the gap is not unbridgeable. There is room in that empty space for something new and different, an alternative to these two options. The Conservative and Reform movements here are growing and fighting for their rights as legitimate expressions of Judaism. Although Conservative and Reform rabbis are not currently considered official, licensed rabbis by the Israeli rabbinate—neither their marriages nor their conversions are considered valid—the Supreme Court here recently ruled that Reform and Conservative rabbis must be allowed to sit on Religious Councils. This decision has resulted in a call to war by the *haredim* against the secular courts, but the fact that the secular courts, at least, are beginning to recognize the Conservative and Reform movements is an important step.

There are others like me who are working to create alternative religious models that do not fit into any of the already existing categories, particularly in Israel, making space for serious Jews who don't want to be labeled in pat ways. Pluralism is spreading here in Israel as well; there are new schools and institutions with a pluralistic ideology. Michal's elementary school has a mixture of both *dati* and *hiloni* children. The Shalom Hartman Institute and Elul are both adult learning centers where people from all walks of Israeli life can come to study Jewish texts together. An organization called Ta Sh'ma (Aramaic for "come and learn") started two years ago to educate about the idea of pluralism. "Tolerance" was the yearly topic for elementary schools in 1998–99. These are only some examples of a growing phenomenon. Hopefully, an attitude of openness will continue to spread.

Along with this will undoubtedly come more divisiveness from those who are fighting against pluralism. We must work our hardest to not let those who are pushing divisiveness win. This is a difficult task, since the people in that camp tend to be louder and more aggressive in their tactics. But we mustn't give up. Our tradition tells us that it was divisiveness that caused the destruction of the Second Temple. In the wake of the assassination of Prime Minister Yitzhak Rabin by a Jew, we cannot afford to be complacent.

I am sitting in the apartment of Debbie Weissman, a religious feminist who has worked for years carving out her place as a woman within the halakhic tradition here in Israel. She is a learned woman who came to Jerusalem more than twenty years ago and has accomplished a great deal in these years. She was among the founders of Yedidyah, a growing progressive Orthodox shul in Jerusalem that has been at the forefront of advancing women's status in halakhah. She is also the director of Kerem, a teacher training center in humanistic Jewish education, and she is active in Jewish, feminist, and humanistic causes.

Surrounding me in Debbie's living room are other religious feminist Israeli women:

◆ Leah Shakdiel, educator, feminist thinker, and the first woman in Israel to sit on a religious community council;

◆ Alice Shalvi, once the principal of Pelech, the first girls' high school to make Gemara part of the official curriculum; founder of the Israel Women's Network, an organization dedicated to fighting for women's rights in Israel; and currently rector of Machon Schechter, a Masorti (Conservative) movement institution;

◆ Penina Peli, who started an organization in Israel to support *mesuravot get,* founded the first women's *tefillah* group in Israel, and coorganized with Alice Shalvi the first feminism conference in Jerusalem;

◆ Rivka Lubitch, who is studying to be a *to'enet rabbanit,* an advocate in the rabbinical courts, which until a few years ago was a position barred to women;

◆ Beverly Gribetz, a learned woman with a Ph.D. from the Jewish Theological Seminary, who is the principal of Evelina deRothchild, a religious all-girls middle school in Jerusalem where the students learn Gemara.

We are meeting here in Israel before we fly to New York for the conference on Orthodoxy and feminism so that we can discuss among ourselves the issues particular to Israeli religious women that should be raised at the conference.

Debbie makes an important point. She is concerned that our Diaspora sisters may think that our situation is more dire than it actually is. Certainly we have a long struggle ahead of us, but a halakhically progressive *datiyah* woman can live a spiritually fulfilling life in Israel. At least in Jerusalem, she says, there is a community for her, a community that she was, in fact, instrumental in building.

"Yes!" I exclaim in Hebrew. "When I told my friends in the United States that I was planning to move to Israel, they said: 'There's no place for you there. Things are even more closed religiously in Israel than they are here. You'll be miserable and alone.' But," I continue, "That's not what I've found at all. I'm no more alone here than I was in New York. In fact, here in Jerusalem, there is probably *more* of a community for me. In Riverdale I was one of three women in my shul who wore a tallit. Here, depending on which progressive *kehillah* [congregation] I choose to pray with, I am often one of several women in *tallitot*. In terms of women's learning, there are many learned women here—so many that there is real competition for the jobs in places that want to hire women to teach Torah. Of course, there are still not many women who teach Gemara, but that is true in the United States as well, and it is changing both here and there. There is a long way to go here in Israel, but there is a long way to go everywhere."

As I say this, I realize that I have found a real home for myself here. True, I have not found a huge community of people just like me, but I have not had that anywhere I've lived. Whether I was on the more conservative and halakhic end of the spectrum in my community or on the more radical and progressive end, I have always felt that I did not quite fit in. It does not seem to be my fate to be part of the mainstream anywhere. If that's to be the case, I might as well make my home here in the Jewish homeland.

In July 1999, nearly 1,000 women came to an Israeli Orthodoxy and feminism conference, cosponsored by Bar-Ilan University and Kolech: Forum Nashim Datiyot ("Your Voice": the Religious Women's Forum), an organization devoted to improving the status of women in the religious Jewish community in Israel. The name "Kolech" expresses the idea that the voices of religious women have often been suppressed, and that the time has now come for us to break our silence and demand a voice. It was an inspiring conference, with many different voices being heard. A wide spectrum of issues was discussed: women's Torah learning; expanding the role of women in the synagogue; women's *tefillah* groups; Women of the Wall; tallit and tefillin for women (a session I presented); teaching the next generation; female rabbis; and much more. Many people were skeptical about whether or not such a conference could take place in Israel—and in Jerusalem, no less. Their impression was that this is too conservative a place for such ideas to get serious consideration. This conference and its organizer, Hanah Kehat, proved them wrong.

I am walking down the street in Jerusalem with my two children. Michal is three and a half years old, and Adin, who is in a stroller, is one. We have just moved here to Israel, and we are exploring our new neighborhood. Michal, with her tzitzit flying, is bouncing along happily, holding onto the side of the stroller, telling me about her new *gan*. She is in a Hebrew-speaking *gan*, and she does not yet understand or speak Hebrew, but she seems to be holding her own. Within a few months, other *olim* (new immigrants) have assured me, she will be speaking fluently.

We are on our way to the park, and we go into a supermarket first to buy some snacks. "*Hi yaldah oh yeled* [Is she a girl or a boy]?" the storekeeper asks me. He says this with a judgmental twinge in his voice, and I understand that he already knows the answer to his question.

"*Yaldah,*" I answer, "*V'hi loveshet tzitzit* [and she wears tzitzit]."

"You know that girls can't wear tzitzit," he tells me in Hebrew.

"No I don't, because that is not true," I argue, also in Hebrew. "The Rambam [Maimonides] says that if a woman wants to wear tzitzit, she shouldn't say a *brachah* over them, but he does say that she can wear them without saying a *brachah* if she wants." I use Maimonides, even though he is not one of the most liberal *poskim* on this issue (according to most, a woman can recite the *brachah*), because I can tell that this man is Sephardi. Maimonides was an influential *posek* for Sephardim in his time, so I think it wise to quote to this man someone who carries halakhic weight for him.

The storekeeper looks stunned. He seems to have gained respect for me—I am quoting Maimonides, and I am quoting a text of which he is not aware. I have taught him something.

"Really?" he says.

"Yes."

"Are you sure?"

"Yes."

That is the end of that discussion. We choose our snacks, pay, and leave.

I am grateful that Michal does not yet understand Hebrew, although I know that soon she will. What will I do when she understands these conversations? Will such interactions undermine the egalitarian worldview I have been trying to instill in her?

I'm on the bus on a Sunday morning on the way to Talmud class. I am reviewing the page of Talmud that we will be studying that day when a young woman about my age who is wearing a full skirt, a loose-fitting, long-sleeved top, and sneakers taps me on the shoulder. Her mode of dress does not necessarily clearly define her as religious or secular.

"You were at the minyan yesterday," she says in Hebrew, "with those two children. I remember you from there." She is referring to a Shabbat prayer service I had participated in the day before that meets once a month, on *Shabbat Mevarchim HaHodesh*, the Shabbat before Rosh Hodesh, when the exact date that the new moon will appear is announced. It is always a very intense and ecstatic service, with hours of singing and chanting and dancing. Women participate in the part of the service where the Torah is taken out of the Ark, paraded around the *kahal* (the congregation), and then read. This *tefillah* is also longer than most Israeli prayer services. A typical Israeli Shabbat *tefillah* begins at 8:00 A.M. and ends by 10:30; this one goes on until at least 2:30 P.M.

I confirm that I was there, and she continues, "It was so wonderful! I've never been to a *tefillah* like it. The atmosphere was something unique. It was holy. Now that was a true *tefillah*!"

I nod my head. "I agree."

"Let me ask you something," she adds. "Do you know how they justify having women read from the Torah?"

I quote to her the source on *k'vod ha-tzibbur* and explain that this

particular congregation decided when it was founded that women reading from the Torah and participating in the Torah service were not
"shameful" to them. She seems satisfied, but not especially interested in
pursuing a lengthy discussion on the legal details. Rather, she wants to
talk about the experience of the *tefillah* itself.

"I enjoyed it so much," she says. "You know, I've been to other
tefillot where women participate, but it always felt forced to me somehow—unnatural, I guess—but not this *tefillah*. There it felt so organic,
as if there were no question that women should participate. The fact
that women did participate made it all the more spiritual."

We talk until we reach her stop, and we say our goodbyes. "I'll see
you next month?" I ask.

"Yes," she says. "*Im yirtzeh Hashem* [God willing]."

As I continue to my stop, I think about yesterday's service. It was a
glorious autumn Shabbat day in the city of Jerusalem, and because of
the beautiful weather we had decided to move outside to pray. The sky
was a bright and deep blue without a cloud in sight, and there was just
enough chill in the air to make me want to wrap my tallit around my
whole body to guard against the breeze.

I was praying, focused inward, listening to the woman who was
holding the Torah and chanting in reverie, "*Shema Yisrael, Adonai
Eloheinu, Adonai Echad* [Hear, O Israel, God is our Lord, God is
One]!" Her voice was so sweet, but not lullaby sweet; it was strong, so
powerful that I could feel its strength lifting my soul upward.

Suddenly, I heard a male voice coming from the street outside the
courtyard in which we were praying. "*Eifo ha-tslav* [Where is the
cross]?" he shouted.

At first I didn't understand. *I must have heard incorrectly or misunderstood,* I told myself. Then I heard it again, loud and clear: "*Eifo
ha-tslav?!*" It was an angry, mocking voice, so strident and certain that
it frightened me.

Is it the women in tallitot, *like me, who have caused this reaction?* I wondered. *Is it the woman who is holding the Torah, calling
out the words of the sacred Shema, claiming them as her own?
Maybe it is the mere fact that we are still praying at this late hour,
and with such rapture.* It was probably a combination of all of those
factors. Anything that this man was not accustomed to seeing at his

own synagogue was not Jewish to him. It was probably as simple as that.

His hatred and fear ruined my prayer moment. It brought my soul back down to earth.

How can someone be so certain that he has a monopoly on the Truth? How can someone be so sure that his interpretation of Judaism is the only valid one that he is willing to call us—a group praying the same words as he, carrying and reading from the same Torah as he— "Christians"? What is it about this (my) country that makes it breed such tension? What is it about this (my) religion that it can espouse loving your neighbor as yourself and also arouse such animosity?

I looked around at some of the faces on the women's side of the makeshift synagogue. Some women were smiling knowingly; others did not even flinch. No one seemed particularly shocked or dismayed by this man's outburst. Only I, the newcomer to Israel, the *olah hadashah*, seemed perturbed.

This, I am beginning to learn, is life as usual in the holy city of Jerusalem, where, our tradition tells us, the Second Temple was destroyed because of *sinat chinam*, senseless hatred among Jews. I have willingly picked up my family and moved to this place. I have left the Land of Freedom and Opportunity to come here to the Land of War and Struggle.

What is a woman like you doing in a place like this? I have asked myself time and time again since we arrived. *What am I doing here, indeed?* I ask myself again now as I ride the bus to Rabbi Strikovsky's Talmud class. Because of his "radical" ideas (such as that women can learn Talmud on the same level as men), Rabbi Strikovsky, a brilliant and pious man, has lost his legitimacy in many Orthodox circles. I am a feminist, a pluralist, a free thinker. I believe in the motto "Live and let live." *Shivim panim laTorah* ("There are seventy faces to the Torah") is a halakhic principle that I have always felt was at the core of my religious belief. So what am I doing here in this place that seems at times to want to spit me out like a piece of indigestible refuse?

I am here because this is my home. I will not let this place disregard me. I will make my voice heard. I am a Jew, and this is my homeland, my Torah, my religion, as much as it is that man's with the voice of hatred.

When I get off the bus at my stop, the air around me feels different than it did when I got on the bus. It had felt heavy with the hatred that I had experienced the day before and the weight of the arduous course that I have chosen for myself. Now the burden is lifted a bit. The air feels lighter. There is hope. At least one woman who was searching, who had felt unsatisfied by the traditional categories, was changed and uplifted by experiencing our minyan, an alternative to the rigid religious categories and labels. For that alone I am willing to confront the hatred of our attackers again and again.

It is fall 1998, Rosh Hodesh Heshvan, often called "bitter Heshvan" because no Jewish holidays fall during this month. I am standing on the women's side of the mechitzah at the Kotel, praying with a group of women. When we entered the Kotel area at 7:00 A.M., some of us with *tallitot* tucked away in our knapsacks, our Torah zipped into a large, green duffel bag, a woman saw us and yelled to us, pointing to the duffel bag, "*Asur! Asur!* [Forbidden!]" before we even began to pray. We are known here by now.

"It's our Torah, too," we told her, gently but emphatically. "It's *your* Torah, too."

I close my eyes and listen to the voice of the *hazanit*, the woman who is leading the prayers. Her voice is like a breeze flowing through me and up to the ancient stones of the Wall, through the cracks in the stone and the weeds that have grown in those cracks. I see the breeze rustling the weeds and then flowing upward, upward. Our voices are getting louder as more women come to join in the singing and as we are each energized and uplifted by one another. Our collective presence makes us brave, gives us the strength to be bold.

As I listen to her voice, I think of the verse from the morning prayers: "How great are Your creations, God; You made all with wisdom." To hear such a beautiful sound coming from a human being honors God, and to hear such a voice uplifting others in the praise of God seems to me the reason this voice was given to this woman. How could God have meant it to be otherwise?

I believe that a woman's voice today is no longer *ervah*. Moreover, there are rabbis today who say that it is permissible for women to sing aloud in prayer (interpreting the legal texts to prove their point), and there are communities living according to halakhah that have permitted women to sing aloud in frameworks such as this. With Orthodox rabbis and a community to back up my position, I feel totally justified in my stance. Finding a way to harmonize my moral intuitions, my study of Jewish legal texts, and my longing for community is my ideal. I will not let those who disagree with the religious choices I have made dictate to me how to pray.

A woman walks by as we sing. She could be anywhere between thirty and fifty and is dressed in navy blue from the top of her neck down; only the skin of her hands and face is exposed. Her head has been shaved, and she has a scarf wrapped around her bald head. "*Asur!*" she says, and she shakes her finger at us. We sing even louder.

"I thank You, for You have answered me and become my salvation," we sing in Hebrew from *Hallel*. "The stone the builders despised has become the cornerstone. This emanated from God; it is wondrous in our eyes. This is the day that God has made; let us rejoice and be glad on it."

A white dove flies down and rests on a stone in front of us. *This is a sign*, I think. This week we read the Torah portion that relates the story of the flood that destroyed the world during the time of Noah. After the rains stop, Noah sends out a dove and it returns with an olive branch, a sign that God has made the waters recede. The world will have a second chance.

There is hope that even our world can be repaired.

*My dove
in the clefts
of the rocks
the secret
of steep ravines*

*Come let me look at you
Come let me hear you*

*Your voice clear as water
Your beautiful body*

— *Shir haShirim* 2:14[1]

I am the dove, looking for the answers in the clefts of the rocks, in the cracks where the weeds grow. I am a weed, striving to push my way in among the rocks.

Someday, I pray, the stone that the builders despise will become the cornerstone.

EPILOGUE

◆

I AM STANDING ON the *bimah* with the Torah scroll open before me. It is my first Sukkot in Israel, and my parents have come to visit us here for the first time.

At the end of Sukkot comes the last holiday of the season, which has two names, Shemini Atzeret and Simchat Torah—literally, "The Joy of the Torah"—and celebrates the Torah scroll and text itself. On Simchat Torah, we complete the final chapter of the Torah and then immediately begin the annual reading cycle again with Genesis. We dance with the Torah scrolls and sing, and each man is called up to the Torah. However, at this shul, one of the congregations to which we belong in Jerusalem, the women are also called up—against tradition, what my parents did, and what their parents did before them, but not contrary to halakhah. In a separate room with separate Torah scrolls, the women lead our own Torah readings, and women from all over Jerusalem come to this place where they, too, can read from the Torah and make a blessing over it.

In the New York neighborhood where we lived for two years before we moved to Israel, our synagogue also had a separate Torah service for women, but my mother never expressed an interest in spending the holiday with us so that she could have an *aliyah*. Perhaps it is the holy air here that has imbued her with the courage to draw closer to her own religious legacy, because last night she announced over dinner that she intends to have her first *aliyah* ever this Simchat Torah.

Last night, we coached her. We went over the blessings with her, gave her directions for kissing the parchment with a tallit and holding the scroll closed while reciting the blessings, and told her where she would stand and for how long. It is not a terribly complicated ritual, but I sympathized with her trepidation. I, too, was nervous my first time. I remember how my hands shook and my voice quivered. If I had been scared, how much more so my mother would be; I had spent only seventeen years without having seen the inside of a Torah scroll. It had taken her fifty-two years to finally draw that close.

When we entered the room where the women's Torah reading was taking place, the *gabba'it* came over to us to ask our names. I told her that I wanted to do the reading from the scroll for my and my mother's *aliyot*, and then we went to our seats to wait for our turns to go up.

As we sat and listened to the woman who was reading, I could feel my mother's nerves like vibrations on my skin. She was sitting in her usual reserved manner, but she was not as collected as usual. I noticed her flip the pages in her *siddur* to where the blessings for an *aliyah* are printed. She was rehearsing.

Soon enough, the *gabba'it* calls out my mother's name—"*Ta'amod, Rahel bat Yechiel Michel v'Chayah, rivi'it!*"—and we both stand.

I, too, am a bit nervous, as I always am before reading from the Torah. It is an awesome experience, not to be taken lightly. A more general stage fright makes me worry that I'll forget every note and vowel and point of punctuation that I have been practicing for days.

The *gabba'it* motions for me to hand the corner of my tallit to my mother so she can use it to kiss the parchment of the Torah. The scroll is considered so holy that we should treat it with extra care; it is a way of reminding ourselves of its sacredness. As my mother uses my tallit for her first *aliyah*, the irony of this event does not escape me. After being an adolescent on my parents' turf, feeling closed out of Judaism because of my inability as a woman to perform mitzvot such as wearing a tallit or having an *aliyah*, here I am in Israel, the place to which I have traveled to establish my new home, enabling my mother to have her first *aliyah* with my tallit. It is a lovely irony, and I am relieved to be experiencing it free of anger or resentment.

My mother's hands tremble, her voice shakes, and she fumbles with the tallit and the wooden Torah handles. She recites the blessing, I read from the Torah, she recites the second blessing, and we both return to our seats. Too busy concentrating on my own role as *ba'alat k'riah*, I did not notice my mother's face during the reading, so I look over at her now to gauge her reaction.

My mother is wiping her eyes with a tissue. Her nose is pink, and her eye makeup is running. I am overcome with affection for my mother in a nurturing way that creeps up on me without warning. I am not used to feeling protective of her.

"*Yishar Kochech*," I say, feminizing the traditional congratulation that I had so often heard said to men in the shul of my childhood after they had finished an *aliyah*.

"That was really moving," my mother says with a sniffle.

"Yes, it was," I say.

I wonder if she knows that I mean for me as well.

NOTES

◆

INTRODUCTION

1 Psalms 36:8–10.
2 BT *Eruvin* 96a.
3 Deuteronomy 6:8.
4 Tosafot on BT *Eruvin* 96a, s.v. *Michal bat Kushi.*
5 Rema on *Shulchan Arukh, Orach Hayyim* 38:3.
6 *Shulchan Arukh, Orach Hayyim,* section 38, *Mishnah B'rurah* subparagraph 13.
7 Hosea 2: 21–22.
8 *Pirkei Avot* 1:14.

CHAPTER ONE

1 Modern Orthodoxy is not a formal denomination but rather a collection of institutions and people who share a religious ideology.
2 Emanuel Rackman, *Modern Halakhah for Our Time* (Hoboken, NJ: Ktav, 1995), p. 63.

CHAPTER TWO

1 Genesis 17:11.
2 Genesis 17:16.

3 Exodus 19:25.
4 Meiri on BT *Yevamot* 46a.

CHAPTER THREE

1 *Shulchan Arukh, Orach Hayyim* 17:2.
2 I can think of twenty women and girls I know personally who wear tzitzit beneath their clothing (some live here in Israel, some in the United States, and some in Europe), and I know there are more, although not many more. When I first began wearing tzitzit, I knew of no other woman who did. This is another example of the slow progress being made in this area, as well as of the gradual building of a global community of similarly minded observant Jewish feminist women.
3 Judith Hauptman also states that this view is common, without a citation, and adds that there is no support for this view in rabbinic literature. See Judith Hauptman, *Rereading the Rabbis: A Woman's Voice* (Boulder: Westview Press, 1998), p. 221.
4 *Perush LaTorah,* on Leviticus 23:43.
5 *Milamed Hatalmidim, Parshat Lech Lecha.*
6 *Sefer Abudraham, Sha'ar* 3, *Birchat HaMitzvot* (Jerusalem, 1963), p. 25.
7 Norman Lamm, *A Hedge of Roses* (New York: Feldheim, 1966), p. 77. Rabbi Lamm attributes this idea to Rabbi Rackman.
8 Saul Berman, "The Status of Women in Halakhic Judaism," *Tradition* 14 (Winter 1973): 5–28.
9 Hauptman, p. 225.
10 Hauptman, p. 277.
11 Noam Zohar, "Women Then and Religious Status." In H. Basser and S. Fishbane, eds., *Approaches to Ancient Judaism,* (Atlanta: Atlanta Scholars Press, 1993), pp. 33–54.
12 Tashbetz, section 270, as cited in Aliza Berger, "Wrapped Attention: May Women Wear Tefillin?", in M. Halpern and C. Safrai, eds., *Jewish Legal Writings by Women* (Jerusalem: Urim, 1998), 75-118. (This is Rabbi Shimshon ben Tzaddok, a disciple of the Maharam of Rothenberg, not to be confused with Rabbi Shimshon ben Tzemach, also called the Tashbetz.)
13 One can infer this from Rabbi Yosef Caro's words in the *Shulchan Arukh, Orach Hayyim* 38:2.
14 *Magen Avraham,* gloss to the *Shulchan Arukh, Orach Hayyim* 38, subparagraph 3.

15 Rema on *Shulchan Arukh, Orach Hayyim* 17:2.

16 BT *Shabbat* 62a.

17 Maharil, New Responsa no. 7. The Maharil's explanation may be closest to the original reason for the exemption. All the positive time-bound commandments from which the talmudic literature exempts women are commemorative of either the Exodus or the establishment of the covenantal community in which women are less than full members. It may be that this is the case because of a given lower social status, but it is difficult to say which came first. I thank Richie Lewis for this insight.

18 See Tosafot on BT *Kiddushin* 31a (s.v. *d'lo mafkidna v'avdina*) where the Tosafot attribute this ruling to Rabbeinu Tam, one of the most halakhically influential *ba'alei Tosafot*. See also *Iggrot Moshe, Orach Hayyim* 49, where Rabbi Moshe Feinstein rules that women should say the *brachah* "Who sanctified us in the mitzvot and commanded us to . . ." even in the positive timebound mitzvot from which they are exempt, since they too receive a reward for performing them.

19 Aviva Cayam, "Fringe Benefits: Women and Tzitzit." In Halpern and Safrai, p. 131.

20 BT *Yoma* 47a.

21 BT *Nazir* 59a; see also Mishnah *Shabbat* 6:4, BT *Shabbat* 63a, and *Torah T'mimah* on Deuteronomy 22:5, note 41.

22 *Targum Yonatan* on Deuteronomy 22:5.

23 Israel Ze'ev Gustman, *Kuntrsei Shi'urim: Masekhta Kiddushin* (Brooklyn: Shulsinger Bros., 1970), *Shiur* 20, section 10, pp. 254–255. I would like to thank Noa Jesselson for bringing this source to my attention.

24 BT *Bava Kama* 87a.

25 Maimonides, *Guide for the Perplexed*, 3:32.

26 For an interesting discussion of this idea see Eliezer Berkovits, *Jewish Women in Time and Torah* (Hoboken, NJ: Ktav, 1990).

27 I would like to thank Rabbi Dov Linzer for providing me with some of the following sources on hair covering for women.

28 See BT *Shabbat* 118b, where Rav Huna says that he is worthy of a reward because he never walked four *amot* without a head covering, the connotation being that covering one's head is a praiseworthy religious practice. *Masekhet Sofrim* 14:15 discusses the practice of wearing a head covering while publicly reciting certain prayers for the congregation. The implication here and in other sources which mention head covering while praying is that praying with one's head

uncovered is disrespectful to God, and therefore covering one's head is a sign of respect for and humbling before God. Today, when observant Jewish men wear a head covering all day long, the practice of head covering has taken on the additional meaning of being a sign of one's religiosity and a personal reminder that one is *always* in the presence of God, which may have been the meaning behind Rav Huna's practice.

29 Rabbi Moshe Feinstein, one of the most revered *poskim* of the twentieth century, makes the distinction between hair and head covering for married women in his *Iggrot Moshe, Even Ha'ezer* 1:58. Based on *Ketubot* 72a–b, which quotes the biblical source for the practice of women's hair covering, Numbers 5:18—"And he [the priest] shall uncover the woman's *head*" (my emphasis)—he maintains that the mitzvah for a woman is to cover her head and not her hair. However, later in the responsum he argues that since the *head* is considered *ervah* (nakedness), and "the laws of covered places of the body make a distinction between a handbreath and less than a handbreath when it comes to seeing without lustful intention," a woman may not allow a handbreath or more of her *hair* to show, invoking, it seems, a statement in the Gemara, *B'rachot* 24a, that a woman's hair is *ervah*. In another section of this work (*Iggrot Moshe, Orach Hayyim* 4:112), he says that the hairs that are outside of one's covering that are not *ervah* can be more than a handbreath. It seems that he is referring to hairs that fall out from beneath a woman's hair covering, but one could perhaps conclude that if he were to agree today that a woman's hair is no longer *ervah* in our society and therefore that the Gemara in *B'rachot* no longer applies, he would say that all hair coming out from a head covering can be more than a handbreath. (It seems, however, from his shifting to hair covering in the previously mentioned responsum, that he considered the *B'rachot* source to still be relevant, and hair to still be *ervah*.)

30 Interestingly, the Gemara concludes this based on the statement of Rabbi Zeira that if it were true that a man could divorce his wife without her ketubah money if she went without her head covered in her private courtyard, there would not be a single "daughter of Abraham" who remained married to her husband.

31 This can be understood from the language of the Gemara in *Ketubot* and *B'rachot*, neither of which refer specifically to married women, but rather seem to be speaking about the common practice of modest dress for all women, unmarried women included. Mishnah *Ketubot* 2:1 says

that if there is a witness that a woman came to her wedding with her hair uncovered, we can assume she was a virgin. This source is later brought by the *Magen Avraham* (see note 36) as proof that unmarried women went with their hair uncovered in the time of the Mishnah. However, it seems from the context of this mishnah that the practice was to uncover the bride's hair especially for her wedding if she was a virgin, meaning that in general it was covered. This reading is based on conversations with Professor Dov Frimer.

32 *Shulchan Arukh, Even Ha'ezer* 21:2; *Mishneh Torah, Hilkhot Issurei Bi'ah* 21:17.

33 I would like to thank Professor Dov Frimer for this historical information. See also *S'ridei Eish*, 3, section 30, s.v. *u-viY'shurun*. It seems that the common practice was for married and unmarried women to cover their hair even in the home, probably because of the source in *B'rachot* and the influence of kabbalistic literature on the subject. There is also a story in the Gemara, BT *Yoma* 47a, of Kimchit, a woman who is said to have had seven sons, all of whom were high priests. When asked why she was worthy of this, she answered that she did not let even the beams of her house see her hair. She was then told that many women did this but did not merit as she did.

34 I would like to thank Professor Dov Frimer for providing me with the historical information about when unmarried women began uncovering their hair and about men praying mostly at home in this time period. See also *S'ridei Eish,* 3, section 30, s.v. *u-viY'shurun*, who says that according to the strict sense of the halakhah, both married and unmarried women should cover their hair outside of the home but inside of the home can keep it uncovered. However, he adds, because of the story of Kimchit (see notes 20 and 33), married women had the additional modesty custom of covering their hair even in the home, while unmarried women did not, which would explain the sentence in the *Shulchan Arukh* (*Orach Hayyim* 75:3) saying that a man can recite the Shema in front of an unmarried woman with her head uncovered, because it was not their custom to cover their hair. According to the reading of the *S'ridei Eish*, the assumption is that the man is reciting the Shema in the home.

35 See Rosh, *B'rachot* 3:37.

36 See *Magen Avraham, Orach Hayyim* 75:3. It may be that these *poskim* understand the Gemara in *Ketubot* as referring to unmarried women in relation only to the *dat yehudit* requirement, since the Torah verse deals with a *sotah*, a married woman accused of adultery.

That, coupled with the fact that *dat yehudit* is subject to change based on what society considers proper, would leave room for leniency in the area of unmarried women's head covering.

37 The Hatam Sofer, Rabbi Moshe Sofer, a late eighteenth- and nineteenth- century European ultra-Orthodox *posek*, seems to hold this way in his responsum, *Orach Hayyim* section 36, saying that even in the privacy of her own bedroom she must keep a kerchief on her head because of *ervah*. He says that he bases his opinion on the Zohar, a medieval kabbalistic commentary on the Bible. Rabbi Moshe Feinstein seems to hold that hair is *ervah* as well (see note 29).

38 See the responsum of *Sefer Yehoshua* 89, who says that the concept of a woman's hair being *ervah* is totally societally based. He even goes so far as to say that if it were the custom for unmarried women to keep their hair covered and for married women to keep their hair uncovered, that would be the halakhic requirement. (It is unclear how he would reconcile this position with the Gemara in *Ketubot*, which states that head covering for a married woman is a Torah law.) The *Arukh HaShulchan, Orach Hayyim* 75;7, takes this position, although it is clear from his dismay at the fact that many women do not cover their hair—calling it *pritzut*, inappropriate sexual behavior, and bemoaning the state of affairs—that he would say that de facto if a woman does not cover her hair, it is not *ervah*, but she should nonetheless cover it—probably based on the Gemara in *Ketubot*.

39 See the responsum of Moshe ben Habib, *Even Ha'ezer* 1, who makes this claim. Rav Yosef Mashash (*Mayim Hayyim, Orach Hayyim* 110), a Moroccan Sephardic *posek* who made aliyah and was rabbi of Haifa in the twentieth century, writes that hair covering is not required at all today, even for married women, based, among other sources, on the responsum of the Maharam Elshakar (no. 35), a fifteenth-century Spanish *posek* who writes that the amount of hair one should allow to show from beneath one's hair covering depends upon the custom of the place. Rav Mashash then extends this to today, when the general societal practice is for all women to keep their hair uncovered, saying that in the past hair covering was required because that was the custom of the times; a woman who went out with her hair exposed, he writes, was considered promiscuous, as opposed to today, when hair covering is often seen as a sign of a lack of intelligence and bad personal hygiene. What he fails to consider, however, is that perhaps the Maharam considered the requirement of a head covering of some sort (like the work basket in the Gemara in

Ketubot, which is said to be required by Torah law) as separate from the idea that hair is *ervah*. One way to reconcile Rabbi Mashash's approach with the Gemara in *Ketubot* is to say that he followed the Mishnah's categorization of head covering as *dat yehudit* and therefore subject to change as societal norms change, as opposed to the Gemara's categorization of it as Torah law. He would therefore have had to have considered the use of "Torah law" in the Gemara to be a loose term, and the verse brought there to be meant not as an actual proof that head covering for women is from the Torah, but rather as an *asmakhta*, a hint that the practice existed in the biblical period. (I would like to thank Rahel Berkovits for providing me with this source.)

40 Although this trend does exist, there are still many observant women today who do not cover their hair at all.

41 Today, at least in modern, open communities, many women do not cover all of their hair, which implies that in these communities hair is no longer considered *ervah* (the concern of the *B'rachot* source). Some women who do cover all of their hair will expose their hair completely in their homes, even in front of men. It is my feeling that in these communities exposed hair in public places on a married woman is also not perceived as sexually improper (the concern of the *Ketubot* source). Some such communities may consider it halakhically or religiously improper, but I would argue that this is not in connection to sexuality, as it seems to be in the Gemara and other later sources. In cloistered ultra-Orthodox communities, however, this is probably not the case, because there an entirely different set of social rules applies. There women keep their hair covered at all times when in the presence of men, and some even in the presence of women. The hair of these women is considered *ervah*, and a married woman going out in public with her hair exposed is considered sexually improper.

42 Interestingly, there is no basis for this symbolic value of the mitzvah in the traditional sources. However, there is no doubt that it has taken on this meaning today, since unmarried women stopped covering their hair.

43 See *Biur Hag'ra* on *Shulchan Arukh, Orach Hayyim* 8, n. 6, *v'nachon*. He calls the practice *"middat hasidut,"* a pious practice. The practice has become so widespread today, however, that by now it is more of a common practice among all religious men than a pious practice only for certain devout individuals. In addition, it has extended beyond prayer and study.

44 These sources are mostly Sephardi, emanating from either Spain or the Middle East. See Beit Yosef, *Orach Hayyim* 91:3, *u-mah shekatav rabbeinu,* who does not distinguish between men and women when he rules that a Jew is required to wear a head covering while praying and reciting blessings. See also the responsum of Rav Ovadia Yosef (*Yekhaveh Da'at,* vol. 5, no. 6), an Israeli Sephardi twentieth-century *posek,* who rules that although it is technically defensible for women not to cover their heads in prayer and study, optimally they should. Also see the Responsum of Rav Mazliach Mazuz (*Shut Ish Mazliach, Orach Hayyim* 24), who says that it was the custom in several lands in the East for unmarried women to cover their heads in prayer and study. Rabbi Yekhiel Weinberg, a twentieth-century European *posek,* also understands the relevant sources to be saying that both married and unmarried women should cover their heads (*S'ridei Eish,* vol. 3, section 30, s.v. *u-viY'shurun*), although he is not speaking specifically about prayer and study.

45 *Shulchan Arukh, Orach Hayyim* 75:1. This source specifies that only hair that she is accustomed to covering must be covered; nonetheless, this text is probably one of the reasons for this common practice— either out of ignorance of the fine points of the wording, or out of a desire to keep at least one aspect of the haircovering practice, even if inconsistently. It is also possible that married women who do not normally wear hats do wear them to shul out of a desire to do what they think is truly halakhically correct at least while in shul. Most probably all three of these factors are at work here.

46 BT *Eruvin* 100b, Rashi, s.v. *atufah k'avel; m'nuddah l'khol adam; v'ha busha b'veit ha'asurin.*

47 At this point in Jewish legal history, polygyny was still legal. Later, in tenth-century Germany, Rabbeinu Gershom outlawed it.

48 Translation from Susan Grossman and Rivka Haut, eds., *Daughters of the King: Women and the Synagogue* (Philadelphia: JPS, 1992) p. xxi.

49 See *Iggrot Moshe, Even Ha'ezer* 1:114, where he rules that since so many observant women today do not cover their hair, this is not grounds for divorce.

CHAPTER FOUR

1 For a good explanation of the "breaking of the vessels," see Daniel C. Matt's *God and the Big Bang* (Woodstock, VT: Jewish Lights,

1996) pp. 79–82, and *The Essential Kabbalah: The Heart of Jewish Mysticism* (New York: HarperCollins, 1996), pp. 13–15.

CHAPTER FIVE

1 See *Biur Hag'ra* on *Shulchan Arukh, Orach Hayyim* 8, n. 6. Since he calls the practice of even limited head covering a *"middat hasidut,"* a pious practice, one could conclude that if one chose, like my father, to cover one's head only while reciting blessings, prayers, and studying Torah, this would be a totally valid application of the custom. In fact, according to the Gra, it would be a pious practice. And even if one were to argue that today, since the practice has become much more common, it is no longer a pious practice but rather an expected common practice to wear a head covering while praying, reciting blessings, and studying Torah, certainly wearing a kippah all of the time would still be considered pious and not obligatory, since the Gra calls even the limited wearing of one a pious practice.

2 Exodus 23:19, 34:26, and Deuteronomy 14:21.

3 *Hullin* 8:4.

4 Torah law, or the written law, is the most authoritative category of Jewish law, attributed to the Bible—even if not written there explicitly, as is sometimes the case. Rabbinical law is a less authoritative category of Jewish law, attributed to the Rabbis. Rabbinical law is still binding, but it is somewhat easier to overturn than Torah law.

5 *Eduyot* 1:5 and 1:6.

6 Genesis 8:21.

7 Leviticus 19:2.

8 Bradley Shavit Artson, "Gay and Lesbian Jews: An Innovative Jewish Legal Position," *Jewish Spectator* (Winter 1990–1991), pp. 6–14.

9 Barry Freundel, "Homosexuality and Judaism," *Journal of Halakhah in Contemporary Society* 11 (1986): 70–87, makes this argument.

CHAPTER SIX

1 A *mesurevet get* is a woman who is "refused" a get, while technically an *agunah* is a woman who is "chained" because, for example, her husband has disappeared (and there is not sufficient evidence that he has died) or is mentally incompetent and therefore unable to give a *get*. Nevertheless, in common parlance the term *agunah* is often used to refer to a woman whose husband refuses to give her a *get* and who

is for that reason "chained" to her husband, and her marriage.

2 This would not automatically include marriages performed outside of the State of Israel that are then registered with the rabbinate. In such cases it would be nearly impossible to require a prenuptial agreement.

3 See *Iggrot Moshe, Even Ha'ezer,* nos. 79 and 80, and *Hoshen Mishpat 2,* no. 113. In these responsa, Feinstein allows for this in cases where it is discovered that the husband is a homosexual, impotent, or mentally unstable. He refers to this as *"mekakh ta'oot,"* or faulty consent.

4 *Mishneh Torah, Hilkhot Ishut,* 14:8.

5 For background on this subject see Irwin Haut, "'The Altar Weeps': Divorce in Jewish Law" in Jack Nusan Porter, *Women in Chains: A Sourcebook on the Agunah* (Northvale, NJ: Jason Aronson, 1995), pp. 45–59.

6 Rachel Adler, *Engendering Judaism: An Inclusive Theology and Ethics* (Philadelphia: JPS, 1998), pp. 196–198.

7 *She'elot Ya'abetz,* Section 2, Responsum 15.

8 Meir Simcha HaCohen Feldblum, *"Ba'ayat Agunot V'Mamzerim: Hatza'at Pitaron M'kifa V'kollelet* [The Problem of *Agunot* and *Mamzerim*: A Comprehensive and Inclusive Proposal]," *Dinei Yisrael* 19 (1996): 207–216.

CHAPTER SEVEN

1 BT *Niddah* 66a.

2 BT *Niddah* 31b.

3 JT *B'rachot* 5:1.

4 BT *Niddah* 12b.

5 *Niddah* 9:1.

6 BT *Niddah* 59b, s.v. *b'mizaneket* and *mizaneket.*

7 BT *Niddah* 59b. The Gemara states that the halakhah goes according to Rabbi Yossi. The reason for this ruling, however, is not that Rabbi Meir's understanding of female anatomy (at least as understood by Rashi) is declared faulty, but rather because when there is a disagreement between Rabbi Meir and Rabbi Yossi, the general rule is to follow the opinion of Rabbi Yossi.

8 *Mishneh Torah, Hilkhot Issurei Bi'ah* 6:1–16 and 7:1.

9 *Hilkhot Niddah LaRamban* 1:1–14.

10 *Tosafot HaRosh, Horayot* 2a, s.v. *horu.*

11 *Sifra (Metzorah, Parshata 5, Perek 8)*. The seven-eleven cycle is here based on the minimum number of days that would be required to fit the circumstances related in the verses of Leviticus. If a woman were to bleed for seven days of niddah (as per Leviticus 15:19), another three days for *zavah* (even after one day with no bleeding, since Leviticus 15:25 says that she is a *zavah* either connected to her niddah bleeding or after her niddah bleeding has stopped), plus another seven clean days after the *zivah* bleeding has stopped (as per Leviticus 15:28), the number of days would amount to eighteen.

12 See Maimonides, *Mishneh Torah, Hilkhot Issurei Bi'ah* 4:2, and Rashi, BT *Shabbat* 11a, s.v. *mipnei hergel aveira*. Both declare it forbidden and punishable by *karet* for a man to sleep with a *zavah*. This is not spelled out in the Torah or the Talmud.

13 After the talmudic period, the minimum number of days that a woman is required to wait became twelve. She must wait a minimum of five days before she can begin counting her seven "clean" days, even if her period lasts fewer than five days, because of the possibility that she may have had intercourse on the day on which she saw blood, in which case she would not be able to start counting clean days for seventy-two hours (which can sometimes span four days), the amount of time the Rabbis say that semen can render a woman *t'meah* (which would then preclude the onset of the seven-clean-day period). We then add a fifth day, in case she had intercourse *ben hashmashot* (during twilight), which is a halakhically problematic time, since we do not know if it is considered day or night. Thus, I would add (against mainstream written opinions, which say that we do not make exceptions, although I have been told that in private oral consultations *poskim* have advised women this way) that if a woman ovulates before twelve days after her bleeding starts, bleeds for fewer than five days, and does not have intercourse with her husband within three days prior to the cessation of her bleeding, she should be told to start counting her seven clean days as soon as her bleeding stops, even if that is before five days have passed.

14 BT *Shabbat* 128b.

15 Maimonides rules this way in *Mishneh Torah, Hilkhot Shabbat* 2:11.

16 Noam Zohar, "*Kors Hakhanah l'Leidah* [A Labor and Delivery Preparation Course]," *Techumim* 15 (1996): 198–202.

17 Leviticus 15:20–24.

18 BT *Shabbat* 13a.

19 *Niddah* 7:4.

20 BT *Shabbat* 64b. See also *Sifra Metzorah, Parshata* 5, *Perek* 9, subsection 12.

21 BT *Ketubot* 61a.

CHAPTER EIGHT

1 *Yoreh De'ah* 197:3.

2 Ibid., 197: 4–5.

CHAPTER NINE

1 BT *Kiddushin* 29b.

2 *Sifre*, Deuteronomy, section 46.

3 *Mishneh Torah, Hilkhot Talmud Torah* 1:13.

4 *Sotah* 3:4.

5 *Likutei Halakhot* of the Hafetz Hayyim, *Sotah* 21.

6 Numbers 27:18.

7 *Mishneh Torah, Hilkhot M'lakhim,* 1:5. Maimonides derives this from the *Sifre*, Deuteronomy, 157:15.

8 I name some of the most well-known rabbis who have been outspoken on this issue, but other rabbis have been supportive as well.

9 Netty Gross, "Breaking Down the Rabbinate Walls," *The Jerusalem Report*, February 20, 1997, p. 36.

10 *Shulchan Arukh, Hoshen Mishpat* 35:14.

CHAPTER TEN

1 Marcia Falk, *The Song of Songs: A New Translation* (San Francisco: HarperSanFrancisco, 1990), p. 10.

ABOUT JFL BOOKS

JFL Books is the book publishing division of Jewish Family & Life! (JFL). Other JFL Books titles include *Living Words: The Best High Holiday Sermons of 5759* and *Beyond Scandal: The Parents' Guide to Sex, Lies and Leadership.*

Further information is available at www.JFLBooks.com. For pricing information on bulk orders of this or other JFL Books, please use the contact information below.

Rabbi Susan P. Fendrick, Editor
JFLBooks@JFLmedia.com

ABOUT JEWISH FAMILY & LIFE!

JFL is a multimedia nonprofit organization based in Needham, Massachusetts. JFL is also the publisher of many Web-based magazines, including SocialAction.com, JewishFamily.com, JewishHolidays.com and Shma.com. *Sh'ma*, one of the Jewish community's leading journals, is also produced by JFL.

Contributions to JFL are tax deductible to the extent allowed by law.

JFL Books
A division of Jewish Family & Life!
56 Kearney Road
Needham, MA 02494
(tel) 781-449-9894
(fax) 781-449-9825
www.JFLBooks.com